Creative Experiencing

SUNY SERIES IN PHILOSOPHY

George R. Lucas Jr., editor

Creative Experiencing

A PHILOSOPHY OF FREEDOM

Charles Hartshorne

EDITED BY DONALD WAYNE VINEY AND JINCHEOL O

SUNY PRESS

Previously published chapters: Chapter Three: Charles Hartshorne, "Negative Facts and the Analogical Inference to 'Other Mind'" In *Dr. S. Radhakrishan Souvenir Volume*, edited by J. P. Atreya et al., 147–52. Moradabad, India: Darshana International, 1964; Chapter Four: Charles Hartshorne, "Perception and the Concrete Abstractness of Science." *Philosophy and Phenomenological Research* 34 (1974): 465–76. Also published as Chapter 9 of Hartshorne's *The Zero Fallacy and Other Essays in Neoclassical Philosophy*, edited by Mohammad Valady, 151–60. Chicago and La Salle, IL: Open Court, 1997. Reproduced with permission of Blackwell Publishing Ltd; Chapter Six: Charles Hartshorne, "The Case for Idealism." *Philosophical Forum* 1 (1968): 7–23. Reproduced with permission of Blackwell Publishing Ltd; Chapter Seven: Charles Hartshorne, "Creativity and the Deductive Logic of Causality." *The Review of Metaphysics* 27 (1973): 62–74. Reprinted with permission; Chapter Eight: Charles Hartshorne, "The Meaning of 'Is Going to Be.'" *Mind* 74 (1965): 46–58. Reprinted with permission of Oxford University Press; Chapter Nine: Charles Hartshorne, "Metaphysics and the Dual Transcendence of God." *Tulane Studies in Philosophy*, "Hartshorne's Neoclassical Theology." Edited by Forrest Wood, Jr., and Michael DeArmey, 34 (1986): 65–72. Reprinted with permission; Chapter Eleven: Charles Hartshorne, "Categories, Transcendentals, and Creative Experiencing." *The Monist* 66 (1983): 319–35. *The Monist: An International Quarterly Journal of General Philosophical Inquiry*. Chicago: Open Court Publishing Company. Reprinted with permission; Chapter Thirteen: Charles Hartshorne, "Politics and the Metaphysics of Freedom." Pages 79–85 in *Enquête sur la liberté, Fédération internationale des sociétés de philosophie. Publié avec le concours de l'u.n.e.s.c.o.* Paris: Hermann, 1953. Hermann: www.editions-hermann.fr/. Reprinted with permission.

Published by
STATE UNIVERSITY OF NEW YORK PRESS
Albany

For information, contact
State University of New York Press
www.sunypress.edu

Production and book design, Laurie Searl
Marketing, Michael Campochiaro

Library of Congress Cataloging-in-Publication Data

Hartshorne, Charles, 1897–2000.
    Creative experiencing : a philosophy of freedom / Charles Hartshorne ; edited by Donald Wayne Viney and Jincheol O.
        p. cm.
    Includes bibliographical references (p. 145) and index.
    ISBN 978-1-4384-3665-4 (hardcover : alk. paper)
    ISBN 978-1-4384-3666-1 (pbk : alk. paper)
    1. Philosophy. I. Viney, Donald Wayne. II. O, Jincheal. III. Title.
    B945.H351V56 2011
    191—dc22   2011003672

10 9 8 7 6 5 4 3 2 1

Contents

Editors' Preface

The manuscript of *Creative Experiencing: A Philosophy of Freedom* was found among the unpublished papers of Charles Hartshorne (1897–2000) that are now deposited at the Center for Process Studies at Claremont School of Theology. It includes a table of contents, a preface, and thirteen chapters.[1] Eight of the chapters are revisions of articles published between 1953 and 1986. The five remaining chapters and the preface were never published. Although the manuscript required minor editing, it was essentially a complete work. Hartshorne indicates in the preface that he planned for the book to follow his *Creative Synthesis and Philosophic Method* (1970) and *Wisdom as Moderation* (1987) and that he considered it his final contribution to "technical philosophy."

One may surmise the reasons why Hartshorne did not see the book through to publication. The manuscript in the form that we have it was put together in his eighth decade. During these years his wife, Dorothy Hartshorne (1904–1995), was in declining health. (The absence of her editorial advice is sadly evident in *Wisdom as Moderation*.) Nevertheless, during this time he published dozens of articles, reviews, and forewords, and four of his books. In addition, Hartshorne contributed to four major anthologies devoted to the analysis and critique of his work—*Existence and Actuality*, edited by John B. Cobb, Jr., and Franklin I. Gamwell (Chicago: University of Chicago Press, 1984), *Hartshorne, Process Philosophy and Theology*, edited by Robert Kane and Stephen H. Phillips (Albany: State University of New York Press, 1989), *Charles Hartshorne's Concept of God*, edited by Santiago Sia (Dordrecht: Kluwer Academic Publishers, 1990), and *The Philosophy of Charles Hartshorne* (volume 20 in the Library of Living Philosophers), edited by Lewis Edwin Hahn (La Salle, IL: Open Court, 1991). Hartshorne's responses to fifty-six scholars fill approximately one-fourth of the pages of these books. Hartshorne's intellectual abilities did not diminish after these volumes, but he did not pursue larger projects on his own. In 1995 he reread his correspondence with Edgar Sheffield Brightman and offered editing suggestions for its publication.[2] His final book to appear during his lifetime, *The Zero Fallacy and Other Essays in Neoclassical Metaphysics* (La Salle, IL: Open Court, 1997), was edited by Mohammad Valady.

While Hartshorne is widely known as a process philosopher and theologian, *Creative Experiencing* shows him in dialogue with the wider currents of both analytic philosophy and phenomenology. The second chapter of the book, which has never been published until now, contains Hartshorne's clearest statement of his views on phenomenology. Hartshorne met and briefly studied with Edmund Husserl and Martin Heidegger during his travels in Europe as a Sheldon Fellow in 1924–1925 and in 1929 he published the first English-language review of Heidegger's *Sein und Zeit*.[3] The meetings with Husserl and Heidegger preceded his exposure to the two men who became the most important philosophical influences on his thinking, Charles Sanders Peirce and Alfred North Whitehead. *Creative Experiencing* also contains essays to which Hartshorne often refers in his other writings but which had never been published in one of his books. Particularly notable in this regard are Chapters Seven and Eight. Chapter Seven, originally published in *The Review of Metaphysics* (1973), presents Hartshorne's analysis of time's asymmetry and its relation to causality; Chapter Eight appeared in *Mind* (1965) and is his most complete statement on the meaning of future tense statements.

We endeavored not to second-guess Hartshorne's editorial decisions and to keep our interference as editors to a minimum. For example, in Chapter Eight, we resisted the temptation to include about a page of material that Hartshorne excised from the original article. We changed his notation for the logical functions of negation, conjunction, disjunction, and conditional to make it consistent throughout. We made no attempt, however, to change Hartshorne's use of exclusive language even though it is clear from his preface that he would have done so had he shepherded the book to publication. There is evidence in the manuscript itself that he was beginning to change from the exclusive use of male pronouns for the creatures and for God to a more inclusive vocabulary. Certainly, he felt strongly about this issue, as the many comments he made in the last two decades of his life make abundantly clear.[4]

We have kept editorial footnotes to a minimum. The main principle we used, only occasionally broken, was that if Hartshorne directly quotes, or seems to directly quote, an author without citation, we provided the reference. Hartshorne obviously quoted from memory. The result was often a slight misquotation, but we believe it is safe to say, not misrepresentation (although see note 2, Chapter Twelve). The irony is that Hartshorne's "remembered" quotation was occasionally more memorable than what the philosopher actually wrote. (See, for example, note 11, Chapter Ten, and note 13, Chapter Eleven.)

The discovery of a previously unknown book-length manuscript by Hartshorne is a scholar's dream. Its publication is a cause for celebration. The leading secondary sources in philosophy and theology testify to the fact that Hartshorne was a central figure in twentieth-century philosophy and that he was the chief representative of process thought in the second half of the century.[5] Judging by the number of books published since his death in which his name figures prominently, it is clear that his ideas continue to be influential.[6] For this reason, we are grateful to George R. Lucas, Jr., and the editors at State University of New York Press for recognizing the importance of publishing this book.

We also thank John B. Cobb, Jr., for his enthusiastic support of this project and his unwavering confidence in our ability to see it through. Steve Hulbert, working in the Hartshorne Archives at the Center for Process Studies, gave generously of his time to assist in a variety of ways to bring this project to completion. Finally, the main editor wishes to offer a special note of gratitude to Emily Hartshorne Schwartz for her invitation to him to help prepare her father's philosophical papers to be shipped to Claremont. It was at that time that the manuscript of *Creative Experiencing* first came to light and began its first steps on its journey to the printer.

Donald Wayne Viney
Pittsburg State University

Jincheol O
Archives Director, Center for Process Studies

Hartshorne's Preface

In a previous book I presented my "neoclassical metaphysics" as a mean between, or higher synthesis of, false extremes.[1] In this book I present it with emphasis on two resources that I take to be decisive in philosophy, appeal to the most concrete aspects of experience (phenomenology) and the appeal to something very unconcrete, truisms of formal logic. Metaphysics is the attempt to interpret concrete experience rationally, in terms of the most general principles of valid reasoning. It is the logic of our most general ideas and ideals.

In the first chapter I derive some guiding principles for metaphysical inquiry from Aristotle, Leibniz, Hegel, and Wittgenstein, and consider to what extent Pierce and Whitehead, Popper, and some other recent writers do or do not conform to these principles. In the second chapter, I offer an approach to phenomenology arrived at by considering some views of Husserl and Heidegger, also Peirce's very different and to my mind basically sounder scheme in his phaneroscopy, plus the view of the immediately given expounded by Whitehead, as well as—without the word—phenomenology. I had begun to develop [these ideas] before reading or knowing any of the above writers.

Chapter Three shows the logic of moving from experience as one finds it in one's own case to the experience of other persons, other animals, and active singulars in general. Chapter Four deals with the problem of relating the scientific description of reality, with its partial neglect of the concrete to the life-world of ordinary experience, and I show that it too is, though in a different sense, only partially concrete. I argue that to understand what concrete reality in principle is one must combine what is positive in science and common sense, ignoring or rejecting their different ways of overlooking, or seeming to deny, forms of concreteness that the two together imply exist. Chapter Five deals with the application to metaphysics of the Popperian principle that we arrive at truth by eliminating erroneous theories. Chapter Six shows how reasons for or against idealism or psychicalism have historically been entangled with reasons for or against other doctrines, such as the unreality of time, exclusively internal relations, and many others, and how psychicalism can be defended when these entanglements are cleared away.

Chapter Seven shows how the Bergsonian-Whiteheadian view of process as conservative of the prehended past logically implies the *partial* predictability of the future. Chapter Eight deals with the relation between the partial openness of the future and the temporality of historical truths, how they are everlasting rather than eternal or timeless. Chapters Nine and Ten deal with the neoclassical form of theism. The last chapters make some application of the neoclassical metaphysics to practical human problems.

Chapters One, Two, Five, Ten, and Twelve are here published for the first time.[2] The other eight essays are slightly modified or extended versions of articles published in six periodicals, a book published in India, and a book published in France. The writing of the thirteen essays spanned a period of thirty-four years, but I am aware of no incompatibility between any two of them. There has been one verbal change: although always pro-feminist, I have only recently become sensitive to the male chauvinism of using masculine pronouns for deity or for human beings generally. I have tried to eliminate most of these. I believe femininity is at least as close to divinity as masculinity. The masculine bias in this matter is one of the worst forms of anthropomorphism. In principle women can do everything men can; the converse statement is less true. Also, motherhood is a more intimate relation than fatherhood. Our relation to deity is more intimate still. "Closer [God is] than breathing and nearer than hands and feet."

With this book and its two predecessors, *Creative Synthesis and Philosophic Method* and *Wisdom as Moderation*, my contribution to technical philosophy may be essentially complete.

CHAPTER ONE

Some Formal Criteria of Good Metaphysics

Hume and Kant are by many supposed to have shown that metaphysics is a vain enterprise, and Wittgenstein to have shown that it consists in misuse of words. My view is that Hume and Kant begged the question by assuming metaphysical positions of their own. On the basis of some bad metaphysics they refuted some other forms of bad metaphysics, and declared the vanity of all metaphysics. Although Wittgenstein was right that some metaphysical views misuse words, he did not even consider the kind of metaphysics that the last ten or twelve decades have seen emerging. The outstanding representative of this new metaphysics is Whitehead. However, Bergson and Lequier in France, Varisco in Italy, the physicist and psychologist Fechner in Germany, and Charles Peirce in my country, are also to be included in the general movement. Before I knew much of Whitehead or Peirce, I was already thinking in somewhat similar ways. In my doctoral dissertation I did not mention Peirce or Whitehead or use their technical terms or concepts.[1] But two years later, as I began to read the writings of these two, I saw that they were the ones from whom I could learn most. Whitehead had the advantage of knowing relativity physics and early phases of quantum theory and knowing a more advanced formal logic than Peirce had arrived at. Also Whitehead had a more fortunate career and worked out his system more fully than Peirce. So I learned most from him, but much from Peirce.

I hold that we now have some good criteria for the distinction between good and bad metaphysics. One criterion was the proposition of Leibniz that in metaphysics the mistakes have been in denials, not in assertions. Metaphysical truth is all positive. By the definition given by Aristotle and Kant, metaphysics seeks "universal and necessary truths" about existence. Hence metaphysical falsity is necessary falsity, impossibility. What is to be denied in metaphysics is itself negative, and such a double denial is positive. "Accentuate the positive" is a sound maxim in metaphysics. All that metaphysical assertions exclude is contradiction or logical absurdity. Metaphysical error *is* misuse of language, but to define metaphysics as such misuse is an illicitly persuasive, question-begging definition.

Another criterion is that metaphysical truth is "the unity of contraries." Hegel was right about this. For instance, possibility and actuality belong together, there can be no such thing as "pure actuality," *actus purus*; no such thing as the merely infinite or merely finite, merely absolute or merely relative, merely necessary or merely contingent, merely subjective or merely objective, merely universal or merely particular. Hegel saw this and Peirce and Whitehead saw it. It is a permanent acquisition in metaphysical thinking at its best. That metaphysics is wholly positive, affirming something and denying only absurdity or words badly used, means that both poles of ultimate contrarieties must be affirmed. Hegelians and Marxists seem to think this means logical contradiction. Not so. For S is P and S is not P is saved from contradiction provided P and not P are affirmed of different aspects of S.

A third criterion of good metaphysics is that, given an extreme position to which there is a contrary extreme, the truth is a mean between the extremes, or a higher synthesis of the two positions. Extreme monism is false and extreme pluralism is false, in both cases because of the extremism. The truth is a moderate monism, which is also a moderate pluralism.

Our three criteria really come to the same thing. One must not affirm one pole of an ultimate contrariety in such fashion that it excludes the contrary pole. Both poles must apply positively.

A fourth criterion is the Principle of Contrast. The function of a concept is to distinguish something from something else. To say everything is necessary and nothing is contingent is to deprive "necessary" of any distinctive meaning. The same with saying everything is contingent. If we set aside all the philosophers that have said one or other of these two empty affirmations, we see that not very many are left. The Stoics and Spinoza, with their necessitarianism, and William James and countless others with their contingentism, were all extremists. The Principle of Contrast is a fourth way of stating the Leibnizian-Hegelian principle.

In putting together these four criteria I have, so far as I know, done something never done before. But the philosophers who come closest to thinking in accordance with the principle are Peirce and Whitehead, in some ways one, in some ways the other. In my opinion neither Leibniz nor Hegel applied the criterion nearly so well as these two have done. I will now try to show this for Whitehead especially.

In most respects Whitehead avoids the contrary extremes: he is not an extreme monist or an extreme pluralist, an extreme subjectivist or extreme objectivist, an extreme partisan of necessity or of contingency, of the infinite or the finite. An extreme monist either denies that there is a plurality of actualities, or holds, as Royce did, that these actualities are completely interdependent, any one implicating all the rest. The opposite extreme is seen in Hume's dictum, "what is distinguishable is separable," implicating nothing else.[2] Whitehead's doctrine is that only relations to *past* actualities are intrinsic to a present actual entity. We depend on our childhood and our ancestors, not on our future states or our descendents. Leibniz held the opposite view about the future. Strict determinism also implies a symmetrical interdependence of events upon both predecessors *and* successors. It destroys time's arrow. Peirce is with Whitehead here in rejecting determinism, not only of human actions, but of all actions. There is, both held, some freedom, some creativity, on all levels of nature. Fechner, Varisco, and Bergson held similar views. But these men rejected Hume's extreme pluralism as true of either the past or future. For them, although the present does not depend upon future particulars, it does depend upon certain abstract features of the future as expressed by the laws of nature, which are statistical or probabilistic, not fully determining of particulars. The present is partly self-determined and partly, but only partly, determines the future.

Whitehead's "reformed subjectivism" does not deprive subjects of their objects; but it implies that in memory obviously, and in perception less obviously, what is on the objective side is previous subjectivity. Memory is experiencing of past experiences, not of mere matter; perception is also experiencing of past experiences. The difference is that, whereas in memory the past experiences are one's own human experiences, in perception they are experiences of a radically subhuman kind, most immediately in the microconstituents of our own bodies (cells or still smaller parts). In physical suffering, not alone do *we* suffer, the living members of our bodies also suffer. Our sensations are sympathetic participations in their feelings.

Note that this new subjectivism, or new idealism, is also a realism. The past experiences we experience really occurred or we could not now experience them. All that Whitehead denies of materialism or dualism is itself only a denial, the notion of *mere* dead, *in*sentient matter, stuff, or process. Materialism as distinctive is essentially negative; what is positive in it Whitehead can accept. Certain negations—such as that tables and chairs, perhaps even trees, do not feel or sense—Whitehead can also accept, but they are not metaphysical negations; they do not entail an absolute zero of feeling in trees or chairs. The cells of the trees, the molecules of the chair, may feel. A trio of people together in an elevator, taken as a single entity, does not feel. What feels as one acts as one, the trio in the elevator does not act, and need not feel as one. So with the chair we sit on. It is a crowd of molecules. This point is Leibnizian, and since Leibniz all idealists who have read their Leibniz intelligently take the distinction between singular and aggregate for granted. Berkeley missed this point as, I think, did Hegel.

Hegel said, and to this Whitehead would agree: in the contrariety subject-object, subject "overlaps." Whitehead, however, analyzes experience as "feeling of (others') feeling," that is, as essentially social in structure; and, as Leibniz did, he generalizes feeling sufficiently to take into account all the differences between an animal, a plant cell, a molecule or atom, all the *singular dynamic agents* in nature.[3]

I will mention briefly a number of other one-sided extremes that White-head avoids. He does not, as he accuses others of doing, focus almost exclusively on *vision*, which tends to give a static and seemingly value-neutral view of nature; rather he takes as the paradigm of direct perception a throb of bodily pain (or pleasure), which shows that something is happening in the body, and something not value-neutral. Similarly, as already indicated, he takes memory as direct awareness of at least the immediate past and interprets perception by analogy with memory rather than the reverse. Rightly, because in memory we know what we are talking about, namely, awareness of past experience, whereas in perception we may have the illusion of being aware only of mere inanimate, insentient matter. For modern physics there is no inanimate matter if that means inactive matter. The idea of inactive matter prevented the Greeks from arriving at a metaphysical, that is, a positive, view of what matter in general is. Common sense and many philosophers have yet to assimilate the discovery that all matter is (partly) self-moved, which by the Platonic principle means that it is not soulless or without feeling.

To some of his critics Whitehead is an extremist in his theory of the changing individual as a sequential society of actual entities, rather than a single actuality with changing properties. Here too, however, Whitehead has a moderate position. The extremes are quite definite. Hume, holding that between successive states of a substance or individual there is no identity at all, only at most similarity, proposed one extreme; Leibniz, holding that the "law of succession of states" in a "monad" is immanent in each state, making the individual completely identical with itself at all times, made explicit the other extreme. Thus, he thought, when Adam was created, all the experiences Adam would ever have were already in him as that monad. Indeed, because of the preestablished harmony, all the other monads were entailed. Either (Hume) no identity at all, or (Leibniz) complete, absolute identity. For Whitehead there is genuine but only partial identity. In each state, there is awareness, "prehension," of *preceding* states. After my first experience as a fetus or infant, I have always been a prehender of that early state in my mostly subconscious memory. So far Leibniz would agree, but not Hume. For Whitehead, later states are not prehended, no matter how subconsciously, as they are for Leibniz. Thus the asymmetry of time is lost by Leibniz but preserved by Whitehead. Hume misses this asymmetry twice over: he holds that, since they are distinguishable, the states are separable, mutually independent; yet, being a determinist in his causal theory, he takes past and future as equally implicated in the present. Here Hume was as wrong as possible. Only an Englishman, I am tempted to say, could be that far from metaphysical insight. Whitehead *was* an Englishman, but so untypical that not many of the English have yet discovered him.

In still another way Whitehead is moderate. For Leibniz there is no interaction between monads, they are logically independent of one another. For Whitehead a changing individual prehends in each of its states, not only preceding states in its own "personally ordered" series, but prehends also, though not in the same way and degree, past states of neighboring individuals in accordance with the principles of relativity physics. In Whitehead's characteristically generalized sense, 'neighbor' includes dynamically singular members of one's own body. Thus Whitehead avoids the artificiality of Leibniz's divinely preestablished harmony that enables us to have the illusion of acting upon our neighbors and being acted upon by them. Whitehead's individuals do have windows through which influences pass.

Aristotle admits no law of succession making it logically necessary that each of a person's states should follow from the identity of the person. On the contrary, things happen to persons by chance interactions with others. Thus, before they existed, Aristotle was (from our point of view) between Leibniz and Hume, and in the doctrinal middle with Whitehead. (No less than the logician Bochenski said so to me once.) What then separates Whitehead from Aristotelianism? The answer is clear: Aristotle supposes that the becoming of experience is continuous. A continuum has no least parts, and in any stretch of it, however short, there are an infinity of lesser parts. Aristotle regards this infinity of parts as potential not actual, and rightly so. Reality is not actually divided infinitely. But this means that the real parts, if any, of a finite portion are finite in number and hence not punctiform or instantaneous but finite in extent. Becoming then is "epochal" or quantized. Not only quantum physics but Zeno-type arguments, independent of physics, are probably partly responsible for Whitehead's view here. The logician von Wright has propounded a similar doctrine, as have the Buddhists for many centuries. The reason for regarding becoming as discontinuous is that becoming involves relations of succession, yet these relations lack terms if becoming is continuous. Points or instants yield no such terms, only least, yet finite, units of becoming can do so. The Buddhists, Whitehead, von Wright, and William James (somewhat unclearly), but not many others, have seen the point. Bergson did not; hence many of his worst troubles. Oddly enough, Peirce also did not. His Synechism, or continuity-ism, stood in the way. He inherited this from his mathematician father. It was Peirce's worst extremism. In some passages he suggests better things. But he had fallen in love with an extreme. Continuity was to be everything. Yet he said himself that continuity is the order of the conceivably possible. If it is the order also of the contingently actual, then it is the order of everything, violating the Principle of Contrast. On this point Whitehead and the Buddhists are the moderates, not the usual Western tradition of reality as a plurality of individuals, each simply identical with itself and simply nonidentical with its neighbors. In Leibniz we have the uttermost caricature of this. For Whitehead the final units of reality are not you or I, but you-now, I-now, and even then our bodies are vast multiplicities of units rather than single units. With the last point Leibniz would agree—with a quibble or two.

Both the Buddhists and Whitehead see profound ethical and religious significance in the quantized view of becoming. For if my or your life is a single changing reality, then, it seems, self-interest must be a simple identity relation; I am I, you are you; therefore, of course I care about me and you care about you, but I may not care about you and you may not care about me. On the contrary, in no case is love a simple identity relation; always it involves partial nonidentity, as well as partial identity. I-now cares about me-yesterday or tomorrow, but I also care about you-yesterday or tomorrow. In the words of the greatest of the Pauls, we are "members one of another." Mahayana Buddhists believed this and so did Whitehead. So also did Peirce. But he lacked a metaphysics to express it adequately.

In another respect Whitehead too is an extremist; and in this respect Peirce is a moderate. Oddly, on this point continuity is again involved and here it is Peirce who is right. Whitehead never denies, and sometimes seems to concede, that possible qualities are continuous, whereas actual qualities are not. The continuum of color can have no definite least parts. Whitehead's own theory of extensive abstraction holds that points are not parts of space or instants of time but are only ways of conceiving the divisibility of spatiotemporal process. Why should this not apply to continuous color qualities? Yet Whitehead speaks of eternal objects as though they formed a definite plurality, and says "blue is *an* eternal object" (italics mine). How small a portion of the continuum between blue-green and purple is this single eternal object? When I put this question to Whitehead he said, "That's a very subtle argument. Perhaps I've missed something." Peirce says that what is eternal about quality is a continuum with no definite least parts. It is a "multitude beyond multitude." And he writes about an "evolution of the Platonic forms themselves," as definite actualities emerge out of the vague primordial continuum of possible qualities.[4]

That Whitehead is no moderate on this issue is clear when one considers the long tradition of nominalism according to which similarities are not to be resolved into partial identities. For one thing, the eternal objects or universals have their own similarities and differences. Similarity and difference are ultimate notions not to be compounded of something else. Whitehead's anti-nominalism is extreme. He too is human and makes mistakes.

Pure nominalism is, of course, an extreme. The point here is not, however, that similarity must be equated with partial identity in terms of eternal objects. The point is in the temporal structure of reality. Becoming is new actualities arising out of past actualities, which are then united into new

syntheses as the present prehends its past. The past consists of definite entities, the future of more or less indefinite or general potentialities. "There are
no occasions in the future," says Whitehead.[5] Peirce says, "the past is the sum
of accomplished facts," and the future consists, not of definite facts with a
later date, but of more or less general, unparticularized tendencies, would-
be's, might-be's, more or less probable may-be's.[6] (Compare Popper's "propensities.") The nominalist can only conceive the future in the same terms
as the past, as a sequence of particulars. There are no such things as future
particulars. Nominalism, Peirce said, cannot understand futurity or possibility. He saw with exemplary clarity that actualization and particularization are
one operation.

We come to the question of deity. The extreme idea that God is wholly
infinite, absolute, independent, immutable, the unmoved mover of all, Whitehead definitely rejects. In principle, actuality is finite and definite; possibility
is infinite and more or less indefinite. The primordial nature of God is indeed
infinite, immutable, independent of all particular creatures; but it is only an
abstraction from the fullness of the divine reality. The consequent nature of
God is God as receiving particular content from the world as God prehends
the world, that is, feels the feelings of the creatures. This is the divine love.
God is, he says, "the fellow sufferer who understands."[7] This statement follows
logically from the requirements of the system, and is no mere concession to
religious feeling.

The long reign of the worship of naked power is over, for some of us. I
grew up in a religion of love, and in the belief (it was my father's) that God is
love in eminent form. Is God ideally powerful? Yes, but in exactly the sense
in which love in eminent or ideal form is also power in ideal form. The key
is love, not power. We should not worship God because besides divine love
there is also divine power. It is the love that explains the power, not vice versa.
Whitehead puts it bluntly, "the power of God is the worship He inspires."[8]
As Whitehead knew, the Greeks had the idea long ago that the divine beauty
or persuasiveness is the secret of supreme power. But the Greeks could not
quite see that love is the most beautiful thing there can be. Why not? Because
they had the idea that love, implying dependence on others and openness to
change, was a weakness, and they supposed that only some deficiency gave
any reason for change. The perfect, Plato argued, cannot change. Implied was
the harmless-seeming but unjustifiable assumption that there could be such a
thing as absolute perfection, taken to mean all possible positive values exhaustively actualized in one actuality.Leibniz saw that not all possibilities of good
are mutually compatible, but he tried to show that this need not apply to God.
Kant rightly rejected his argument here but failed to revise the idea of God
to take this "incompossibility" into account. Whitehead was the first great
thinker to take it clearly into account in thinking about God. The actualization of all possible good is impossible; hence the only thing for God to do is to

go on endlessly actualizing more good. Since possible value is inexhaustible by any actualization, becoming, not being, is final. Even God changes, but only by increase. God does not become more righteous, loving, or holy but does acquire additional creatures to love and appreciate. Ethical good, righteousness, is abstract compared to aesthetic good, beauty, or happiness. The latter has no possible absolute maximum, in spite of Plato.

Another extreme that Whitehead avoids is the one-sided emphasis on moral goodness compared to aesthetic values, the enjoyment of beauty—especially the beauty of friendship and love. Ethics comes in as we take future as well as present values into account, and values for others as well as for ourselves. In Whitehead there is nothing of the idea that we should live to receive rewards or escape punishments after death. There is little of Dante in this religion. So much the better, say some of us. Yet Whitehead agrees with Dante that it is love that moves the world.

For Whitehead the final service God does for us is also the final service we do for God, that our ephemeral, mortal lives on earth shall have abiding significance as ideally prehended in the consequent nature of God. In this philosophy the aim of life is quite literally to enhance the glory of God, meaning the beauty of the creation as enjoyed by God. If this is extremism, it is a very old one. The ancient Jews had it and so did some of the Hindus. I think it is the most moderate view that makes much sense out of our human condition—or of any nondivine being's, actual or possible.

Whitehead's belief in God is based not only on the idea that without God our mortal lives could have no value from a long-run point of view, but on several other difficulties with a nontheistic view of reality.

One such difficulty is the following. Since there is freedom in every creature, the orderliness that any going world requires is an inexplicable mystery unless the freedom of the creatures is inspired by a cosmically influential ordering power. Either the creatures conspire to maintain a minimal order, or they are all ordered by the same universal Influence. Since the order is contingent, there being other possible cosmic schemes, it is as though a cosmic decision had been made. Neoclassical theism says there can be a cosmos of free creatures only because all the lesser freedoms are influenced by the supreme freedom, whose decisions determine the basic laws that are the rules for the game of life. The rules obtain not for eternity but for some cosmic epoch. If other laws are possible, with their own aesthetic possibilities, they too should be tried in good time. Only a sublime imagination could have thought up this idea of an infinite succession of cosmic epochs with God the architect, not of the detailed structure of the epochs but of the basic styles, the laws that make them possible. Whitehead implies a few other reasons for belief, but these two are the obvious ones. I think myself there are half a dozen that fit this type of philosophy.[9] If any other philosopher since Plato has made so magnificent a contribution to philosophical theism as Whitehead, I do not know his name.

That "subject overlaps object" illustrates a basic asymmetry or directional order. In formal logic one-way relations are the principles and two-way or symmetrical relations are special cases, as equivalence (or the biconditional) is of simple conditioning. Again, the contingent includes the necessary, not vice versa; in every basic contrariety there is such one-way inclusion. I seem to be the first to make a list of these asymmetrically inclusive polarities (under the label of "ultimate contrasts," in Chapter VI of my book *Creative Synthesis*). I claim to do there what Hegel should have done but failed with any clarity to do. And the key is formal logic, not his pseudo-logic, as in the *Logik*.

Whitehead has a "dipolar" conception of deity, as compared to the main one-sided tradition, yet in treating God as a single actuality rather than the eminent form of personally ordered *society* of actualities I think he introduces difficulties that can be mitigated by preferring the latter analogy, emphasizing of course that the "supreme exemplification" of the categories is bound to be mysterious for we who are nonsupreme examples. I also view as a mistake Whitehead's scornful rejection of the Platonic analogy of a divine World Soul, of which all else is the cosmic body.[10] The justification given for this rejection I find invalid. If the human mind–body relation is not a clue to the way mind relates to inferior levels of reality, what is? Even Hume made this point. As Consequent, God analogically has a body, and Whitehead's categories work better if applied to God in that way. I argue elsewhere that Merleau-Ponty's generalized idea of "flesh" supports the position.[11]

CHAPTER TWO

My Eclectic Approach to Phenomenology

The term *phenomenology* seems to have been invented by Hegel. Its use in recent times has been for a somewhat different idea. Almost wholly independently of one another, two philosophers came to use it for a way of doing, or a branch of, philosophy. Peirce (born 1839) was the first of these; Husserl (born twenty years later) was the second. Peirce's "phaneroscopy"—later he used Hegel's word, possibly influenced by Husserl's usage— was designed to do something like what Husserl had in mind. This was to base philosophizing on direct inspection of the data of experience, on what is given to us. Here one also recalls that Bergson (born two years after Peirce) wrote his first book on *The Data of Consciousness*. William James (born 1842), who was praised by Husserl and who influenced Whitehead (Husserl's contemporary, who knew something of his work) also needs mentioning. Whitehead, who once said, "Metaphysics is a descriptive science," meant by this that it gets its basic concepts from the most general aspects of experience as directly given to us. Whitehead also said that philosophy was a "critic of abstractions," criticizing them partly in terms of concrete data of experience. His favorite "fallacy of misplaced concreteness" makes the same point.[1] His impression of Husserl was that Husserl scarcely reached the concrete in his "intuition of essences," a conclusion I (and others) had reached while in Freiburg in 1924.

A chapter of my 1923 dissertation at Harvard discussed—without my using or knowing the word—the phaneroscopic question, "As what are sensations experienced?" The answer I gave to this question caused me, when I later encountered Husserl (still later, Whitehead and the writings of Peirce), to disagree sharply with Husserl and agree most with Whitehead on a basic issue concerning experience, the nature of sensory qualities. However, I also saw in Peirce's phaneroscopy in some respects the best approach to the general nature of experiencing and reality as experienced. Now, after more than sixty years of reflection since I first heard Husserl lecture and began to read him, I attempt to sketch my own phenomenology. It has some common ground with all the writers just listed, but as a whole is close only to Peirce and Whitehead.

A phaneron, something given or apparent, to or in an experience, must, it seems, be distinguished from the experience as a whole. Experience-of-x is x plus something. But the relation of the two is no mere *and*. Experience-of-x includes x. Whitehead uses 'prehend' for this inclusion. The word is not new, but the meaning is definitely distinguishable from any concept that had been equally clearly set forth by anyone else, so far as I know. I shall try to show some of the ways in which one can fail to arrive at Whitehead's meaning, which I regard as the best approximation yet attained to the truth about the idea of givenness or of having data.

As usual, errors here come in pairs of opposites. One can suppose that experience and its datum are mutually independent logically. In that case, there seems no reason why in general the experience should agree with, be true to, its datum. Something appears but its nature may be *entirely* different from what it appears to be. This is the paradox, I think really contradiction (or nonsense), that appearance can wholly hide the something that appears. Then, I say, the something simply does not appear. The opposite extreme is: appearance exhibits completely and clearly the nature of what appears. A theist who means business should see that this is the way reality must appear to deity. The view claims infinitely too much for our kind of experience, or any animal experience. The opposite view claims too little—Kant, for example, with his thing-in-itself wholly hidden by appearance. The moderate or wise view clearly is: our experiences *to some extent, or with some limitations*, exhibit to us realities as they are in themselves. Our experiences do not "mirror" nature with ideal fidelity and clarity. To that extent, Rorty is right. But the opposite extreme does not follow, and I see no reason to join Rorty in his limiting us to what current discussions encourage us to say about nature or ourselves.[2] What then are the limitations of our experience as true to nature? They are principally three.

First, we are the imaginative and linguistic animals. We live largely in our imaginations, not just in our perceptions, and our imaginations are stimulated, inhibited, and partially expressed by our verbalizations. The given, if particularly attended to, is not simply accepted; we immediately begin to tell ourselves or others what we perceive. The given *symbolizes, indicates,* or *iconizes* for us much that is not given to any noticeable extent. The red traffic light is not just red, it is a danger or prohibition signal. It would often not be safe to respond merely to the redness or the red something as it is in itself. All animals of the higher sort must respond to signs of the not then and there given. It is artists, not scientists or philosophers, who cultivate the ability to respond to the given apart from, or in addition to, what it pragmatically indicates. Heidegger and Whitehead, even Peirce, take this into account much more than Husserl does. Coming to philosophy, as Whitehead partly did, via

Wordsworth and Shelley, also through music and musicians (I later married one), I found that only some philosophers and some psychologists thought of the given in a way that made sense out of aesthetic experience and gave support to a doctrine I shall come to presently.

The second limitation is that, as animals, we experience reality as having three basic levels, (a) ourselves (and other people or animals) as experiencing subjects, with our own experiences as ever-present samples of such subjectivity; (b) our bodies as not simply our experiences; (c) the rest of nature, including plants and the inorganic, seemingly mindless, merely physical processes or things. That this threefold or fourfold complexity of experience can and often does cause confusion in our philosophical thinking seems to me obvious. Nature is not designed to make things easy for philosophers, this we know. (And why should it be so designed?)

As to (b): if we experience physical pain, we may take this as an appearance of something physical going on in our bodies, which indeed it really is, as doctors understand better than some philosophers seem to. Or, is what is then going on in the body just our human suffering? In that case why does the doctor, aiming at our bodily health, bother to ask us about it? "Oh," some say, "because our suffering must have a *cause* in bodily process and the cause may mean danger to our physical health and survival." But this seems to change the subject from that of arriving at an understanding of the experience–experienced relation to that of the effect–cause relation. Since Hume we ought to know that causality itself is a basic philosophical problem. Perhaps the relation of givenness is the key to causality, rather than, or as much as, the other way around. (Hume on causality scarcely took pain as an example.) Is what physically causes us to suffer something wholly different from the suffering? If so, is only the suffering given and the wholly different cause not given? Is the doctor asking about two totally unlike things, the suffering and something entirely mindless and insentient, a merely physical process? I say that this is a vicious extreme in the question about mind as mirroring or not mirroring nature. With Whitehead (also, less clearly Bergson and Peirce) I say that our sufferings do to some extent mirror what goes on in the body.

Physical pleasure presents the same issue. Philosophers scarcely dare, it seems, to consider the nature of sexual pleasure theoretically. Are the bodily conditions of this pleasure wholly different from pleasure, mere physical processes, with only the qualities, really structures, of spatiotemporal–causal configuration that physics and physiology know about? The cell theory of the body has yet, I suggest, to be generally accepted and reflected upon by the learned public in its bearings on the psychophysical problems. Cells resemble ourselves in being highly organized creatures. Either cells can or they cannot have feelings, some of these remotely akin to what in us is called pleasure and some to what is called pain or suffering. If cells can have such feelings, then the natural way to interpret our physical sufferings or enjoyments is to suppose that they do mirror, with whatever qualifications or distortions (mirrors can distort) as may be necessary, their bodily conditions. The bodily conditions of our feelings are, I confidently believe, themselves feelings, but on a subpersonal, cellular level. If you say you know that this is not so, I ask, how do you know it? I know no such thing.

Consider now our perceptions of the inorganic portions of nature. These we experience largely through our distance receptors of sight and hearing, also those of touch. These perceptions are taken by some to relate us directly to things outside the body. Yet science seems to show that the most direct conditions of the experiences are all inside the body, no less so than the conditions of pain or physical pleasure. In a dark room one can "see stars," experience color. I used to be able to do this, before going to sleep, in the dark. I can no longer do it, but I did do it. The colors were patterned and beautiful. They kept changing. And a psychologist once showed me how to experience brilliant visual sensations in a suddenly wholly darkened room as afterimages of intense light-induced sensations. Why resist the evidence that the immediate conditions of those sensations were inner-bodily? (The retinal cells did not immediately stop acting after their overstimulation by light.) If, in our pain, the bodily basis is a cellular feeling akin to our suffering, then, by parallel reasoning, our sensing of brightness and color is not wholly dissimilar to some feelings in the cells of the optical system. Peirce hints at something like this. That we as adults have such a strong impression in vision of directly intuiting extra-bodily entities rather than inner-bodily ones is not hard to explain. Our animal existence forces us to begin at birth, if not before, leaning how to take the sensorily given as exhibiting, for practical purposes, what is going on in as well as around our bodies.

That all sensation is human feeling of some subhuman or nonhuman level of feeling was a conviction I reached long ago as answer to what I later learned to call a phenomenological type of questioning of my own experiences. I then knew no philosopher who had expressed this conviction. When, eight years later, I found Whitehead's formula for "prehension" (of concrete actualities) as "feeling of feeling," rather than just feeling, I at last found said what I had believed, and said better than I had said it. Bergson and Peirce also, I found, hint at some such idea.

That sensory qualities are intrinsically, and not by mere association, feelings has been the view of quite a number of philosophers, for instance, Berkeley, Goethe, Bradley, Bosanquet, and Croce. But it was Whitehead who not only said this but combined it with the recognition that what is given in having a sensation is not just *our* feeling, *our* subjectivity; rather it is the microconstituents of our bodies (of which the Greeks and the Scholastics knew nothing) that are themselves given (in blurred, indistinct fashion—of this indistinctness more later) as sentient. We feel their feelings. This is one of the basic forms of our human prehending.

A second such form is what we call memory. Remembering is one's present (indistinct) prehending, feeling, of one's own past prehending or feeling. True, the body is involved in this, but as Bergson brilliantly points out, since what is not effectively, *distinctly* remembered at a given moment is always incomparably more than what is effectively remembered, the function of the brain is to largely filter out the irrelevant aspects of our past experiences; otherwise we would be utterly overwhelmed and confused by the plethora of mnemonic material.

If memory is, at least in part, present feeling of one's own past feelings and sensation is feeling of some feelings of one's bodily constituents, then in either case it is prehending as involving an emotional duality. *No feeling is solipsistic*, a subject merely aware of itself. All feeling, all sentience, is social, and involves some degree of sympathy in a literal sense. The commonplace dogma "no subject can feel the feelings of another subject" is wholly question-begging if used against this doctrine. What is true is that prehension is, strictly speaking, asymmetrical. If X prehends Y then Y does not prehend X. My past self did not prehend my present self, but my present self does prehend my past self.

The reader may be wondering how the things just said are known. Does the present self prehend itself as prehending the past self? We come here to the question of "introspection." Peirce, Whitehead, and Ryle have all indicated that for them this is not a third form of awareness over and above memory and perception. It is rather a way of using memory, especially very short-run memory. I keep prehending my just previous feelings or prehendings. I also keep prehending some of my bodily constituents. These two forms of prehension constitute together the core of one's awareness of selfhood or personality. Each moment my feeling of my past feelings and of my "bodily life," as Whitehead calls it, acquires an addition, but normally only a very slight one. So of course I am for myself the same person. But go far back; look at a very old diary. Or consider the time when I, for example, in early infancy had no conscious selfhood, a state I therefore cannot with any distinctness remember. To say I simply am that so slightly personal individual, identically that remote past actuality, seems remarkably close to pure nonsense.

We have still not sufficiently distinguished prehension from other conceptions of givenness. Memory seems to be experience of the past; perception, primarily at least, experience of the present. Memory gives us time, whereas perception, especially vision, gives us space. Yet in fact both give us time and space. We see stellar events as they happened in the more or less remote past, and we certainly hear sounds as they occurred in the past. We see lightning before we hear the thunder, similarly with explosions. At most, only events in the body could be perceived simultaneously with their happening. To admit this complete simultaneity is, Whitehead holds, a mistake. It makes memory and perception different absolutely in temporal terms.

Introspection as simultaneous experiencing of that very experience looks like a truly vicious regress. The present is itself; it does not have to prehend itself. The now prehending self will be prehended by the next self-state. In any case the main mass of memories that make up one's sense of self is prehended and that is enough. The present self now enjoys its long-term selfhood, it does not have to enjoy that present enjoyment as datum to have that enjoyment. It has it as its "subjective form of feeling" but not as its objective form, in Whitehead's terminology.

Our prehending, or feeling of feeling, is, it was said earlier, indistinct, both in perception and in memory. This is the chief of the limitations of the mirror model. The best mirrors are almost as distinct in their results as direct sight. Human prehensions are far from that. They lose a vast amount of fine details. The Greek atomists shrewdly guessed this; Aristotle missed it. Plato was in between. Leibniz agreed on this point with the atomists. What we see consists of masses of for us imperceptibly small moving items. Our direct awareness of our own bodies is of active cellular organisms that we can't quite discern individually. All this we learn indirectly, partly by using instruments. But even armchair considerations can tell us that our senses, and our memories as well, give us mostly vague outlines. Seen from a distance details are lacking in the seen as seen; as we move closer they come out more, but as we get very close the reverse change occurs. Only microscopes give us still "closer" vision, but this too has its limits. We experience *nothing concrete* in its richness of detail.

It is the same with memories. How vague they mostly are. Our memories and our perceptions can give definite answers to some questions, but language always abstracts from a great deal. We know neither ourselves nor any other animal with anything like our or its fullness of aspects or details. We not only do not know everything, we know nothing in an absolute sense. Husserl's brave talk about *Evidenz* failed to take this into account. He once wrote in the margin of a passage where he had dealt with *Evidenz*, "*Vielleicht ist dies nur ein Ideal.*"[3] Then he crossed this out. He was more nearly right the first time. The ideal here is theistic or nothing.

There is, I hold, another form of prehending, and that is prehension of the human by the subhuman, our cells as sensitive to our feelings. If our feeling of their feelings has its limitations, much more limited are the cells' abilities to feel ours. This helps to soften the difficulty some scientists feel with admitting that our experiences can influence our bodily processes. They can, but not so much that physiological explanations of what happens lose their relevance. In deep sleep our cells manage largely without us. Our experiences are at such times not harmless epiphenomena, rather they are apparently nonexistent. So to that extent our body is indeed a self-running machine, or better, a society. But so is an ordinary machine a society—of molecules. A waking human being is, however, more than just a society. It is a society subtly influenced by a dominant personally ordered (or single-line sequential) society of human experiences. This society is dominant in the sense that it influences and is influenced by a great mass of cells each of which is appreciably influenced at a given moment by only a few others, perhaps a thousand out of billions.

Two more forms of prehension are of the human by the radically super-human form of experiencing that which is deity, and prehensions by human subjects of the divine subject. These are extreme cases, by the very definition of God. Yet to assume them is not a theoretical extreme in a sense that, by our criteria, can therefore be ruled out. There are some genuine extremes. The radical difference between a high-grade animal and an atom is not our invention. However, it is no absolute difference. The atom has self-movement, and this was Plato's definition of "soul." Greek dualisms of mind and mere matter were based on an illusion. Descartes' dualism was based on another illusion, that soul is wholly without spatial character. He declared this; he did not, and one cannot, prove its correctness, as various philosophers have since maintained.

Apart from these two false arguments for dualism, what is there that really stands up to analysis? Leibniz either was or was not right in holding that the merely inert objects we seem to perceive in nature are really collections of active entities. And the sense of spatiality that does not apply to human experiences is the sense that implies a multitude of entities imperceptibly small and hence with no motions perceivable by us unless the entire collective changes position. A rock falls for us if the mass of its particles changes location downwards grossly enough for us to see the difference. Its shape is the locations, very roughly sketched and taken as relatively unchanging, of its invisible constituents. Mere matter *ist ein Massenphänomen*, as one German Swiss writer says, and its singular members are not soulful unless on a very simple, low level.[4] They are trifling taken individually. This adequately accounts for the popularity of a more or less explicit dualism in human thought. Nevertheless, the notion of an absolute vacuum of mind anywhere in nature is a zero for which no non-question-begging evidence seems possible. I agree with Peirce, Whitehead, Bergson, and how many others that we do not need it. Mere matter explains nothing; not, for instance, how there can be causal influence from past to present, or from one part of space to another. Mind as prehensional does explain this. In any case it is mind or experience that we have to be concerned about.

The readers who know Husserl's work will not need to be told how different my phenomenology is from Husserl's. In some ways it is less different from Heidegger's. That our basic experience is of being-in-the-world is common ground, for our prehensions relate us not only to our own previous experiences but also to our bodily histories and through them to the world's history. In vague, indistinct fashion we feel ourselves in a vast whole. Through manipulation of things we feel our *Umwelt* and through our sense of kinship with others like us we feel our *Mitwelt*. Ortega Y Gassett and Merleau-Ponty agree roughly with Heidegger that the directly given is not limited to "hyletic data," but includes concrete processes that are as actual as one's own experiencings. Husserl's form of idealism, surprisingly close to Berkeley's, was for these three students, and for me, a clear mistake. Ortega and I saw this from the outset and for this did not need the others mentioned. I accepted epistemological realism before my European studies. The whole idea of an experience without independent data that are more than mere qualities, mere adjectives, has never been convincing to me. In addition, I (later) accepted Peirce's, "What we believe in our hearts we should not pretend to doubt in philosophy." Or again, "As if doubting were as easy as lying!"[5]

If phenomenology means taking a "presuppositionless" stance, then I think it repeats Descartes' mistake long after we should have learned better. Bracketing the world, setting aside all beliefs, would mean ceasing to talk or to think. Infants and apes have perceptions and memories, but they cannot philosophize. To get answers one must have questions, even if the answers are to concern the immediately and concretely given. Here Peirce's phaneroscopy is nearly exemplary. He started with elementary reflections upon some mathematical truths. Number theory arises from the ideas of one, two, three, or first, second, third. With a stroke of genius Peirce saw that 'second' presupposes 'first,' but not vice versa. Many a couple's first child has been their only child, but no couples' second child has been their only child, except in the sense of their only still living one. Counting thus illustrates two basic relationships, independence and one-way or nonsymmetrical dependence. With 'third' we have as presupposed a first and a second in their proper relationships. Here is the idea of a whole and its parts or constituents: $X \& Y = Z$. Given this we can combine wholes and reach any finite complexity.

Having these extremely abstract ideas, the point is to see how concrete experiencing embodies them. Here I incline to think Peirce made a subtle mistake. A particular second presupposes a particular first *that did not presuppose it*. Thus dependence and independence are both required. In experience as such, how is this illustrated? Is it not clear: present experience depends upon, requires, preceding experience. In memory this becomes manifest. But the previous experience did not require the successor that in fact has remembered it. Peirce's tychism establishes that. He is not a determinist. Thus both the first two categories are embodied in experiences as such, considered in opposite temporal directions. Yet Peirce refuses to allow this. Instead he defines Firstness as dependence upon no other thing "being what it is regardless of anything else." And Secondness he defines as being what it is relative to (dependent upon) just one other thing. Here Peirce takes too literally the numerical aspect of his concept, and fails to see that the non-numerical idea of dependence is the more general idea. Absolute independence of *everything* else is an extremely special case of independence. So is the idea of depending upon just one other thing. When we count things we are considering them from a special point of view, abstracting from various concrete differences. But phaneroscopy is seeking to understand the concrete.

In saying that an experience depends upon preceding experience, we are considering the experience as a unitary whole, not just in some limited aspect. Dependence upon one or more others is the general idea, the category; independence of one or more others is its negative. Experience in general suggests the idea of dependence upon one or more, perhaps all, predecessors but not on any successors in their full concreteness. This gives us the natural intuitive idea of causation. I required my ancestors to exist; they did not require me. Their having been is an aspect of my world, but my "going to be" was or is an aspect of their world only for a strict predestinarian or determinist. Peirce definitely (at the age of nearly forty) gave up classical determinism fifty years before quantum physics. (Somewhat earlier still the great Clerk Maxwell had strongly hinted that he did not believe it.) But in his theory of the phaneron Peirce failed to make full use of the asymmetrical view of becoming that in fact he was vigorously espousing in other contexts.

By taking independence of everything rather than independence of one or more things as the embodiment of Firstness, Peirce was forced to look for something extremely abstract rather than a concrete aspect of experience. In medieval or Aristotelian thought God was often defined as absolutely independent of all else. Oddly, Peirce does not usually mention this when he reiterates his definition of Firstness. What he does do, and one can see why, is to cite possibility as the independent. An actualization of a possibility presupposes the possibility, which did not depend on that actualization; granted indeterminism, many actualizations might never have taken place. But the present is precisely the real possibility, the causal condition, of the future!

Having gotten the idea of one-way dependence from the idea of counting, Peirce failed to see that this idea in its more than numerical meaning is what we need in interpreting experience as such. Living is incomparably more than counting. Dependence on zero other things is an extremely abstruse notion and remote from concrete actualities. But depending on ancestors, or on previous experiences, is precisely what concrete experience confronts us with all the time. Dependence on just one other thing is another abstruse idea of no obvious relevance to the concrete. For all we know we depend on an infinity of other things, if the creative process had no beginning.

If experiences are second to their predecessors and first to their successors, then what is Thirdness? Peirce says it is dependence on just two other things. Given that, we can combine thirds into superthirds and get any complexity needed. Peirce here seems to make a leap that lands him into the realization that a *universal* is a third something of which more than one, at least two other things are instances. Somehow from the transition from two to three he derives the idea of an abstraction. I was long puzzled about this. But suppose we return to the concepts, dependence–independence, and drop the question of *how many* other things are involved. There is still need for a third idea. Events, experiences, do not depend on their successors as they do on their predecessors, but still they depend on something besides just their predecessors. Our independence of the details of the future need not imply that we could be what we are were this the last moment of becoming, were there no future at all to work for or contribute to. Peirce defends in other contexts the idea of *probability* as a third between yes and no. Besides absolute dependence on past events and absolute independence of future events there can be a third relation also expressed in temporal terms; dependence on real possibilities and probabilities for the future. Since for Peirce the future does not consist of definite events and all definite events are past, particularization of the more or less vague possibilities for the future is for him the same as their actualization and becoming past. He says that no nominalist can understand the future. Its reality is generally, "objectively vague." Possibility and futurity are one. "It is the past that is actual." The future as given is phenomenal Thirdness. A purpose or plan is the paradigm universal. If its full particularity were included in it there would be nothing for realization to add. Universals are above all purposes for the future. Prehending the actuality of the past and helping to prepare for, decide, or bring about the actuality of the future is what life essentially is.

Peirce shows that he is slightly confused when he raises and *does not answer* the question, "Is Secondness basically symmetrical or asymmetrical?" Obviously the relation of second to first is one-way in the manner shown earlier. So Peirce on the one hand stayed too close to the numerical clue he started with, and on the other hand forgot the clue just where he needed it.

It remains true that Peirce's three categories represent a momentous contribution, as Peirce thought they did. His Firstness at least settles one basic issue of the time and of all time: are there external relations? The clearest, most useful definition of external relations is precisely in terms of independence. Peirce defined Firstness as a thing's being what it is "regardless of anything else." Change 'any' to 'some' and this gives us the not necessarily absolute independence we need for categorial generality. So, with his first category Peirce dismisses extreme internal-relations doctrines like those of Bradley, Royce, and Blanshard.

Peirce does not use the word "depend" as I have been using it, but he uses "relative to" or "with regard to"—meaning, I think, what I mean by "dependent upon." And his "regardless of" is my "independent of." Where he says Secondness is "a mode of being of one thing which consists in how a second object is," he is defining a constitutive or internal relation. Thus with his second category Peirce is dismissing extreme external relations doctrines like Hume's, Russell's, and so many others.

By admitting both categories Peirce allies himself with Whitehead and all those who see the twin absurdities of extreme monism and extreme pluralism. William James could be counted here, though he never succeeded in reaching a very clear generalization of the nonextreme doctrine so far as it concerns nonhuman individuals or dynamic singulars in general or as such.

With his Thirdness, Peirce did in some passages come close to saying what I want him to say, that Thirdness is basically futurity as neither wholly determinate nor wholly indeterminate. Consider the following.

> If the prediction has a tendency to be fulfilled, it must be that future events have a tendency to conform to a general rule. "Oh," but say the nominalists, "this general rule is nothing but a mere word or couple of words." I reply, "Nobody ever dreamed of denying that what is general is of the nature of a general sign, but the question is whether future events will conform to it or not. If they will, your adjective 'mere' seems to be ill-placed . . ." This mode of being which *consists*, mind my word if you please, the mode of being which *consists* in the fact that future facts of Secondness will take on a determinate general character I call Thirdness.[6]

In this passage Peirce dismisses nominalism without committing himself to a doctrine of similarity as partial identity, and without Whiteheadian eternal objects as I understand and criticize them. Compared to what any number of philosophers in this century have written, including even so wise a thinker as the mature Bergson, I think Peirce in his phaneroscopy comes closer to the truth about the logical structure of reality than anyone else except Whitehead, and in some respects surpasses even him. If Whitehead excels, it is by the doctrine of quantum actualities and the doctrine of prehending. Also by his coming much closer to a formulation of theism in terms of a coherent system of categories.

Bergson's best contribution to the analysis of the phaneron is also the one least noticed. It is his account of dreams, where he, first of all the philosophers that I know about, pointed to the two chief traits of dreaming that are common to it and waking experience. These are the positive functionings in both cases of personal memory and the sensing of the dreamer's actual bodily condition. The dreamer hears sounds that are actually sounding around him, is cold and the cold appears in the dream, is sexually excited, which also appears. Bergson gives a number of examples; I have experienced these and still others. The commonest perhaps has been needing to urinate and dreaming of that condition. As for memory, of course it is there, for one's sense of identity is (indistinctly) there and memory is a principle component of that. The importance of these facts is this. An argument against realism has been that in dreams nothing other than the dreaming itself is given as actually there and is there; hence perhaps waking experience could occur without any independent reality being given. So we have Berkeley's account (virtually Husserl's) of perception as merely of one's own "ideas," but constituting a world because of their orderliness and (partial) predictability. Descartes prepared the way for this, as is well known. The argument from an unrealistic view of dreams prepared the way for an unrealistic view of waking experience. The argument collapses if even dreams give us actual bodily conditions.

The irony is that Norman Malcolm defines realistic dreams out of existence by declaring they are not really dreams because the one having them is not really asleep. Either this is a viciously "persuasive" redefinition of dreaming or it is such a redefinition of sleeping. I say it is real dreaming and real sleeping.

Malcolm makes it clear that his motive is to destroy the skeptical argument against realism. But Bergson had shown how to do that. Had Malcolm read Bergson on dreams? He told me he had not. When I read Malcolm on the subject, I immediately went to Bergson and found the truth—yes, various relativists, the truth, not simply what it is currently fashionable to accept. Indeed, it is not very fashionable to accept the truth here. But it should be, now that Bergson has written so well about it.

Bergson's famous description of becoming, confused by declarations that it is indescribable, or describable only in irrational terms (such as by using a symmetrical term like "interpenetration" to express an asymmetrical view of a past retained in unconscious memory and a future that does not in advance exist even as a wholly definite possibility) is, so far as it is true to the phaneron, better said independently by Peirce and Whitehead. But neither of these hit the target on dreaming. Bergson did. However, Peirce came to the equivalent of Bergson's view of the permanent reality of past events, as did Whitehead (probably in this case influenced by Bergson).

The writer of these lines has been criticized as going through the history of philosophy looking for agreements and disagreements. As my two most historical books tried to show, I have gone through the history of philosophy trying to find out who had shown what.[7] I am an anti-compatibilist because of James's cogency in "The Dilemma of Determinism." I believe in a changing deity, rather than a wholly changeless one, because my teacher Hocking gave me a convincing argument for this view. He came to it largely through James. I came to a realistic interpretation of dreams because of Bergson's arguments. I am a psychicalist because of the arguments of Leibniz and many others, plus the fact that before knowing any of these writers I found direct experience was pervasively of feeling, akin to pleasures and pains, and later found philosophers who also intuited experience in that fashion.

I was looking for truth before I was looking for agreement. Much of what I believe is rather reasonably read into Plato or Aristotle, or both. Epicurus was an anti-compatibilist, I think for the same reason as James was. Each great philosopher has had some things right, or nearly right. I do not recall ever thinking, after my early teens, that any thinker has had everything right. I believe in the pervasiveness of chance because of Peirce's admirable arguments for this view, which I thought quite odd when I first heard about it (from the logician H. M. Sheffer, one of my teachers). I believe that becoming is quantized because of the Whitehead–von Wright arguments plus my knowledge of the trouble Peirce and Bergson both got into by trying to defend complete continuity, not only of pure or logical possibility but also of actuality. I believe, however, in the non-quantizability of logical possibility, and hence disbelieve in Whitehead's eternal objects (as a definite multitude) because of Peirce's reasons on this point. If this way of using the history of ideas is not one good way I should like to know why.

One of the ways in which philosophers differ widely is in the use they make of their predecessors or contemporaries. Some, early in their development, find one philosopher particularly congenial to themselves and then judge all the others largely by the standards proposed and more or less realized by that one philosopher. It may be Hume, it may be Kant, or one so far back as Plato, Aristotle, or Aquinas; or it may be one so recent as Husserl, Heidegger, or Wittgenstein. Other philosophers find a number of thinkers congenial in some aspect of their views but uncongenial in other aspects, and form a habit of expecting to agree *and* disagree with other thinkers more or less equally emphatically, depending on which elements in their thought are in question.

The differences between the two classes of philosophers are not absolute. Plato seems to have begun as a disciple of Socrates but more and more tried to take all his predecessors into account. Aristotle began as a Platonist but also tried to take the others all into account. It happened that my very early hero was Emerson, and then Royce (in one book) but before I knew much about other writers than these two, I arrived at some elements of my own incipient system by which, from then on, I tended on some issues to judge philosophers.[8] I had ceased to be an Emersonian or Roycean, and soon thereafter began to take a number of other thinkers somewhat seriously for diverse reasons. This stage lasted four or five years. Then came Husserl, Heidegger, and several others, none of whom became really central in my thought. Then, at one and the same time, Peirce and Whitehead came home to me in a way no one since Emerson had done before.

In Peirce and Whitehead both I found writers whose sources of inspiration seemed even less centralized in some one thinker than was my own. They both seemed to have learned from most of the great philosophers. Peirce, a creative formal logician, even tried for a while to take Hegel seriously and did take Aristotle, Scotus, Occam, Descartes, Leibniz, Kant, and some British and American empiricists seriously. Whitehead wrestled with the pre-Socratics, Plato, Aristotle, and the theology of the Church Fathers; with Descartes, Spinoza, Locke, Hume, Berkeley, Kant, some Hegelians, James, Dewey, Santayana, Russell. I deeply distrust those contemporary thinkers who largely dispense with the philosophers of other centuries than our own. This may work fairly well in physics, but not so well in philosophy. I think that the best philosophers are eclectic in a good sense and take intellectual history as a principal source of ideas and arguments.

As an eclectic phenomenologist, I can say the following. Husserl was right in seeking the source of meanings in concrete experience as such but dismally wrong in trying to conceive experience in abstraction from an actual world, without any genuine givenness of dynamic agents other than the experiencing or experiencer itself—in short, to abstract from the social structure of experience. Nothing is left with this abstraction. Husserl was also wrong to look for "evidence" of a kind that only God could enjoy. Heidegger was right to distinguish the *Umwelt* from the *Mitwelt*, but failed to take sufficiently into account the possibility that the "around-world" really is a "with-world" so far as singular agents, dynamic singulars, are concerned. The mere with-world is a world of collectives, with no active singulars other than animals as awake and experiencing.

Merleau-Ponty was right to reject the notion that minds could operate without bodies, and his generalized idea of "flesh" has truth in it. Even God has a body, as Plato said long ago. However, it is *the* body, the cosmos.

Peirce was right that there are external relations (independence of some things from some other things), also internal relations (dependence of some things upon some other things), and that futurity and possibility belong together (as he knew Aristotle had seen). But Peirce tied down the dependence too closely to the particular number of things toward which there is or is not dependence. And he did not focus sharply enough on the asymmetry of the basic dependencies.

Bosanquet, Bradley, Croce, Berkeley, the psychologist Spearman (and some others), and most recently Whitehead were right in stressing the inseparability of sensation and certain kinds of feeling, as is most obvious in pains, pleasures, sweet tastes and smells, bitter or sour tastes or smells, but is more subtly discernable even in colors. Heidegger hints at the idea in *Sein und Zeit*. Heidegger was also at least partly right to say that we understand the qualities of nature apart from ourselves "by diminution" of our own qualities. Fully worked out this should get rid of an absolute dualism of mind and mere mindless matter. The diminution is not to a zero of anything and everything psychical. A zero of thought in any usual meaning there may be (apart from ubiquitous divine thoughts functioning as laws of nature), but not of feeling and a sense of the past and the future—memory and anticipation—though these elements can be indefinitely diminished in scope and complexity of distinct details.

There are philosophers whose talents seem not to involve much phenomenological insight. Perhaps the most widely influential recent American philosopher is Quine, the logician. I see him as an example of this limitation. Richard Rorty, much cited for his criticisms of modern philosophy, and remarkably aware of most of its recent phases, seems to me another. In his view the most important philosophers of this century are Dewey, Heidegger, and Wittgenstein. In Dewey I see something of a phenomenologist, especially in his treatment of ethical, aesthetic, and religious experiences. He has a sharp sense for what I regard with him as the superstitious (I would say idolatrous) exaltation of the eternal and immutable in theory of values. Heidegger I have dealt with this. Wittgenstein's contribution to phaneroscopy I find chiefly in some remarks of his about the necessary relations of color qualities. There seems some overlap with what I wrote on this subject in my book on sensation.[9] Dewey was aware that experience, naturally interpreted, refutes compatibilism, an artificial doctrine accepted by Rorty. Quine (like Carnap in this) gave up determinism, if at all, only because of what physicists had been saying on the subject.

I have found no very clear indication in Wittgenstein on the subject, but I think he was not a determinist. My acid test of a thinker's insight into experience as such is his stand on determinism. By this test the founders of pragmatism, all three, pass, but Rorty, who admires two of them, does not. Among linguistic analysts, Austin stands out. He asked Isaiah Berlin, "Does anyone really believe in determinism as we all believe we all die?" The pragmatists (Rorty calls himself one) believed in some degree of tychism, some qualification to classical causality.

My own nomination to the status of greatest of living philosophers is Karl Popper.[10] Is he a phenomenologist? His concentration on physics and biology is one reason for his limited interest in this aspect of philosophy. A factor favoring such an interest is his intense musicality. Another is his unusual early exposure to Christianity, his parents being Jews who converted to Christianity in order, he says, to avoid antagonizing members of the major religion of his society. He respects religious people but avoids definite religious doctrines. He is not a disciple of any definite other philosopher, but an eclectic in what I call the good sense. He is not a compatibilist, which argues sensitivity to the difference between the actual past and possible-probable future as the only past or future that is really believed in, or lived by. He realizes the positive value of unpredictability, as vividly illustrated in music and in the scientific enterprise where the aim is not finally to predict the detailed future but to falsify alleged predictions in order to come closer to the mixture of order and disorder that is reality. I think he would not quarrel with Whitehead's "disorder is as real as order."[11] He told Einstein that God, if one must use that word, would find a world with an open future more interesting than a world in which only ignorance explains inability to predict everything.

That Popper never accepted positivism is another sign of his closeness to actual experience. He clearly holds that what experience discloses is being in a world, not mere sense data or hyletic data, either as mere appearances of the unknowable or as the only reality.

I have not so far used the sacred term *intentionality*. In Husserl's use of it I find a momentous ambiguity. It is one thing to have a conscious hypothesis, a supposition; it is another thing to have a *given* actuality. In memory we have actual past experience itself indistinctly given, not a mere thought that there was this experience. In perception we have cellular feelings indistinctly given, not merely supposed to have occurred. What Husserl calls *intending* is not what I (or Whitehead) call *having a datum* or *prehending*. Whitehead's "symbolic reference" takes care of intending, and so does Peirce's theory of signs. The given is commonly taken as a sign in adult human experience. That which something given is taken as a sign of may not exist or occur, but the given did exist or occur. I define the given in an experience as the independent causal conditions of the experience. Givenness *is* causal conditioning, where experiences are the effects. To intuit, feel, or prehend something is not to infer it from the given—that is symbolic reference. The lower the level of the experience the less of such reference. Givenness is important, not to furnish a definite and secure starting point for inference but to explain in principle the causal structure of the world, to furnish what Hume asked for, an "impression" of "necessary connection," where the necessary is strict only as from effect to cause, not as from cause to effect.

Husserl sometimes called himself a Cartesian; I incline to think he was also far too close to Berkeley, and to Kant, but without things in themselves as wholly inaccessible—a doctrine that almost reduces Kant to Berkeley, apart from the theistic question. Certainly there was much originality (and ingenuity) in Husserl's work. Originality, of course, is not identical with truth. I cannot see that the Europeans, with Husserl and Heidegger, were as fortunate as we in my country, with James, Royce, Dewey, Santayana, Peirce, and Whitehead. My Harvard teachers included three of the most brilliant students of James and Royce: Perry, Hocking, and Lewis. The last was well aware of Dewey. By good luck I also encountered Husserl and Heidegger. So perhaps I know something of what the whole development comes to.

CHAPTER THREE

Negative Facts and the Analogical Inference to 'Other Mind'

I wish to focus on a little-noticed implication of the pretended skepticism that says: perhaps other human beings are mere behaving bodies, and I alone am a behaving and experiencing (feeling, sensing, thinking) person. I suppose the "skeptic" to concede that, behavior for behavior, others are not observed to be in principle less adaptable, less able to reach the goals their behavior suggests to observation, than he is himself. Under "behavior," I also include physiological structure, even microscopic. My point then is, the skeptical hypothesis entails the notion of a mere privation, a purely "negative fact." The proposal runs, "My neighbor's body and behavior are just what they might be if he did have thoughts and feelings, but for all I know the thoughts and feelings simply aren't there." The hypothetical absence of experience would, thus, be a sheer privation with no positive significance whatever. But is such a *merely* negative fact so much as intelligible?

How do we detect "negative facts"? The question has been much discussed, but not always with sufficient clarity concerning its exact meaning. Am I happy? No, because I feel intense anxiety or mild annoyance. Is there anyone in the room? No, because whichever way I look I see something I should not see were there a human being in that direction. Thus I see the opposite walls, and people are not transparent: I see the chairs with a completeness, which would be impossible if anyone were sitting in one of them. In all cases of verified negative judgments, the verification depends on *positive* characters, which are incompatible with some proposed positive character. We do not see simply "not blue," but various other colors; we do not see merely "not round," but various other shapes, or perhaps a homogeneous expanse with vaguely delimited boundaries. Similarly, I suggest, "not conscious" or "insentient" is meaningful only if some positive character is incompatible with being conscious or sentient. But the skeptic is not affirming such a character, even hypothetically.

27

He is saying, granted a perfectly good human body, equivalent to mine, still perhaps feeling is absent. I suggest that he is here talking nonsense, in that no such purely negative trait of a situation is ever observed, nor can we conceive how it might be observed. One may simply fail to experience X, being perhaps dead or asleep (states that themselves are partly positive); or one may, if you wish, experience "the absence of X," but this itself is a positive act, and it requires a partly positive datum. We are offered no such positive datum, even hypothetically, for the supposed absence of feeling in normal bodies.

It is to be noted, also, that whereas my feelings are given, at least for me, in memory or retrospection, and your feelings for you, an absence of feeling (including sensation) in me could only be observed by someone else. But, according to the theory we are considering, this is impossible (so long as I act as a waking person). One would have to observe in my alert and active body a sort of hole in reality, a vacuum, which might have been filled with feeling, but in fact is not. However, vacua, in the sense in which they do exist, have positive characteristics. Things go on in them that would not go on if any bodies, e.g., air molecules, were present. But the supposed vacuum of feelings releases no positive possibility, which the presence of feeling would curtail. Therefore, we are dealing with a meaningless idea.

The "skeptical hypothesis" concerning other minds, then, confronts us with the disjunction: *either* the "argument by analogy" to other minds is cogent *or* the notion of mere privation is legitimate. But is the notion legitimate? In the light of this question, the contention "'other mind' is unobservable" loses some at least of its terrors. For X's mind is observable, at least by X, but a mere privation of mind in X, by no one!

I do not at all wish to imply that X's mind is observable *only* by X. This notion seems to arise partly from underestimating the relative truth in behaviorism, and still more from an arbitrary restriction of "observer" or "experiencer" to the human case. (Nor am I thinking merely of a divine observer.) But in this chapter I am arguing: *at worst*, the unobervability of X's mind (his body being normally active) is relative, while that of the absence of his mind under these conditions must be absolute. Hence this absence has no standing in speculation.

We must, no doubt, grant that there could be entities whose effects upon the world were too subtle for our means of detection: however, this possibility cannot be relevant to my neighbor's mind, for the "expression" of feeling and purpose in one's own behavior includes many aspects that are not especially subtle. The positive meaning of an "absence" must be somehow appropriate or proportional to this absence. Otherwise it would not be the positive meaning of just that absence.

A possible objection to our argument might be the following: suppose there were "no world," what could this be but a sheer privation, a complete vacuum of being? I reply, What indeed, and for that very reason should we not suspect the idea of being nonsensical—even though we are thereby committed to holding that the existential statement "some world or other is real" is necessarily true? Here we recall the current dogma that *all* existential statements are contingent. The dogma perhaps commits a category mistake. Existential statements mentioning particular or specific existents—men, lions, Churchill—are contingent; but existential statements of such a form as, "The most general class of concrete particulars is not empty," are not only on a high, but in a significant sense, the highest, logical level, or level of abstractness, and they commit one to no proposition on any lower level, even though they say that there are some on lower levels that are true. There is thus no reason why the contingency of the lower levels must carry over to the highest. Each particular, or special class of particulars, may be contingent, even though "there are *some* particulars or other" is not: just as, "You must do *something*" does not say that there is any particular thing you must do.

A theist, of course, might suppose that "No world exists" means, "God enjoys his own solitariness," or "He knows that he has not created anything." This is in a way positive, but is it self-consistent? It implies that creating is something deity might or might not do, whereas perhaps any coherent meaning of "deity" includes an activity of creating, not necessarily this world, but some world or other. And is not the notion of a knower knowing only himself absurd? Could even God observe a mere privation? I hold that we have no right to suppose this, since we have no idea what he would be observing as the objective situation. "Nothing" is not a situation. In any case, even if there could be divine knowledge of a mere privation, this knowledge itself (that God has not created a world, though he might have done so) would be a positive fact, and a contingent one. Hence if "world" means something existing contingently, even a theist cannot consistently maintain that all contingent facts might be purely negative.

I have elsewhere argued at length that "the nonexistence of God" could have no possible positive meaning, and that this suffices to render it logically null and void. Whether this justifies "God exists" depends only upon whether this apparent assertion is more than verbally positive, and upon whether it is self-consistent. But if it really asserts something and something noncontradictory then, since its denial is meaningless, it must be true. This is Anselm's great discovery, persistently misunderstood. Anselm failed only to make sure that "God exists" is in better case than "no God exists" with respect to its positive character and consistency. Indeed, with his type of theism, I maintain that consistency is in truth lacking. But if another type can avoid this defect then his argument becomes valid, in support of that type.[1]

A thoughtful reader may wonder if I have not contradicted myself. For I have said that "God exists" may be necessarily true, while in a previous paragraph it is said that statements asserting the existence of "particular or specific existents" are contingent. Is not God a specific, indeed a particular existent?

I answer, certainly not.[2] He is individual, but to confuse this with specific or particular is another category mistake, which is only possible because theistic philosophers have done their job so poorly. I say this bluntly because I have strong feelings in the matter. It is tragically true that the theistic problem has been mishandled precisely by those supposed to be its most masterly exponents. Specificity, particularity, and individuality are irreducibly distinct ideas, all three, and it is above all in dealing with the idea of God that their confusion is most fatal. Ordinary individuals are close enough to particulars and species to come under the same rule of contingency, but even with them there is a real distinction between all three aspects, and the uniqueness of God includes a uniquely vast gap in him between particularity on the one hand and individuality on the other, and by virtue of this infinite gap (for it has no finite measure) the rule forbidding the necessity of particulars is quite compatible with the necessity of the divine individuality, or of God's bare existence as God. God is just not a "particular individual"; this phrase is sheer absurdity in his case. Yet he is individual, and he is particular. I have explained this elaborately elsewhere and shall not repeat the entire analysis here.[3] In my view, what is particular about God's existence is not who exists or *that* he exists, but only *how*, or in what concrete "state," he exists. The state itself is particular and therefore it is contingent: what is necessary is only that *some* state *or other*, expressive of the divine individuality, will be actualized *no matter what* else is actual or inactual. I hold that the divine individuality differs from others not in being less flexible in its capacity for alternative states, as some of the supposed masters of doctrine tell us, but the exact opposite, in being infinitely flexible, precisely and incomparably the most variable of all individualities. But just as we remain "ourselves" through a certain limited range of variations, so does God, but through an unlimited range. God is not the least but the *most* "movable" of all movers of others, the most able to be himself through absolutely infinite variations in concrete detail.

I think that Indian philosophy has been closer to seeing this, in some of its many traditions, than the main stream at least of European philosophy. It is, however, a plain implication of Whitehead's doctrine of the Consequent Nature of God.

The almost universal neglect in the literature of the requirement that all fact have its positive aspect, and of the immense consequences for metaphysics of this requirement illustrates, to my mind, how rudimentary current analyses of "metaphysical statements" mostly are. In my opinion, nearly all the energy has been put into analyzing the aberrations of metaphysicians, not the essential meaning of the metaphysical enterprise. That "we cannot know the past," or other minds, and the like paradoxes are egregious failures in the trial and error business of groping for the metaphysical truths. The acceptance of the impossibility of merely negative facts, with its implications and applications, and other sober logical (and axiological) truisms, and their implications, will be among the successes of metaphysics, when it begins to have success. Perhaps it has already had some, but the writers who have contributed most to it during the past one hundred years are not at the moment being read very widely.

Assuming the axiom of positivity, the argument by analogy to other minds, while not indeed the full explanation of how we know "other minds" (this would be a task for another occasion), appears nevertheless cogent, since skepticism concerning it depends upon an idea of mere privation, which has no standing in experience and no positive coherent meaning whatever.

The reader will also note that phenomenalism is likewise cut off by the same type of argument. If the positive character of actual and potential experience is entirely *as if* there were an independent world, then there is (only, however, in the sense of "independent," which has positive meaning in some mode of experience!). For the contrary view asserts a hypothetical absence, which would be simply that, and this no one could conceivably experience or genuinely conceive. Nor are manifestly skeptical doctrines the only ones cut off by the principle "every fact must have positive aspects." Certain forms of dualism also fail to meet its demand. It is one of the most powerful of truistic axioms. Yet I believe it really is a truism—that is, not open to well-considered denial. (The attempts to deny it sometimes fail to distinguish between partly and wholly negative facts. Our axiom does not say, "A factual statement must, or even can, have *exclusively* positive implications"; it merely denies the possibility of the contrary extreme, that it can have exclusively negatives ones.[4])

When Heidegger, echoing Schopenhauer, asks, "Why is there something rather than nothing?" he seems to suppose the question has a consistent meaning. But does it? (Perhaps he does not intend the query to have a literal meaning.) "There is something" is incapable of falsity. "There" already implies something.

Lest it seem intolerably suspicious that so much be held to follow from a mere truism, I must add that the propositions thus derived are all capable of cogent support in other ways, without employing the axiom of the positivity of fact. Certainly, in the present instance (the belief in other human minds), one need not have connected this belief with the axiom in order to be perfectly and reasonably confident of its validity. Nevertheless, appeal to the axiom affords welcome confirmation,[5] here and elsewhere; while no "counterintuitive" consequences appear to follow.

CHAPTER FOUR

Perception and the Concrete Abstractness of Science

It is a truism that science gives us an abstract description of reality. Ryle has compared this description to the financial accounting of a college in contrast to its actual life. It is easy to see why this analogy should have occurred to him. A chemical formula for sugar omits the sweet taste we enjoy when we eat sugar; a physical formula for redness, whether of a light-reflecting object or of light itself, omits the sensory quality we enjoy (or suffer) when we see red things. Science uses the sensory ("secondary") qualities as mere indices of abstract structures such as vibration rates. The colorful rich world of daily experience (the *Lebenswelt*) makes the scientific picture seem rather empty, a result of wholesale omission. And so there is naturally resistance to the pronouncement often made that the scientific objects are the realities and the sensory appearances of these objects are subjective, real only so far as human or animal experiences are real. However, I think we should equally resist the converse statement that the life-world is the concrete reality and the scientific picture but an abstract catalogue of the things manifest in that world. Nor is it enough to say that both worlds are real. The correct view is more complex and more subtle than any of these three propositions even begins to express.

First, science does not simply abstract from, omit, certain of the *positive* features of the perceived world; it also adds enormously to those features. To the obvious macroscopic organisms in nature it adds microorganisms, a whole subworld to itself, including the cells of which all visible plants and animals are composed. To the obvious stars in the sky it adds galaxies and island universes. To the obvious stones, bodies of water, and diaphanous air it adds molecules, atoms, and particles. To water waves it adds air and light waves and a vast system of kinds of waves. To the obvious cases of motion it adds many forms of movement of which mere common sense knows nothing, e.g., the Brownian movement, or that motion that is one aspect of what heat is, apart from the sensations of animals. To the obvious contrasts between parents and offspring it adds very unobvious and far greater contrasts between living species and their extinct ancestors and predecessors.

Second, and in part as a corollary of the foregoing, it is not only science that abstracts; our very sense perceptions do this for us. Sense experience is an enormous *simplification of* the perceived world. Where there are billions of individuals (cells, molecules), direct experience gives us only gross outlines of quasi-individual groups of these individuals. Where there are complicated rapid motions, perception gives us only a statistical averaging out or neutralization of these motions, as in the sensation of heat. Where every cell in the retina has its own unique processes and each of the still more numerous molecules in the seen object its more primitive processes, we may experience but a small number of shapes and colors. What is this if not an extreme form of abstraction, though one performed not by but for us as conscious beings—partly by our bodies and partly by mental functions that escape conscious introspection?

Of course we all know the ways in which the implications of the foregoing paragraphs can be evaded. 'Molecule,' we may be told, is but a conceptual device useful in predicting or controlling experience. Or in Dewey's terms, it is our recognition of certain possibilities of interaction between organism and environment. I wonder where we are to stop in explaining away the discoveries of science about the individual constituents of nature. Are cells only conceptual devices? I admit that what Dewey says is close to what some quantum physicists say. This raises questions I have not succeeded in judging with any approach to competency, because of my limited mathematical abilities. Still, I venture to say, in the words of Whitehead, "Science is not a fairy tale."[1] Nor is it mere adaptation to an unknown reality. When physicists speak of atoms, they do not normally mean a concept, or concepts, but particular items in nature as nature might be (and once was) without any animals similar to man. But no such items are directly and definitely encountered, one by one, in the life-world.

Leibniz, not Hume or Kant, first gave the clue to the double character of science just considered—that it enriches as well as impoverishes our world picture and is at once more and less abstract than common sense. The Leibnizian clue is that all our perceptions are "indistinct." (Leibniz also used the word "confused.") Kant was right in objecting to one feature of this doctrine as Leibniz intended it, namely, the contention that the perceived world is merely represented or "mirrored," rather than actually given. As Kant said, the given is the concrete or individual in contrast to the abstract or universal. It does not follow, however, that the individual is *distinctly* given. Individual constituents of inorganic nature are all imperceptibly small, as the great Greek materialists correctly surmised. And not even other macroscopic animals, nor oneself, as individuals can be perceived more than relatively distinctly by any of us.

Our memories of our own pasts are mostly very indistinct, with a few patches standing out less unclearly than the others. *All* human or animal intuitions, whether perceptual or mnemonic, must fail to exhibit concrete individuals in their full concreteness or definiteness.

Science and perception are both abstract; but there are two forms of abstractness. In one form details, special cases of some general property, are left out of account; in the other form one or more general properties are omitted. Science is abstract in the latter sense, for it sets aside the entire class of what are often called secondary and tertiary qualities and substitutes the so-called primary qualities, which are really structures rather than qualities in the distinctive sense. Perception yields both structure and quality, but neither one with distinctness and sharply individual detail.

What is the conclusion? I think it is this: where direct perception yields positive qualities, there (or somewhere in the situation) these qualities exist; but where (as everywhere in [so-called] inorganic nature) perception fails to exhibit individuals as possessors of the qualities, while science has valid evidence that the individuals exist, there and to this extent it is science that reveals the reality. It is tautological that no one can visually perceive the "nonexistence of invisibly small individuals"; all one can do if they exist (and why not?) is to fail to perceive their existence. Consequently, it is mere logic that direct perception cannot be the criterion for the existence or nonexistence of individuals other than those above the threshold of the resolving power of our vision and touch. What is left if not scientific inference from perception? Accordingly, to condescend to science as essentially and exclusively abstract, as Ryle and many others have done, is a blunder. Only science can decide what very large (but less than [cosmic or] divine) or what very small entities there are. Mere perception has to be limited by the capacities of the sense organs and the degree of distinctness of the human modes of intuition. On the other hand, it is perception, not scientific inference, at least as science is now constituted, that reveals qualitative aspects of reality.

It may seem question-begging to term perception indistinct simply because it misses individuals whose reality is established only by science, taken realistically. However, the indistinctness is apparent, even apart from the theories of science. Consider *transitive* relations such as qualitative sameness for perception, as when we perceive no difference between color samples A and B, or between B and C, or C and D, but do perceive a difference between A and D. Consider the speckled hen the number of whose specks cannot be counted. Consider, as the level-headed Greek atomists did, the many indications in ordinary experience that the visible qualities of things tell us next to nothing directly about the things' possible or probable behavior. One white powder will explode if ignited or pounded; another white powder will do nothing of the kind. Color seems beautifully irrelevant to the dynamic natures of things. Vision gives no direct clues as to weight, hardness, magnetic features, and many other behavioral properties. Again, why do smells come of themselves to the sense organ, while colors require light? Neither sense gives any direct answer, nor do the two together do so. The world of sense appearances is obviously hiding much of what matters to civilized humanity about the things appearing. Therefore, I cannot be persuaded that Aristotle was being very bright, or Leucippus, Democritus, and Epicurus anything but *very* bright in their thinking about this matter. What a feeble attempt it was when Aristotle tried to derive from touch qualities (warm, cold, wet, and dry) the explanation of physical transformations!

If sensory appearances are hiding so much, what is the means of this hiding? Is there some film of stuff, or largely opaque veil, between us and nature? Rather, "appearance," as contrasted to "reality," is essentially negative. It is not something experienced but a partial failure to experience. The stuff between us and things is, with one *qualification* to be noted in the next paragraph, simply the indistinctness of our sense intuitions themselves. Not that we are merely intuiting our own intuitions. No, we intuit independent realities, but in some only of their real qualities, and we intuit these qualities abstractly with individual outlines drastically blurred. In short, there is no veil; but direct experiencing is limited in its capacity to appreciate details. This limitation is to be taken as an ultimate principle. Moreover, the idea of an unlimited or perfect capacity to apprehend details and individual qualities is remarkably like one of the many ways of defining deity. That our direct experience is only more or less distinct may be a way of putting the point that we are not God.

One other distinction is required. Granted that in perception we directly experience independent reality, it is a further question whether this reality is (at least chiefly) inside our own skins or around us in the environment. I hold, with Spinoza and Whitehead, that the primary physical data are inside our skins. To this extent there is indeed a stuff, a veil, between us and the "external world." But this veil is physiological. By perception we normally acquire much reliable knowledge of that external world, but we have been learning how to do this since infancy, or even since fetal stages. So of course we form perceptual judgments about the environment extremely rapidly, easily, and in many respects accurately. The realism that forgets the generic development encapsulated in this fact is indeed "naïve." Appearance as veil consists of physiological processes translating (of course not perfectly or without "noise") some external events. What we most directly possess in sensory experience is essentially the physiological surrogates or analogues of external structures. Science is finding out how these analogues are produced, and why, for normal purposes, they are quite reliable. But all physical process, whether inside or outside the skin, involves vast complexities that we cannot distinctly intuit. Hence the physiological account cannot of itself explain the basic failure of perception to directly reveal the fine structures of the world. The explanation must be found in experiencing itself, or mind as such (apart from any eminent or divine form).

If we now return to the other side of science, its genuine abstractness, its impoverishment of the world picture, we can, I think, see possibilities for a synthesis of science and ordinary life as each in its way revelatory of the natures of things. We know our own experience not merely as having certain spatiotemporal structures but also as having certain qualities, sensory or emotional—a rich treasure that is not described in books on physics, chemistry, or even physiology, so far as they stick austerely to their subjects. A blind or deaf man can understand these sciences, but he misses a part of the ordinary *Lebenswelt*. Whether or not the sensory and emotional qualities are confined to animals more or less similar to ourselves, they are certainly *in nature*, unless nature is arbitrarily limited to what is outside the skins of such animals. The qualities are at least in us, and we are in the spatiotemporal scheme of things. "Idealistic" arguments to the contrary seem to me weak.

Three questions remain. (a) Are the qualities merely in our minds, or are they also in our bodies? (b) Do the qualities, or qualities more *or less* similar, occur elsewhere in nature than in high-grade animals? (c) How far down the scale of individuals, from man to atom or particle, is there something at least remotely like such qualities (in the sense in which a vibration rate is not even remotely like blue or sweet—indeed there is a logical-type difference)? Leibniz was the first to put this third query sharply; since his time Peirce and Whitehead have considered and somewhat revised his answers; most philosophers, so far as I can see, are pre-Leibnizian in not clearly seeing even what the problem is. For they never reckon carefully with the evidence, apparent long ago to Democritus, far stronger now, that conscious sense experience omits and abstracts as genuinely as science does, though in a different way. Only a combination of thought and sense can give us such awareness of the concreteness of things as falls within our capacity.

Whatever may lack sensory qualities, experiences do not lack them. To deny that red is in the experience of red is to talk nonsense, as G. E. Moore did in his famous "refutation" (later, on this point, rightly repudiated).[2] But it does not follow, in spite of Ducasse, that the redness is *only* in our experience.[3] If we are aware of a red something or process, then there is, in our experience, not simply red but a red something. And this something is not merely our experience of it. Experience, awareness, is never simply of itself, but is always a more or less transparent response to a given.

Husserl's disciples in general unluckily missed and obscured this truism by their ambiguous or question-begging term "intentionality." One can mean or intend a mere possibility, but experiencing is never merely intending. It is always a having of a given, and this given cannot be a mere "claim" that something is actual; it is always an actuality. Nor can it be a mere quality, a "hyletic datum." Rather, to intend is to use a *given* qualified actuality as sign

of something not effectively given. Nor can the given depend upon the experience. It is always independent. The reflective experience for which an experience is itself given is, as Husserl almost says but seems not to grasp clearly, an
immediately *subsequent* experience, and is thus a special form or use of memory,
what Husserl first called "primary memory" and then later "retention." His first
usage was best, since the contrasting term is not mere memory but recollection
(*Wiedererinnerung*), remembering after forgetting. Simple memory, not complicated by intervening forgetting, is just memory. Thus it can be held that
every experience has something other than itself as simply possessed, rather
than merely intended, claimed, posited, inferred, or what have you.

What is this given something? It has two main forms: (a) previous experience by the same person, and (b) other types of events that are not obviously, but are perhaps really, also experiences, though not experiences by the
same person. The first form occurs in what we normally call memory; the
other in what we call perception, the data of which *always* include events
in the members of one's own body. In being aware of these members one
is not a self aware of that very self. One is, at least at a given moment, a
single individual; one's bodily members are a vast *multitude* of other (though
only relatively independent) individuals. The longer philosophers neglect this
elementary distinction between self as knower and the self's body, the longer
will confusion about the structure of perception persist. In sensory experience
vast numbers of individuals are (indistinctly) given. These individuals are not
the experience; there is a subject–object distinction, and while the subject (the
momentary experience) is one, the objects are numerous.

Consider a pain. One experiences the pain; however, the pain is not the
experience, but the datum of the experience. (It is an element in the experience, but inclusion is not identity.) Nor can the given be produced by the
experience, for what an experience produces is precisely what is not given to it.
Experience is a partly free, self-creative response, not to that very experience
but to something else that must be there to make the experience possible. This
is why we cannot avoid pain simply by refusing to produce it, and cannot turn
it into physical pleasure simply by producing that.

An old controversy about pain derives partly from a failure to recognize
the duality in all experience, its subject–object structure. In experience of red
(or of pain) the red (or pain) quality belongs *both* to the experience and to the
experienced. It belongs to the former, for otherwise what is the difference
between experience of red (or pain) and that of green (or pleasure)? The contrast in object qualities becomes derivatively also a contrast in experience (or
subject) qualities. Now the controversy referred to is this: some say pain is a
sensation, some say it is a feeling, others say it is a sensation to which normally
a certain feeling is attached. Normally pains are disturbing, that is the feeling;
but indifferent or masochistic experiences are possible in which pains seem
either neutral or even enjoyable.

I think the truth is more subtle than any of these descriptions. The pain as independent datum is not *my* feeling, for that would be dependent. The pain as *my* disturbance is of course my feeling, and dependent on me as subject, but this is the pain quality as an attribute not of the datum but of the experience. There is a to-me-painful awareness of a painful datum. What is this datum? We have sufficient evidence to locate it somewhere in the bodily processes. Just where in these processes is a secondary question; the point is that the processes are somatic, belonging initially to human cells, not to human experiences or minds. Put simply and roughly, certain of my cells suffer; as aware of their suffering I, too, suffer, normally speaking. For sympathy with somatic processes is just one main aspect of the mind–body relation. Hurt my cells and you probably hurt me. However, I can to some extent neutralize this somatic sympathy, or give it a perverse turn. After all, there is usually much more than pain in my experience; unless the pain is massive and intense, the rest of the experience may give such satisfaction as to cause me to say that I do not mind or even enjoy the experience. What in some cells may be overwhelming misery may in my vastly more complex and capacious experience be but a trifling speck of suffering, which may have a certain value, perhaps of contrast with other elements in that experience.

If pain is taken as intrinsically neutral, then the fact that it is normally disturbing is a mystery. On the contrary, if it is intrinsically negative, a suffering but—as given, as object—a suffering by what, for all we know, may be certain cells, then—though there may well be a range of possibilities as to how one appropriates this cellular suffering into one's own momentary suffering-enjoyment, one's happiness-unhappiness—still, the normal way must be to suffer with the cells, to accept their naïve verdict of negativity as valid for me. For plainly an animal had better, normally, take the side of its own members, favor their weal not their woe. I submit that this view fits the facts, as no other can.

One obvious consequence is the falsity of the alleged axiom that one can be immediately aware of no feelings but one's own, or that "other mind" cannot be a direct datum of sense perception. On the contrary, sensation in a multicellular animal just is its feeling (some of the) cellular feelings, the latter feelings having their own independent reality. Here we have Whitehead's "feeling of feeling" instantiated in a crucial case. This is but the beginning of a long story, which future science and philosophy should be able to elaborate, correct, and complete in a fashion of which many have not the faintest suspicion.In this way we may finally recover the concreteness of the life-world as integral to our overall picture of reality as a coherent whole whose vague outlines are given to direct experience, but whose specific and particular details are largely hidden from that experience and from mere common sense.

One clarification is needed. If the datum is independent, and the datum in sensation is chiefly somatic, it follows that the given somatic processes are independent of our awareness of them, while the awareness itself is dependent upon the processes. In Spinoza's two-aspect view, neither aspect, mind or matter, is independent of the other, since they are but two ways of conceiving the same substance. According to interactionism, mind and body mutually influence each other. But we are looking for a one-way influence of bodily upon mental processes.

To speak of influence or action is to speak causally; causes precede effects, according to physics, and I believe according to any clearheaded philosophy. So the bodily conditions of givenness must precede the experiences in or to which they are given. Whitehead asserts just this. He, unlike almost every other Western philosopher (some Buddhists appear to have preceded him), has drawn the correct conclusion from the one-way influence essential to a realistic conception of experience: experiences must follow, not be simultaneous with, their data.

At once three basic problems are illuminated. (a) We see how experiences can depend upon independently occurring actualities; (b) we see that the standard puzzle, "How can past events be experienced since they are past, gone out of existence?" is wrongheaded; (c) we see the answer to Hume's query about causal connections. (a) If events depend only upon preceding conditions and not upon subsequent ones, and if the data of perception are precedent, then of course they are independent. (b) So far from its being a paradox that the past is given, anything else is indeed paradoxical. Only that whose becoming is finished can be given, i.e., only past events. Also simultaneity is a mutual relation; therefore, it is unfitted to explicate the relation of givenness. And it is paradoxical to suppose that future events, those which have not yet happened, can be given. (c) If givenness can itself be given, and personal memory is just that, the givenness of past cases of givenness, then we can furnish Hume with an impression of causality. It is memory as *impression of previous impressions*, the givenness of previous cases of givenness.

But is there not interaction between the mental and the bodily? I believe that there is, but the action of the humanly mental on the bodily is not the relation of human experience to its data. When I feel an occurrence of feeling in some of my cells, the cellular exhilaration or disturbance has already happened by the time my exhilaration or disturbance, my sympathetic participation, occurs. It is then too late for the participatory feeling to influence the feeling participated in. Only a later stage of bodily feeling can be open to influence by the present state of my human feeling. A bodily response to the humanly mental must follow it temporally; and this will be (retrospective) cellular sympathy for the human, not human sympathy for the cellular. This reverse influence of mental upon bodily may well be slight (epiphenomenalism says nil), since the capacity of cells to sympathize must be very inferior to that of human beings.

Nothing is easier than to understand the skepticism many feel toward any such view. What I call the "prosaic" or "apathetic" fallacy is almost as naturally human as the poetic or pathetic fallacy. The world is neither the fairyland of primitive cultures nor the great machine of early modern science. Nor is it merely a vast but mindless organism. It is rather a vast many-leveled "society of societies." Enormous imagination and courage, combined with careful weighing of rather complicated chains of evidence, are required if we are to arrive at much of an idea of this cosmic society. There is no easy path, whether sentimental or cynical. But we are not even fairly started on the right path if we overlook or deny the *pervasive indistinctness of human experience or the evidence in direct awareness of two levels of feeling*, the second derivative, logically and temporally, from the first.

I return once more to the abstractness of science. Structures can be traced from experience to bodily process, from that to the environmental process, far out into the universe; but qualities can reach us only across bridges of feeling that at each stage lose most of the individual distinctnesses of the previous stage. Hence it is that science must focus upon *group structures* rather than individual qualities. Most of the universe is and must remain qualitatively mysterious to us. What does it feel like to be a fish, a paramecium? We can know much of the spatiotemporal patterns of what goes on in these organisms, but their feeling qualities, how shall we know them?

The view I have defended is a "causal view of perception," but it is the last type of view that seems to be meant by most of those using this phrase. I hold that close to the most important and original contribution of Whitehead is his discovery that, instead of using an otherwise explicated doctrine (what doctrine?) of causality to characterize givenness ("prehension"), we can use the natural realistic conception of givenness to explicate causality. Then we have both an answer to Hume and a truly realistic conception of experience. And, by taking to heart the indistinctness of experience, we can understand that the concreteness of the life-world is somewhat illusory and in need of help from science; also, why science, to transcend common sense, is compelled to set aside (not deny but subordinate) the qualitative side of the life-world, and why our knowledge of qualities is incapable of definite, intersubjectively valid extensions to keep pace with the structural extensions that science can effect, so that our wish to know things as they are is only to a limited degree realizable.

Our comfort is that what we cannot know we do not need to know in order to plan our lives and find our role in the creative advance that is reality. Moreover, we know what, in principle, it is that we are missing, and why, no matter how our knowledge increases, we are bound to miss it. The fish and the paramecia enjoy, though they do not objectively know, their to us inaccessible feelings. As for the question, "Can these feelings, along with the rest of the concreteness of reality, be adequately and distinctly known?"; that question is purely theological, so far as it makes sense at all. It is God "to whom all hearts are open"—God, or no one!

The position taken in this chapter can be summed up by expanding its title so that it runs: "the abstract *concreteness* of perception and the concrete *abstractness* of science." Perception is essentially concrete in that it exhibits all the general categories of reality, but it is in detail abstract by failing to exhibit distinctly most of the individual instances of the categories; science is essentially abstract in that it systematically sets aside some categories (because they are not interindividually measurable), but in detail it is concrete by its power to detect otherwise hidden individual cases of the categories it employs. To use science to remedy the defects of perception it is necessary to expand the catalogue of *individuals* far beyond the deliverances of direct perception. To use perception (or what perception and memory have in common) to remedy the defects of science, it is necessary to expand the list of cosmically applicable categories to include generalized versions of the basic dimensions of experience as such, e.g., qualities of feeling, and personal and impersonal memory (i.e., perception). In carrying through this program one discovers that the distinction between "appearance" and "reality" is ambiguous: it may mean the contrast between the physiological and the extrabodily processes generative of perception; it may mean the contrast between the indistinctness or indefiniteness of all perceptions (other than divine) and the definiteness of independent reality, or reality as omniscience would experience it.

The inclusive function is experience of (past) experience, or feeling of (past) feeling, in its two forms, personal and impersonal. This inclusive function Whitehead calls prehension. The structure of the life-world is in principle the basic structure, but it must be seen as more intimately, subtly, and variously social (and temporal) than is obvious to common sense, yet in fair agreement with those philosophers, prophets, and poets down through the centuries who have held that love, or social relatedness, is the key to the great problems.

CHAPTER FIVE

Metaphysical Truth by Systematic Elimination of Absurdities

I define metaphysics as the rational search for universal, nonempirical, and necessarily true statements about existence. Mathematics seeks universal, nonempirical, and necessary truths, but not about existence. It studies patterns that might conceivably exist and the necessary relations between such patterns. But metaphysics, if successful, affirms categorical but nonempirical, necessary statements about what exists. By nonempirical statements I mean, as Karl Popper does, those that no conceivable observations would *falsify*. However, unlike Popper, I limit metaphysical statements to extremely general ones, whereas Popper allows a certain class of particular statements to be included. This class is those statements that refer to the universe in its entirety yet also in its details, as when one says, somewhere in the universe there is such and such, for instance, a planet within 5 percent of the earth in basic specifications: mass, circumference, amounts of various elements. No human observations could disconfirm this. However, divine observation conceivably could. So I do not classify it as metaphysical.

That not all existence can be contingent was I think the classical position from the ancient Greeks down to Descartes, Spinoza, and Leibniz. At any rate, actual statements like "there might have been nothing" seem relatively recent. Even Hume, who I hold implies the idea, does not explicitly formulate it. Its modern appeal, and the general distrust of metaphysics as such, can be partly explained by several factors. The prestige of empirical science is one of these. Another is the long reign of the deterministic ideal of causality, only recently challenged in science. By making causal necessity, given the actual past, apply to ordinary events, so that the past collectively became as all-determining as divine omnipotence (as some have conceived it), determinism made it impossible to have an intelligible theory of contingency (which is rooted in freedom) and therefore made it also impossible to have an intelligible theory of necessity. For the modal contraries, like other extremely general contrasts, mutually require each other. Still another closely connected factor unfavorable to metaphysics was the exclusion of mind as such from the account of nature as given by physics, chemistry, and much of biology—even of psychology so far as behaviorism is carried to an extreme. The connection of this with determinism is that, as Plato dimly saw, we detect the presence of mind, at least partly, by its creative freedom in precisely the sense in which determinism excludes freedom. Without the ideas of creativity, or genuine freedom, as belonging to awareness, experience, mind, the psychical in a broad sense, metaphysics is so dismally limited that the insistence in science upon determinism, and at least methodological materialism, goes far to explain the failure of early modern metaphysics. Moreover, many theologians, by their way of construing divine omnipotence and omniscience, sometimes implicitly, sometimes explicitly, have taken a deterministic, materialistic view of inanimate, and even much of biological, nature, and thereby helped to further dim the prospects for metaphysics— therefore also for theology, since theism, the assertion of God's existence, is, as we shall see, a metaphysical doctrine.

What the foregoing account comes to is that science and theology have for several centuries been in an unconscious conspiracy, as it were, to foist a bad metaphysics upon the educated public. Determinism and materialism are not empirical scientific discoveries, but metaphysical doctrine. Since science and theology are both showing signs of realizing that neither unqualified determinism nor materialism are necessary, if in the long run even helpful, for scientific or religious ends, the present situation is hopeful.

A curious historical fact is this: the British tradition, more than any other, has been addicted to a one-sided contingentism or rejection of existential necessity (such as metaphysics by definition requires) yet the same tradition has been exceptionally wedded to determinism. Hume affirmed both these extremes, little congruent as they are together. Nothing, he held, can exist by necessity, yet, he also held, science shows us that causes completely determine what happens. John Stuart Mill, great exponent of political freedom and critic of metaphysical speculations, was also a determinist, as was Herbert Spencer, the dedicated evolutionist. Yet evolutionary biology is the least deterministic natural science in its actual practices and theories. Peirce therefore said that Spencer was only a semi-Spencerian. McTaggart and some other Anglo-Hegelians had no good word to say either for creative freedom, or for a genuine theism.

Metaphysical necessities favor indeterminism. What is strictly necessary is not what actually happens or what particular things exist, but only that the most general abstractions, such as being, becoming, actuality, possibility, relation, individual, should all have some positive instances. This is the meaning of "there must be something."

The reason necessity applies only to extremely general or abstract ideas is clear. It is a logical truism that no step from a more to a less abstract concept is deductively necessary. If there are foxes there are animals, if animals then living organisms, if the last then there are concrete things or processes. Going in the reverse direction is at every step nonnecessary or contingent.

Leibniz, by defining the necessary as what all possibilities have in common, implied, without realizing it, that the necessary can only be extremely abstract, and that the very meaning of becoming is its piecemeal contingency. Evolutionism gives concreteness to all this. Every species, and every individual within a species, is a partly free creation, not a necessary consequence of what went before. It is a possible consequence, and causal explanation is not of why exactly what happened did happen, but of why what happened was then and there possible and something more or less closely like it at least probable. The real laws of nature are statistical or approximate, allowing for individual freedom, however slight in many cases this may be.

Every student of philosophy is likely to have heard of two theories of truth, truth by coherence and truth by correspondence. My position is: metaphysical truth is indeed truth by coherence. With universal concepts alone only necessities can be stated—given coherence, necessary truths, given incoherence, necessary untruths or impossibilities. I am here in partial agreement with Rudolf Carnap, as against Quine, except that I generalize somewhat Carnap's doctrine of L-true. But I generalize also (without, I believe, invalidating it) Carnap's reason for the doctrine. With more specific concepts than those of metaphysical generality, coherence is only a necessary not a sufficient condition for truth. There must also be correspondence, as shown, at least indirectly, by observation.

Absolute idealists tried to stretch truth by coherence to cover all truth. This one-sided, extreme view excludes freedom, and violates the Wittgensteinian Principle of Contrast too obviously to appeal to very many nowadays. But the opposite extreme, that there is no truth by coherence even when universal categories alone are used, also violates the Principle of Contrast. If there must be both contingency and necessity, then there must be truth by coherence. It is very abstract truth, but as a common feature of any and every possible truth it is significant. (Bad metaphysics means an element of unconscious absurdity in all our thinking.) In this, as in so many issues there are more than two positions to choose among. The two extremes are: (a) All truth is by coherence and is necessary; (b) all truth is by correspondence and is contingent—these are false extremes. A century ago the extreme of necessitarianism was somewhat popular; now the extreme of contingentism is popular. I reject both, partly for the same reason, the Principle of Contrast. Plato and Aristotle are also largely on my side in this.

An example of an important metaphysical truth is the principle of incompatible positive values. In every concrete decision something good is ruled out. This is so not because of any contingent features of the world, but for purely conceptual reasons. Specific ideas coming under universal categories are contingent in their application because they come in *mutually incompatible but positive options*. Under *quality* take a color of a definite hue, say, a saturated red. This is one of four basic forms of color quality, each of which has a multitude of possible variations. All of these are positive, but any one of them in a given time-place or locus in experience rules out all the others. Choosing is not between a positive and a merely negative, but among positives. The notion that there might be a heaven where nothing good would ever have to be decided *against* is, I believe, a form of confused metaphysics. Actualization is contingent because it is creative, adding to the definiteness of the world. If there were a uniquely right addition to make to that definiteness, it would not be an addition, for its unique rightness, as determined by what is already actual, would be there already as part of the definiteness of reality. What is already there *partly* particularizes what would constitute a good addition, but it cannot fully particularize it.

Consider the ideals of equality and freedom. Why wish for equality? Because friendship is a great good and friends are ideally equals. In an equalitarian society there can be much friendship. But how is equality to be obtained? If there is freedom, hence an aspect of chance or randomness in reality, complete equality will be infinitely improbable or impossible. And without freedom there is nothing. Life as such *is* freedom on some level. Whitehead's analysis of experiencing as prehension, or feeling of (other) feeling, makes this clearer than anyone else had ever made it. The prehensive unity that an experience is could not, logically could not, be dictated by the items prehended. It is a creation! A world of free beings, and I hold there can be no other, will produce inequality among individuals of a species. The attempt to evade this in some absolute way will lower the level of freedom for all, without achieving what it seeks. Some will be coercing others to keep them from getting ahead of their fellows, and this will be an inequality, perhaps an ugly one. One can see this in Russia and China. (In China Confucius made women grossly inferior.)

Suppose there were "nothing," then all positive affirmations of existence would be *contingently* false (unless absurd), and all negative ones would be contingently true, though without anyone to do the affirming or denying. There would be no animals, no plants, no atoms, no God, and no nondivine beings either. Of course we might take 'nothing' in 'nothing exists' as a special kind of something, and so the statement would be positive. But this is like supposing that if nobody knows a certain truth then that truth would still be known by that special something called nobody. I hold, on various grounds, that total nonexistence is a mere set of words with no coherent meaning.[1] The most general concepts employed are not coherently employed in saying, "There might have been nothing." "Language is here idling," not saying anything. I suspect Wittgenstein would have agreed. If so, he should not have *defined* metaphysics as misuse of language, a viciously "persuasive" definition if there is one.

Negation presupposes something to negate, and something more than a mere proposition. "There are no elephants in the room" is not made true by nothing being in the room. What shows us the absence of elephants is the presence of other things, people, furniture, or air enabling us to hear, and light enabling us to see, the contents of the room more completely than we could were elephants occupying large parts of the space. The *merely* negative cannot be experienced. The business of concepts is to explain positive observations. Karl Popper makes this clear in his carefully positive account of observation statements. The word *positivism* is traditionally used in an odd way. I am, with Popper and some others, indeed a positivist, as I have just shown. To assert absolutely nothing is not to assert; one can only assert something. Bergson makes this clear, oddly enough in his partly wrongheaded book about evolution. To merely deny is not even to deny.

Granted then, for the sake of the discussion at least, that 'something exists' is a necessary truth, we have the question: what if anything can be said about this necessary something in a universal, but still positive sense? We cannot find the answer in observation. For that only shows what in fact, not what necessarily, exists. Metaphysical truth transcends observation and is justified only by relations of concepts so general that to deny them exemplification would make the something that must exist indistinguishable from nothing.

Various candidates for the status of necessary existential truths have been proposed. God has been said to exist by necessity; Aristotle held that the world in its most general features, as well as God, exists eternally and necessarily; Spinoza held, or seems at least to hold, that God and even the details of the world exist necessarily. Some have said that the something existing necessarily must be entirely unitary, an undifferentiated reality, nonspatial and unchangeable, and that the notion of a world of change and plurality is mistaken. Others have said that what exists can only be a plurality of things each of which might exist without any of the others. This is the doctrine of exclusively external, nonconstitutive relations. Hume and Russell, also Quine and many others, have held or not clearly enough denied it.

Some have said that what exists is only *matter* that, in many cases at least, is totally without any kind of sentience or awareness, any feeling, memory, anticipation, thought. Others, I among them, hold that the something that must exist can only be some form or forms of awareness, feeling, thought, or physical functioning.

I propose the following strategy for selecting, among metaphysically universal statements, those that make coherent sense and those that do not, or—the same thing—between those necessarily true and those necessarily untrue. We are looking for rules or principles by which we can distinguish sense from absurdity in the way universal concepts are related to one another. We cannot assume that the truth is obvious here, for nearly thirty centuries of recorded disagreement in such matters show that it is not obvious. My proposal is twofold.

1. We must divide the combinations of universal concepts into *exhaustive* sets of mutually exclusive combinations—small sets, too, for otherwise life is too short to make a decision possible.
2. We must look for rules or principles by which we can eliminate some of the combinations as violating the meanings of the concepts combined.

We are looking for conceptual absurdity, necessary falsity, in the hope that only one of the mathematically possible combinations in each set will be left when all the absurd ones are eliminated. If this is not, and I think it is not, the way metaphysics has been done in the past, then metaphysics is still a young discipline. For, I submit, this is the rational way to do it.

One rule for eliminating absurdity is to beware of extremes, such as extreme monism, plurality is unreal; extreme pluralism, there are many mutually independent realities and no inclusive reality somehow uniting them all. Russell, oddly enough, thought one must choose between these extremes, and nowhere does he even seriously consider the idea of a moderate pluralism that would also be a moderate monism, a higher synthesis of, or medium between, the extremes. I talked to him about this; someone interrupted our talk by telephoning Russell.

In ethics, as Aristotle pointed out, virtues are means between contrary extremes, thus courage between rashness and cowardice. I believe I have shown elsewhere that beauty is a mean between extremes in at least two dimensions.[2] In all fundamental matters there are reasons for rejecting extremes. Take pluralism: there are many things. This implies relations among the things. These relations may be supposed mere *additions*, wholly extrinsic to the things, really an additional set of 'things' in the broadest sense. Or relations may be supposed wholly intrinsic to the things related. Extreme pluralists—Hume, Russell, Carnap, Quine—say the former; extreme monists, if they admit plurality at all, say the latter—thus Spinoza, Bradley, Royce, Blanshard. All of these eight writers illustrate how not to do metaphysics in our time, that is, after these philosophers have already shown the limitations of so doing it. These dead horses, so to speak, flogged each other; if we want to stop flogging them we must find a third position.

In truth there is a clear possibility of a third position. A relation between X and Y might be extrinsic to Y but intrinsic to X. All relations might be intrinsic to some thing or things and extrinsic to some other thing or things. If then we examine the arguments by which monists sought to refute pluralists, and those by which pluralists sought to refute monists, we shall find, as I have shown in many writings, that the arguments in the one case as in the other collapse if we reject the assumption, common to both sides, that relations must be either all extrinsic or all intrinsic to both (or all) terms.[3] No argument for this assumption is given by either side. How can we hope to settle metaphysical controversies by so careless a procedure? Yet my criticism applies to Nagarjuna, the great Buddhist of long ago, Bradley of this century, Hume of two centuries ago, and Russell and Quine of our time. The remedy is in the twofold procedure I propose.

The rule, beware of extremes, may be closely related to another rule, beware of positions that take symmetrical ideas as first principles. That related terms symmetrically contain their relations is the extreme nonpluralistic position, for as Bradley shows, it makes relations and plurality unintelligible. That terms symmetrically fail to include their relations is the extreme pluralistic position. Both positions may be, and I hold are, false because the essential form of relatedness is that of one-way inclusion and one-way noninclusion of a relation, taking two or more terms into account. Thus we, as related to Plato, contain our relations to Plato; he contained no relation to us, for we did not exist to relate to. Symmetry is not the key to temporal relations, though it is to spatial ones. Moreover, as Milič Čapek keeps telling us, time is the key to space, not vice versa. Spatial symmetry is a special complication in temporal (causal) relatedness.

We now have *three* closely related principles of elimination among metaphysical doctrines: extremes tend to be absurd, first principles are asymmetrical, and the Principle of Contrast. If all is necessary, as Spinoza seems to say, then necessity loses its contrast with contingency and therefore its distinctive meaning. If all relations are exclusively external, or exclusively internal, then in both cases the contrast on which the two ideas depend collapses and therewith the ideas, and so nothing is being said by asserting either of them. The violation of this principle defines not metaphysics, but only *bad* metaphysics. *These* it goes a long way toward defining.

Consider the problem of the identity of a changing thing or person. According to Hume, there is no identity at all between you (or me) as of today and you (or me) as of yesterday. (Russell took this view also.) The reality of a thing or person is a stream of states, events, happenings, or processes. Each new momentary state is simply an addition to the earlier moments or states. There are similarities but no identity. According to Leibniz, on the contrary, a person, at least the person as a single sequence of mental states, a single monad, is at all times strictly the same entity in different temporal parts of its career. At all times I have been the person that would at this moment have exactly the experience that I do have at this moment. All my career follows from the "law of succession," which is my identity. Neither of these two extreme doctrines is common sense, or really good sense. Aristotle and Plato both knew better, as did Epicurus. Yet there *is* some individual identity. Successive moments may be partly identical and partly nonidentical. Each of us is a rememberer of his or her childhood in a way no other person can remember *that* childhood. Memory of X somehow includes X, for otherwise it is not X that is remembered. Whitehead's theory of prehension takes this into account. I now prehend, that is, intrinsically relate myself to, a certain childhood in a way in which no one else relates himself or herself to that childhood. Yet in a different way some others do or did relate themselves to my childhood. On the other hand, that childhood did not relate itself by prehension, or any other intrinsic relation, to my or anyone's present experience. There was no such experience to relate to. Thus we have a one-way partial identity by which the past enters into the being of the present but not vice versa. Still further, the partial identity of me now with myself in the past goes with a partial identity of others, as of now, with me in the past. Persons are *only partially identical with themselves through time and only partially nonidentical with others in space.* Some of them perhaps, if old enough, prehend, in a somewhat different way but genuinely, my childhood.

As the Buddhists have seen for two millennia and Whitehead saw recently, the notion that all motivation reduces to self-interest presupposes a false metaphysics of individuality. Moreover, Whitehead is not the only Westerner who has seen this. Hazlitt in England saw it but had so little luck in convincing his English public that he gave up philosophy for literary criticism. Thomas Nagel seems to see it. I came close to seeing it before I knew about Whitehead, Buddhism, Hazlitt, or Nagel. I did get some help from Royce, who, however, gave a falsely monistic interpretation of the idea. He thought there were only internal relations among states of an individual or among individuals, whereas the moderate monism or pluralism (they are the same) takes relations to the details of the later moments to be external for the earlier moments. Hence, as Nagel and Hazlitt and even Quine have seen, it is just as directly rational to act for the future of others as for one's own future. Concern for self is no mere identity relation and concern for others is no mere nonidentity relation. Pure identity is symmetrical, personal identity is not. All this shows how ethics depends on metaphysics. A false notion of individuality makes a sound ethics needlessly difficult. Theoretical egoism is a superstitious view of the self, if it makes sense at all.

Note also that not only memory, but perception also is retrospective and gives us the past—in some cases the near, in others the remote past, as when we look into the starry heavens.

Take the issue of materialism versus idealism or spiritualism. Is this division exhaustive? Some say there is also dualism. Most materialists today are really emergent dualists, according to whom there is mere insentient matter, then there is matter somehow endowed with sentience. Materialism claims to be nondualistic, but it can be accused of being a crypto-dualism or emergent dualism. The sentience that previously insentient matter acquires is not really shown, in a more than verbal sense, to be a property of the matter that was there before the emergence.

Suppose, however, we can show that what is called insentient matter is a complex whose constituents (cells, molecules, atoms, etc.) are, for all we could ever know, primitive forms of sentience. Leibniz was the first to see clearly that, by exalting the constituents of matter *above the zero* of mind or the psychical, we achieve a nondualism that is genuine and yet can accept all the results of natural science.

Materialism and dualism share a common assumption, that there is some non-question-begging *positive* criterion for the *total absence* of sentience from a portion of nature. A merely negative criterion, e.g., inactivity, begs the question. We all admit that tables do not feel, but then neither does a crowd of persons, taken as a single thing, feel; its members feel. So with a crowd of molecules or atoms, as in waves, winds, waterfalls, a gas, or a piece of metal. Tables are, as unities, inactive, what feels acts. Waves, winds, clouds are in a sense active, but they do not act as one and so do not feel as one. Trees are cell colonies that cannot be proved to act as one; hence they may not feel as one. But a live plant cell, or something in a cell, acts as one and it may feel as one. What non-question-begging sign shows otherwise?

To avoid an unintelligible dualism, the supposedly insentient must either be elevated at least above the zero of sentience or else the sentient must be reduced, in a way many of us find unintelligible or merely verbal, to a special form of the otherwise *absolutely* insentient. Like many other absolutes this one too is *unobservable*, and in no positive way intelligible. What we need from it is derivable from a sufficiently generalized concept of sentience itself. If matter in its everyday cases taken as wholes does not feel, its invisibly small constituents may do so. To neglect these constituents is to proceed as though science had discovered nothing much about nature. Aristotle had no established atomic, molecular, or cellular theories; we do. We know that nature is everywhere active, and that the seemingly unitary may really be composite, not a single agent but a crowd of agents.

The history of ideas strongly supports the hypothesis that it was largely the apparent lack of activity in some parts of nature, as given to perception and so-called common sense, and the lack of unity in some other parts that seem active, as in fire or winds, that misled people to simply deny mind to much of nature. In addition we know that the idea of mere, or strictly insentient, matter is largely a product of science in its ancient and early modern forms. Many peoples living close to nature tend to think of nature in a vague way as pervasively animate and sentient. If egoism as a theory is a superstition or metaphysical confusion, why not materialism also? The real or sound *common sense* must be common to all human beings, not unique to some especially sophisticated cultures. I can appeal to Charles Peirce in this contention.

Still a third source of the materialistic or dualistic notion (the basic error is what the two have in common) is the apparent lack of free action in much of nature, plus the hypothesis, falsely supposed to be confirmed by scientific data, that causal determination of events by the past is absolute. Quantum physics now shows to many scientists what Peirce and Clerk Maxwell, two superb geniuses, over a century ago guessed—a well-educated guess—that causal laws are really statistical and do not absolutely exclude individual freedom in the genuine sense of doing *this* when doing *that* instead was also causally possible, given the entire psychophysiological past.

After centuries of strict determinism taken as almost obligatory for science and philosophy, and agreed upon by Kant and Hume, for example, and at least not denied by Newton, we have, for about a century now, been moving into a new kind of science, philosophy, and theology. We begin to take seriously the suggestion of Maxwell that determinism is a "sophism," arising from the long delay in the formulation and full understanding of statistical laws—as in thermodynamics and the study of gases. We come back to the old formula of Epicurus, "chance *and* necessity," rather than the mere exclusion of chance. Chance is the negative side of what positively is creative freedom, enriching reality by the production of definite actuality out of partially indefinite potentiality. It is significant that Epicurus's formula was recently taken by Monod, a famous French biologist, as the title for his major work.[4]

Returning to our rules of elimination from sets of metaphysical options, I remark that the rule against taking symmetrical ideas as first principles is supported by elementary formal logic. We explain equivalence as two-way implication, biconditioning by simple conditioning; we do not explain normal implication as one-way equivalence, for that is contradictory. Similarly, we define the symmetrical relation equality as the *double negative*, neither term greater (or better) than the other, whereas we cannot define or assert greater than by merely asserting or denying equality. X is unequal to Y does not tell us which is greater.

A wise rule, I believe, is this: given a symmetrical idea, look for the non-symmetrical one in terms of which the symmetry can be defined; or, in general, look for one-way relationships, since any two-way ones will be special cases of these. Thus interaction is a two-way relation, but it is explained as a complex of one-way actions. For example, I-now influences you a moment later, you-now influences me a moment later. Neither of these actions is strictly symmetrical. But they are all there in any interaction between us. Or suppose we love each other. It does not follow that there is one relation that read one way is your love for me and read the other way is my love for you. Surely there are two relations here, not one. Symmetrical expressions always abstract from the full actuality described, only one-way ones can do justice to the reality.

Space is the dimension (or set of dimensions) of symmetry in relatedness, time the dimension of one-way relations. Hence time's arrow should be taken seriously and not explained away. Physics is only now beginning to come to grips with this matter (Prigogine). Space is a complication of time, not time of space.

Another logical truth relevant to metaphysics is an axiom of modal logic: $N (p \cdot q) \equiv (Np \cdot Nq)$. If a conjunction of propositions is necessary, so is each of the conjoined propositions. The inclusive modality cannot be necessity, but must be contingency.[5] That 3 and 4 are 7 *and* it is now-and-here not raining, this truth as a whole is contingent, although the arithmetical truth is necessary. Reality as a whole cannot be necessary unless everything is necessary. And that would violate the conceptual Principle of Contrast: with universal categories, both sides of such pairs as necessary–contingent, infinite–finite, absolute–relative, must make sense and have application if either does. Spinoza's "all is necessary" deprives the term 'necessary' of any distinctive meaning. This alone should rule out Spinozism, though there are plenty of other principles that also count against the doctrine.

If only contingency can be inclusive, then reality in its fullness must be contingent and the necessary factor must be an abstraction. It is the concrete that includes the abstract, not vice versa (another basic asymmetry). If I think an arithmetical truth, that truth is in me, I am not in it. This is the Aristotelian principle that forms are in individuals, not vice versa. And as Leibniz saw, necessity is defined as what all the possibilities have in common, what is left when all differences are abstracted from. How then can this residuum be concrete? Yet God was often defined as the wholly necessary being. Aristotle was the first to give this definition, and he correctly deduced from it that God's knowledge cannot, on the assumption, include contingent features of the world. The entire Middle Ages tried to make sense of the combination: God is wholly necessary, God knows the contingent world, from which it follows that God's knowledge cannot include what God knows. If the world is contingent, then knowledge of the world is either something contingent in God or something contingent not in God. But what is a knowledge that is not in the full actuality of the knower? No medieval thinker gave a rational solution of this puzzle. Leibniz and Arnauld, two fairly high authorities in the matter, virtually admitted that they could not do so, but they failed to draw the appropriate conclusion that the medieval theistic metaphysics was a failure.

The only solution is to admit, with Socinus of Italy (c. 1600), that there are in God qualities that might have been otherwise, i.e., contingent qualities. Moreover, if we have any genuine freedom, power of self-determination, vis-à-vis God, then we decide something in God who knows our decisions. We partly decide what God is to know and hence something in the knowing. *We change God.* This abrupt break with a long tradition was the first; but by now the same step has been taken by many, mostly without knowledge of Socinus. Whitehead is one of these. A dozen names could be given of those who preceded him, but he may have scarcely known any of these predecessors. I had taken the step before I knew anything of Whitehead's metaphysics. So had a teacher of mine, Hocking at Harvard. So had my father and one of his teachers in the last century. Theology in our time is simply not what it was in the Middle Ages. Our problems are partly quite different.

CHAPTER SIX

The Case for Metaphysical Idealism

By 'idealism' I shall mean, in Ewing's phrase, the attempt or claim to "interpret reality in terms of mind."[1] Or, it is the doctrine that reality is essentially psychical. The terms 'panpsychism' or 'psychicalism' can also be used. "Psychical" means having such functions as feeling, perception, memory, volition, thought. For idealism, whatever lacks all of these functions is only an appearance of or abstraction from what does possess some or all of them. In still other words, reality, or what there is, consists of cases, forms, aspects, kinds of "experiencing," and of nothing else. This I take as the central affirmation of idealists. Ewing gives many samples of idealistic writing, omitting Leibniz for no apparent reason, also omitting Peirce and Whitehead, among others. As a result, his selections, though most useful, scarcely begin to cover the variety of forms that idealism has taken. Yet his book makes wonderfully clear why idealism has fallen into disrepute, considering the strange aberrations with which it has historically associated itself.

Idealists deny any literally insentient, thoughtless matter taken as more than an abstraction from things that in their concreteness, and taken one by one, are at least sentient. Schopenhauer is a marginal case, admitting only "blind" will as coextensive with reality. Kant is also marginal, since he refuses to characterize things in themselves as either psychical or not psychical. But he does limit the knowable to appearances, i.e., experiences. Moreover, the only hints—ethical or religious—he gives concerning the noumena favor idealism.

In the foregoing deliberately broad definitions it is not assumed that such terms as 'feeling,' 'experience,' 'memory,' 'thought,' refer only to human instances, or even only to vertebrate animals—or to these plus some supreme, "absolute" or divine form of mind or spirit. All such restrictions upon the scope of psychical terms raise issues more specific than I intend by the option, idealism or not idealism. The same is true of views restricting idealism to one side of such alternatives as monism versus pluralism, internal versus external

55

relations, optimism versus pessimism, determinism (even if by final causes) versus various gradations of indeterminism. It is indeed remarkable how many metaphysical and epistemological issues (I have counted fifteen without trying to be exhaustive) divide so-called idealists from other idealists.

As some use words, an "idealist" is one who believes that all relations are intrinsic to both or all their terms, or that everything depends upon everything else. But many idealists (by my definition) deny this. For some writers, an idealist is a person who thinks that, in knowing, one knows only one's own mental states, or at least knows only these directly. Or, that physical objects are only human, or human and divine, ideas. Yet some idealists reject this view, and by a reasonable definition of terms are epistemological realists. Some psychicalists declare the "unreality of space and time"; others do nothing of the sort. Idealists have been theists or atheists, Christians, Hindus, or Buddhists, nominalists or realists, a priori rationalists or empiricists, dialectical philosophers or anti-dialecticians. They have held causal theories of perception or acausal theories. They have been essentially literary or artistic in their interests, or essentially scientific, even distinguished contributors to physics or biology. They have thought in terms of 'substance,' or (Buddhists, Whitehead) have objected to this concept, taking events or momentary actualities as reality in its basic concrete form. They have been deeply agnostic (Kant) or startlingly gnostic (Hegel).

What follows from this immense array of internal differences in the idealists' camp? One thing follows immediately: one cannot refute (or establish) idealism as such by refuting (or establishing) one or more of the many doctrines upon which idealists have disagreed—unless these doctrines can be shown to follow from (or to entail) idealism itself. G. E. Moore, a noted opponent of idealistic claims, said once that he "devoutly hoped" that idealism (the view that reality is essentially "spiritual") was true. He contended only that it failed to follow from any evidence offered for it.

What can be validly inferred from the idealistic thesis, and from what can it be inferred? These are the crucial questions, and it is amazing how seldom they were clearly discussed by either the proponents or opponents of historic idealistic systems. One thing does follow from the thesis that reality and mind (i.e., experience or the psychical) are the same. This is that either reality is easy to understand or mind is not easy to understand. The history of thought refutes the first supposition; so the second only is left. But then is it surprising that idealists have had trouble agreeing as to how the "mind" that they equate with reality is to be conceived? Idealists may have differed because their doctrine forced them to face the genuine, concrete, ultimate reality, not some artificial, abstract simplification. They have rightly located the central mystery, but its mysteriousness remains.

On both sides of the historic controversies one can see the wish to make things simple and obvious. For Berkeley, it is enough to point out that nature is thinkable and perceivable only as human (and divine) ideas. His critics are happy to see that 'idea' may mean *either* a case of thinking or perceiving *or* something thought about or perceived, so that the argument rests on an ambiguity. For Green, one has only to see that 'reality' means a system of relations and that "relations are the work of thought," to which James replies that relations are perceived or felt and are no inventions of "intelligence." For Bradley, the proof of idealism is that relations are contradictory, hence unreal, and that the only model of relationless reality we have is feeling. For Russell, the point is that relations are indispensable, and so also are terms, which must be independent of the relations. For Blanshard, the clue is the insight—"to understand is to see to be necessary." But Ernst Nagel finds it plain that this is a false view of understanding. None of these writers has clearly shown the truth or the falsity of idealism as such, or the logical connection between this issue and the others mentioned.

Perhaps at long last it is time to consider dispassionately the logical rather than merely historical relations of the idealistic thesis to other doctrines debated among philosophers.

The idealistic question essentially concerns the mind–matter distinction. To reject idealism is to raise the question: dualism or materialism? (The theory of "neutral stuff" can, by a suitable definition of matter, be included under materialism.) Idealism, in short, is one of the two forms of antidualism, materialism being the other. What connection has the joint rejection of dualism and materialism in favor of idealistic monism (not opposed to a pluralism of individuals) with the other topics discussed earlier? Clearly it depends, at least in part, upon how the structure of mind or experience is conceived. If, for instance, this structure is deterministic, then idealists should be determinists, if not then not. If and only if the apparent plurality of minds is genuine should idealists be pluralists. If mind is immutable, then so, for idealism, is reality. But is mind immutable? This seems anything but obvious. If it is the function of mind in knowing to create or alter the known, then of course the things we know are, insofar, creatures of our thinking or perceiving. But, as Santayana pointed out, in now being aware of our previous experiences, we can hardly be creating these past experiences. So, as applied to memory at least, the supposedly idealistic doctrine of knowing is untrue to mind or experiencing itself. Yet how can this show the falsity of idealism as such? Some idealists agree entirely on this point with Santayana.

Many critics of the psychicalist theory have thought to show, if not its falsity, at least its problematic status, by finding fallacies in many of the arguments offered by idealists. And certainly a good many are fallacious. But do they exhaust the possibilities?

How would one show that a certain idea is adequate to explicate "reality"? Would it not be by showing that the idea in question can take all the forms that reality is known, or even can be conceived, to take? Thus if mind can be concrete and also abstract, extended and also inextended, dependent and also independent, singular and also plural, valuable and also trifling, simple and also complex, long-enduring and also momentary, fixed and also changeable, actual and also potential, with quantity as well as quantity (and with as great a range of qualities and quantities as you please), contingent as well as necessary, conditioned as well as unconditioned, a part of reality and also reality as a whole—if mind can be on both sides of every genuine contrast, in the sense in which reality can be so (even unrealities are at least mistaken but really occurrent ideas, fancies or what not), then there is no need to assume some additional principle. What is in no sense psychical will be what is in no sense real. How 'psychical' can retain any useful meaning, in spite of this equivalence with 'reality,' we shall consider in the following.

Opposition to idealism must consist in attempts to put mind on one side only of "genuine contrasts" (such that reality is on both sides). Descartes' denial that not mind but only matter can be extended is the paradigm of anti-idealism, calamitously accepted by many idealists. When Aristotle contrasted mind as actuality of an organic body to its matter as potentiality he was taking a somewhat anti-idealistic position. But when, for instance, he said that the soul was "in a manner all things" he was taking an almost idealistic one. Similarly, when Plato defined the soul as the self-moved, and the source of all motion, but implied a contrast with matter as incapable of self-motion, he was stopping short of complete idealism. For idealism, either every reality is self-moved or mind is not in every case or form self-moved. An idealist does not view mind as what is left over when one abstracts from behavior or matter in motion; rather, he takes matter in motion to be also mind in some form. When (if he did) Plato associated soul with eternal ideas *rather than* with changing bodies, he was insofar anti-idealistic. If mind is reality, then it has all the forms of reality, not just some of them. It is [wholly] inextended only if nothing is extended, wholly actual only if nothing is potential, pure form only if nothing is anything other than form. If mind needs something to mold, control, or form, something potential for further determinations, then for idealism mind itself must be the form, the forming, and that which is formed. It may not be the same individual mind, or the same kind or aspect of mind, that is on both sides of every contrast, but it must be mind in some case, kind, or aspect.

If the foregoing is sound, there are two opposite strategies for an idealist. He may hold that mind is on one side only of at least certain seemingly basic contrasts, but urge that the other side is "unreal," i.e., that these contrasts are not what I have been calling "genuine." And this procedure may seem to be helped by the consideration that the unreality in question is a problem only because there is at least an appearance of its presence, appearance being something mental. The objections to this strategy, however, are widely recognized, especially in the West. I cannot see it as a valid procedure, with one exception to be discussed presently.

The other strategy is to resist every attempt to confine mind to one aspect, corner, or species of thinkable reality. I believe that this strategy is capable of great power.

Consider the contrast concrete–abstract. Experiences are concrete events, if by an experience we mean, say, all the human experiencing—sensation, perception, feeling, thought, memory—in a person at a given moment. But in such an experience abstract thought can be a feature, so that in this example of mind we have room for the function of abstracting and for abstract objects as such. Similarly, in experience there are certainly quality as well as number, and also geometrical forms. And so, I believe, with every contrast whatever, apart from the verbal and question-begging contrast: mind and (in every sense) not-mind. 'Mind' is no more subject to limits of generalization than is 'reality.'

Of course *human* experience has but limited scope, and so has experience as a property of vertebrate animals only. Hence I do not believe it made sense when Berkeley tried (if or so far as he did try) to treat worms, plants, and rocks as mere factors—"ideas"—in minds on the vertebrate level or higher. Only experience much less like the human than any vertebrate's will account for the objects of our perceptions of the lower levels of nature. To look to God for the experiences required is to look in the wrong direction. It is experiences much more subhuman than a fish's that are needed. Here I think Leibniz, Peirce, or Whitehead should be our guide, not Berkeley or Hegel.

I conceded earlier a certain limited validity to the strategy of dismissing some contrasts as not genuine, or as mere cases of the contrast real–unreal. It is obvious that a psychicalist is forced to explain away some features of the perceived world, at least as often interpreted. Rocks, winds, and waters do not seem to be sentient individuals; indeed, trees scarcely seem so. Idealism is thus bound to be in some tension with common sense. It may be partly for this reason that so many of its exponents have gone so far—so madly far, I am tempted to say—from common sense. They could not enjoy an effortless harmony with the views of "the plain man," or with ordinary language, as Berkeley wanted to do. So they perhaps felt that they might as well be hanged for a sheep as for a lamb. But another attitude is, I think, preferable.

Not only should one economize on departures from good common sense, but one needs a clear principle for such departures. I think the principle we need is simple: the plain man is apt to draw *negative* conclusions from his failure or inability to observe something, especially where positive views would make no difference for ordinary purposes. In such cases idealism may be within its rights in preferring more positive conceptions. The rationale of this is: what we experience as present is thereby shown to be present (though we may have mislocated it, perhaps taking it to be outside when it is inside our bodies), but what we do not consciously experience as present in some, for us, imperceptibly minute, subtle, or trifling form, or in some, for us, incomprehensibly vast or superior form. Thus to observe motion is to know that some sort of physical change really occurs (if only in our own bodies); to fail to observe motion or change is not to know that what is physically present is strictly immutable. Its changes may be too slight, on too minute or vast a spatial or temporal scale, to be apparent to our perceptual powers.

The usual classification of natural things as inanimate, vegetable, or animal—or: lifeless and mindless, living but mindless, living and minded— rather obviously derives from a neglect of the preceding caution. For our raw observation, much of nature seems to consist of "inert" stuff, moving only if something else moves it, hence not plausibly taken as feeling or thinking. Even plants scarcely move, save in the imperceptibly slow fashion of growing, and this is analogous to forms of change in us that occur without our feeling them. Also, where—apart from animals—we do observe lively activity, it seems entirely without individuality. If moving waters, winds, or molten lava feel, what individuals participate in this feeling? Is it each wave, an entire ocean or river, each cloud, all the atmosphere, the volcano? Our perceptions of inanimate nature disclose no definite agents, even for the activities we do detect. But if this justifies denying that there are such agents, then it justifies denying that the seemingly static rocks are full of invisibly small motions; and so the kinetic theory of heat is refuted by common sense!

Who has really answered the Leibnizian argument: reality is essentially activity, appearances to the contrary being due to negative illusions (failure or inability to observe being taken as observation of absence); reality is essentially individual, appearances to the contrary being similarly illusory? We know that we and other animals are individuals, active and sentient; we do not know but rashly guess that the failure of our perceptions to discover activity, individuality, or sentience in much of nature means their absence. And this in spite of the fact that the whole sweep of modern science implies the inadequacy of these perceptions to reveal directly more than gross mass movements of invisibly small but active agents—such as molecules or cells— analogous, however remotely, to animals, as rocks, rivers, and even trees are not. Science disproves the apparent lack of activity and of individual differentiation. Yet these are the only non-question-begging criteria of the presence of feeling and mind in some form, however lowly or far from the human species of mind. Leibnizianism fits current science in this respect far better than it did the science of three centuries ago when Leibniz began to think about this problem.

Einstein stressed the exact similarity of any electron to any other. But Bohm and others now reject this as not the whole story. Relations to the environment enter into electrons as though they prehended their neighbors, and indeed many remote entities. And the environment is always unique in some degree.

Animal experience, our accessible sample of experience, is but an item in the world, true enough. But this same animal experience, first of all our own and that of our human fellows, is also our most accessible sample of active, individual reality. Of course we must generalize beyond the sample. But how? By generalizing simply beyond experience as such, or by generalizing the idea of experience itself?

If reality simply is mind, in various forms and aspects, the word 'mind'— or 'experience,' 'the psychical'—must, some will object, lose all distinctive meaning. Are not ideas essentially contrasts? If just everything is psychical, then is not "psychical" a synonym for "something, anything you please"? In a sense, yes; in a sense, no. There are three aspects of the 'no.' First, the doctrine is not that everything is, *in the same sense*, psychical. For instance, if 'X is psychical' means 'X at least feels,' then obviously many things are not psychical. A crowd of persons does not literally feel, only the persons in the crowd feel. Also abstractions—for instance, feeling as such—do not feel. The idea of a triangle does not itself think. Concrete reality *concretely* instances the psychical, abstract reality *abstractly* instances it; individual realities are *individual* instances, aggregate realities *aggregate* instances. Or, actual reality is actual feeling or experiencing, potential reality is potential feeling.

The second reason why it is not a meaningless duplication of words to equate reality and experience is this: the equation reminds us that every concept, even so general a one as 'reality,' must be related somehow to experience. The most general ideas are still ideas, and experience gives them their sense. If we cannot take 'experience' to have a sense as general as 'reality,' what meaning can we attach to this latter word?

We understand that there is more in the world than we ourselves experience partly by taking into account what others experience. If we are to believe that there is more than any human being experiences, can we do this otherwise than by implicitly grasping a meaning for 'experience' or 'knowledge' wider than the human? The escape from the egocentric predicament is not by dismissing the very idea of a subject, but by recognizing a variety of subjects, actual and possible. The alternative to egoism is altruism; the remedy for self-centeredness is sociality. We transcend species-centeredness (if we do) by recognizing a society wider than the human. What is wrong with phenomenalism or Berkeleyanism (also materialism) is its arbitrary cutting off of the social conception of objectivity at the limits of humanity, or of terrestrial animal life—whether or not God is added. Indeed, if the idea of mind or "spirit" can span the gulf (in some sense infinite) between humanity and God, how can it fail to cover the finite though vast difference between a human being and a molecule? And how can even the least creature fail to exhibit some lowly degree of that which in eminent form is deity (assuming we can distinguish deity from the mere unknown)? A dualism of mind and mere matter, as Berkeley and Leibniz both saw, is subtly incompatible with theism. But so is the notion that minds can deal directly only with ideas, rather than with other and in some cases vastly different minds.

Epistemic Transcendence is most clearly grasped in the social case. *You* are not merely idea or feeling in me, for you have your own ideas and feelings. Who can establish limits to the generalization of Transcendence in this social sense? Or prove that there is any other kind? Or that any problem is illuminated by supposing that there is? I admit I see no such problem. A third reply to the appeal—in itself entirely in order—to the "Principle of Contrast" is that mind has degrees. Experiences vary in intensity, complexity, spatiotemporal scope, extent of creative freedom, and awareness of alternative possibilities. The lower limit of diminishing degrees, for idealism, coincides with nonentity. No experience at all, human or nonhuman, means no concrete reality at all. But very low degrees will, for many purposes, be equivalent to none at all. Idealism can claim to find a place for all the contrasts we have any need to make.

Anti-idealism implies a criterion for the total absence of experience in some parts of nature. I know of no such criterion that is both non-question-begging and conceivably applicable in experience, except through the confusion spoken of earlier between 'not observably present' and 'observably not present.' For example, it is arbitrary to say that, since our feelings require nervous systems, without such systems there can be no feeling. Of course there could not be our specific kind of feelings, or even the metazoan animal kind, in single cells or molecules. But there are structural and behavioral analogies between metazoan response to stimuli and an amoeba's response or even an atom's. Moreover, the push-pull, purely mechanical account of physical action has been shown to be what Leibniz held it was, a myth due to the grossness of our perceptual discrimination, masking vast numbers of nonmechanical relationships. On all levels environmental changes influence internal changes in individuals; and this is the general formula for perceptual behavior. To say that the formula is more general than the idea of experience can be is merely to declare idealism false by definition. For *idealism is the doctrine that mind is as protean and multiform as the reality that mind is trying to know.*

Idealism has sometimes been defined as the equation "to be is to be perceived." If the phrase means that supposing A perceives X, X could not have existed if A had failed to perceive it, realists have shown how implausible it is. This is especially clear in the case of human memory, which is our way of perceiving our own experiences. The remembered events are presupposed, rather than produced, by the remembering. Moreover, there is little interest in perceiving things unless more than one person can (at least indirectly) perceive the same things. It is counterintuitive to suppose that perception gives a merely private world. On the other hand, there does seem to be a connection of meaning between reality and perceivability. If, then, it can be shown that the implied possibility of being perceived cannot remain unactualized, perhaps to be is indeed to be perceived—but by whom? By someone or other, or some set of subjects or other, no matter which, so long as they are capable of perceiving the thing. Thus the reality of anything may require that the class of perceivers of that very thing should not be empty, but it does not require just this perceiver or that, or even that the perceivers be human. Things are there, not solely for human beings, but for birds, insects, who can say what else?

The requirement that a certain class be nonempty, though the particular members are indifferent, is not without analogy. A respectable doctrine of universals is that they are real only if there are particular instances, or, at least, instances of someone thinking the universal. But most holders of this doctrine have not supposed that the very instances there actually are were necessary. Thus happiness is real if there are happy beings. But any happy beings will do. Another and in a way closer analogy: persons eager for fame require for their satisfaction that people praise or be interested in them. What people? Any people, able and willing to furnish the right sort of praise or interest. The example is less remote than it may seem from our problem. For who is entirely without something like the need to be attended to by others? We all look to the future to take some interest in, get some value from, what we are now. First of all our own future selves are looked to for this. Also other human beings. Every human experience expects to constitute part of the past for subsequent experiences. Idealism, as some of us construe it, suggests that this be generalized for all experience and all concrete reality.

Events are real only as past or about to become past; but pastness is a relational affair, no event being past in and for itself. Also, the only clue we have to pastness as a relational status is in *experience* of past events, as, for example, in memory. I say "for example" because it can be argued, and I believe it is true, that perception also gives us the past, rather than the absolute present.

In the light of the foregoing, perhaps the famous formula should run "to be is at least to be destined to be perceived." But by the time an event has really happened and can be talked about, it is past for some present, and idealism interprets this as equivalent to, remembered, or perceived by some subjects. Everything concrete and singular is first subject and then object for other subjects. But no particular "other subjects" are required; merely whatever subjects subsequently come along, able to do the objectifying. The future alone will determine what subjects, i.e., what concrete particular experiences, do the remembering or perceiving of things now coming into being.

It might be thought that for a theist one subject in particular is required as perceiver of each actuality, namely, the divine subject. However, my view is that God is not a particular simple subject or psychical actuality. God's awareness of a particular worldly actuality is a particular awareness, as a free synthesis of data it could have been otherwise and yet have been the awareness of those very data. Actualities must be divinely apprehended, but there is no particular divine apprehension that is uniquely required for this. Thus theism need introduce no violation of the principle that objects of an awareness never imply that very awareness. What is required is that there be a real distinction between the divine essence-and-existence and the concrete acts of divine awareness in or by which the essence is actualized. Like so many dichotomies, 'essence and existence' is inadequate to express reality; the triad essence, existence, and actuality is needed. From "necessarily some actualization" to "this actualization," the step is by decision, not by necessity.

An important distinction is that between 'what is experienced is *in* the experience' and 'what is experienced *depends upon* the experience.' Of course, if *A* experiences *O*, *O* is in *A*'s experience. Otherwise *A* would have experience of nothing, or of no particular thing, not experience of *O*. Yet it does not follow that *O* has no other and independent status besides that of qualifying *A*'s awareness. Even if one renounces both naïve realism and the usual form of sense datum theory, there is still a third locus for *O* besides the experience and the extrabodily object, namely, the neural process, which for some idealists is psychical—not in human but in subhuman form.

The notion that what qualifies an experience is thereby reduced to a mere adjective of the experience is the fallacy that leads to solipsism. The traditional subject-predicate logic obscures the truth here. True, the inclusion of the object is normally, or in nondivine experience, in a sense incomplete. It does not do full justice to the thing experienced, but this deficiency or "abstractness" of objectification does not alter the concrete object experienced as it is, or was, in itself. That is the very point of the "deficiency," that the object is the independent target, only some aspects of which are attained in the sense of being in the distinctly conscious portion of experience.

No doubt this is a subtle and difficult point. But in any case, there is no standard logical rule according to which entering into a complex entity necessarily alters the item entering the complex. Hence realists should not feel forced to deny the inclusiveness of experience in order to preserve the independence of particular objects from particular subjects. 'In the mind,' some of them said, was only a misleading paraphrase for 'present to or apprehended by the mind.' But how misleading is it? If experience is not a unity inclusive of its data, I, at least, have no idea what it is. And Moore in the end virtually conceded that he also had none. Take a case of aesthetic enjoyment. What makes it *that* concrete enjoyment is lost if we abstract from the objects given in the experience. Moore's "diaphanous" awareness to which the data are mere additions is only awareness in general, or merely as such, an extreme abstraction. It is no concrete instance of this abstraction. But Moore's realistic contention stands, just the same. The data are included, but their existence did not require just *this* inclusion, i.e., inclusion in just this experience.

We are now ready to consider what theory of relations idealism requires. In the relevant sense relations are "internal" to those terms, if any, which could not exist except in the relations in question. They are external to those terms, if any, which could exist not in the relations. In other words, a term to which the relation is internal depends upon the relation, hence upon the other term (or terms) involved, while a term to which the relation is external is independent of the relation and the other term. $Ra^ib \supset Dab$ (if the relation R of a to b is internal to a, a depends upon b); $Rb^ea \supset {\sim} Dba$ (if the relation of b to a is external to b, b does not depend upon a). By these expressions we avoid the ambiguity in 'depends upon the relation,' which might mean depends upon the relation to the other term mentioned; or it might only mean depends upon the relation (say, being perceived) to *some* suitable term, not necessarily b. In the latter case, dependence upon the relation would not entail dependence upon b. I have argued that things perceived depend upon being perceived, but not by any particular actual perceiver rather than other possible ones. However, so far as a particular pair of perceiver and perceived is concerned, the relation is internal to the former, though external to the latter. Thus idealism ought to hold that relations are for some terms internal and for some external. Internality and externality, or dependence and independence, both occur, and they can combine in one and the same by no means unusual instances. There is no formal contradiction in "$Dab \cdot {\sim} Dba$," any more than there is in saying that p entails q but not vice versa.

Why suppose that symmetrical cases exhaust the possibilities? The very definitions of "internal" most commonly given, e.g., by Bradley, Russell, and Ewing, imply or strongly suggest symmetry—thus "grounded in the natures of the terms." And so, by carelessness at the start the controversy was almost condemned to miss the truth. The thesis that reality is essentially mind neither requires nor permits us to assert that all things are mutually dependent upon one another. Nor does it require or permit us to assert that they are all mutually independent. These two contrary symmetries are alike anti-idealistic. They also equally conflict with a realistic epistemology. Only if independent realities influence the formation of particular experiences can there be knowledge. Granted an independent thing to know, say, O (which can be another, independent experience), we can then readily distinguish experience of O—or EO—from O itself, even though E is essentially $E(O)$, or E-including-O. A whole necessarily includes its part, but is not necessarily identical with it. (Such identity is a degenerate case.) Bradley's arguments can all be answered, provided one takes asymmetrical cases into account, which he fails to do.

Where relations are external to both terms, they are "relations of reason," relations in the mind of some spectator, as a third entity over and above the two terms. Where they are internal to both terms, the latter are merely aspects of one and the same thing, as in the right and left sides of one's visual experience, for example. Thus all relations are internal to something, and all are external to something. But merely from Rab nothing at all follows as to the dependence or independence of either term with respect to the other.

Another mistake of "absolute" idealists was to put primary emphasis upon mere relations of comparison, such as likeness or difference. Here indeed a certain symmetry is found. But (as Ernest Nagel rightly urges) a symmetrical relation of dependence is not thereby implied. Suppose A is six feet tall and B is five feet; the difference in height of one foot is not thereby shown necessary to A, say, unless it is known that A could not have existed with his height of six feet without B existing with his height of five feet. And this is the very question at issue. Perhaps A needs no relation to B, either as alike or as different; for there might, so far as A is concerned, have been no such thing as the referent of 'B.' Of course, things can have definite height or other properties only in relation to *some* context; but things can have their definiteness without being contrasted with everything whatever, no matter where or when in space-time. Washington's thoughts and feelings, for example, were what they were, no matter what some later historians have said about them. It is the historians and not Washington for whom the contrast between themselves and Washington is or was an intrinsic relation. After all, the historians knew about Washington, but not vice versa. To try to settle the question of independence by arguing from relations of comparison is thus question-begging. Only after we know what dependencies there are can we be in a position to ascertain how far relations of comparison are constitutive. If and only if A depends upon B does A depend upon the difference between A and B.

It might be thought that the independence of Washington from us is, after all, a kind of relation to us, and that, since Washington is either dependent upon or independent of us, relationship to us is a necessary property of Washington. Hence independence is contradictory. Now independence is, I grant, a real property essential to individuals. But the independence of Washington was with respect to *any* individuals, no matter who they might be, coming after his time. This independence is completely stated in the previous sentence. Nothing whatever is added to Washington's independence, as a real property, by specifying which individuals have come to fill the role of 'persons upon whom Washington did not depend.' To suppose that something is added is to contradict the assumption that he was independent of no matter what persons might come after his time. Independence is not a relation specifically to actual individuals but to a set of possibilities, a neutrality as to what determinate actualizations of these are effected.

It favors idealism that the causal relation, like the temporal relation, and also the relation of complex wholes to at least some of their constituents, are all, when interpreted naturally, cases of one-way dependence analogous to the one-way dependence of experiences on their given objects or data.

With all these counterexamples, we need not take to heart Hume's "What is distinguishable is separable."[2] The letter X is clearly distinguishable from the letter pair XY, but, while the single letter can occur without the pair, the pair cannot occur without the letter. Thus the symmetry of the comparison relation does not carry over into the dependence relation. Hume's dubious theory of "simple" impressions (repeated in essence by Ayer and Russell) obscured the importance of this point. In the memory of a previous experience, the later or remembering experience is complicated by the earlier in a one-way relation of dependence. It is instructive that while Bradley argued against, and Hume for, symmetrical independence, both were reasoning from the same relation of comparison—difference or distinguishability. They drew the two possible opposite conclusions, given the false assumption that the logical structure of comparison relations must be the same as that of dependence relations.

Strictly speaking, even comparison relations are symmetrical only so far as we abstract from the specific ways in which the two items are distinguishable. Thus of two experiences one may be the more, the other the less complex; one with more sense of red or yellow; one predominantly visual and the other auditory. The most concrete relations of comparison are never symmetrical. Always the partisans of symmetry obscure issues. They commit the fallacy of misplaced concreteness. Even in physics this can be seen, and not alone in the parity matter.

The neglect of the asymmetry in all specific relations of comparison is apparent in the arguments of Nagarjuna and also those of Fa Tsang in India and China long ago. Nagarjuna asks, "Is an effect similar, dissimilar, both similar and dissimilar, neither similar nor dissimilar?" He then deduces absurd consequences from each of the four options. The attempt to exhaust the possibilities is in principle admirable. But since each of the four is stated in symmetrical terms the real options are missed. And the absurd consequences all derive from the neglect of the asymmetrical aspects that have been ignored. Of course, effects are both similar and dissimilar, compared to causes, but what makes the connection is the *how* of the similarity or dissimilarity, and this differs in the two directions, cause–effect, effect–cause. The effect, concretely specified, resembles and differs from its causal conditions (they are always plural) as a creative synthesis resembles and differs from its data. The data are necessary conditions, while the synthesis is the logically sufficient condition from which the other end of the relation is derivable. Nagarjuna's dialectical proof of the impossibility of a rational cosmology begs the question.

Fa Tsang urges that just as "second" presupposes or implies "first" so "first" implies "second." Here the asymmetry is in the distinction between actual and possible. If X is the second to perform a certain feat there must have been a first; but Y can be the first to perform a feat even though no second has occurred and perhaps may never occur. First implies the idea of a *possible* second but that is all, while second implies an actual first. Fa Tsang's mystical monism is not proved by his argument. By ignoring the possible–actual contrast he begs the question. Any pluralist who understands himself affirms that contrast. The first person to land on a small sea island might be the last, if the island then sinks into the sea. It is remarkable that similar sophistries were committed by the two founders of Mahayana Buddhism, and much later by Hume, Russell, and Bradley, to mention only a few of those who have been blind to the one-way dependencies of existence.

Since idealism implies that mind must be on both sides of every genuine contrast, it is not enough for an idealist to say, with Bosanquet, that the nature of mind is to include and the nature of objects to be included, from which he infers only that reality as a whole or in its full concreteness is mind. One must also say that experiences can be included as objects in other experiences, so that it is the nature of mind to be included as well as to include. By taking also into account abstract aspects and aggregates of experiences, one can conceive experience to have as many forms as reality.

It is time to face the Cartesian (really Augustinian) dictum, often put forth as self-evident, that mind is inextended. This has been deliberately rejected by men with every conceivably relevant form of competence concerning both space and mind. Thus—to mention a few—Fechner, James, and Troland were psychologists of note; Clifford, Varisco, Peirce, and Whitehead were philosophizing mathematicians; Burger is a physicist; Sewall Wright is a great geneticist, a mathematician with a fine knowledge of natural science in general. Many others could be named who see no need to deny the reality of extension in order to explain the world idealistically. I myself reached an idealistic view of the physical world at the age of twenty, and it did not then, and does not now, seem to me that I was in effect declaring spatiality to be unreal. Whatever the status of the Cartesian dogma, self-evident it is not. Only careful argument will do on a question discussed with such immense care as, for instance, Whitehead has discussed it in *Process and Reality*, or Peirce in volumes I and VI of the *Collected Papers*.

Naturally, one can find abstract aspects of mind of experience that cannot be supposed, in any direct clear sense, to occupy space. Thus virtue has no definite, unique, size or shape. Concepts in general are like this. But an actual concrete experience, including elements of thought, perception, memory, desire, is not nowhere, nor yet somewhere in a point. Where then, if not somewhere in a region? Experiences have spatiotemporal relations, for in the modern view space is simply a network of cause–effect relations; and if one rejects (rightly, I think) epiphenomenalism and mere materialism one must see even human experiences as entering into such relations, with both temporal and spatial aspects, as truly, though not as obviously or simply, as any events whatever.

If the proper strategy of idealism is the one I have suggested, those critics of historical idealistic systems who have attacked one-sided doctrines of interdependence, or of the exclusive reality of the inextended, eternal, or absolute, have been idealism's friends in disguise. And those idealists who have tried to explain away one side of categorial contrasts in order to leave the field to mind were anti-idealistic in spite of themselves. Immense confusion has resulted from the failure to distinguish clearly between the two essentially opposite ways of defending the idealistic thesis. To explain basic contraries through mind is one thing; to explain them away as unreal is another. Only the latter has had much attention from the critics.

Idealistic speculation began about three centuries ago in the West with Leibniz. More than a thousand years earlier another form of it had reached fairly sharp formulation in Asia, especially in Mahayana Buddhism. In all that time the question concerning the equivalence of mind and reality was argued only as an issue entangled with others whose necessary connection with *this* issue was never made clear. I have attempted in this sketch to show how confusion resulted from this procedure, and to suggest the direction in which a remedy is to be sought.

Like every philosophical view, idealism needs to be tested by its compatibility with the principle that meaning implies contrast, and hence that the truth is not to be looked for in crassly one-sided positions, such as extreme monism or pluralism, doctrines of universal interdependence or universal independence, absolute optimism or absolute pessimism, eternalism or temporalism, a priorism or empiricism, rationalism or intuitionism.

The subject of Moore's "devout hope" deserves more balanced and adequate refection than it could receive in the battles of the first quarter of [the twentieth] century by which the hold of an extraordinarily one-sided and counterintuitive form of idealistic metaphysics was broken.

CHAPTER SEVEN

Creativity and the Deductive Logic of Causality

A number of writers, sometimes called "process philosophers," have held that becoming is both creative and cumulative—"creative" meaning that the new in any moment of process was not wholly contained in or strictly implied or entailed by the previous moments, the initial conditions, and "cumulative" meaning that these conditions are in some sense contained in or strictly implied by the new. Each instance of becoming is a "creative synthesis" of the previous instances. Causality, on this view, is one-way inclusion or entailment. Bergson's snowball image of duration neatly expresses the idea. The rolling ball acquires new layers while retaining the old ones. Or, to use a more literally applicable formula, an adult remembering (mostly with very indistinct consciousness) his childhood presupposes and somehow implies his childish experiences, though the child was in no comparable sense aware, or implicative, of the adult life of that individual.

It is less obvious but, according to Whitehead or to my "neoclassical" version of process philosophy, no less true that even in perception it is past, not absolutely simultaneous, events that are given.

It seems not to have been noticed that deductive logic can show how, from the creative-cumulative view, it is intelligible, that, although exact and unqualified prediction of future events is in principle impossible, still much about the future is predictable. Partial though not complete predictability, I shall show, is an entailment of the creative-cumulative view. This is the logical structure (not made explicit by him) of Whitehead's "answer to Hume," which I regard as the only answer that need have impressed Hume very much.

It may be well to say here that I assume, against Hume and also Einstein, but with Peirce, Bergson, Boutroux, Dewey, Montague, Whitehead, Popper, and many physicists that the genuine causal laws are all approximate or statistical, not deterministic in the classical sense. I believe that the arguments for this view are very cogent. Moreover, I am confident that quantum uncertainty is not the only aspect of nature in application to which classical determinism is at best useless. I believe Wigner is justified in expecting that the laws of organic systems, especially on the higher animal levels, will turn out to be more complicated than those of inorganic systems. We shall, it seems likely, have to go further from classical concepts than Heisenberg has done, rather than be able to relapse into Newtonian rationalism, as even Einstein wanted to do. Moreover, the "dice-throwing God" that Einstein could not believe in is the only one Peirce and some of the rest of us could or can believe in. I should also say that while we must take the theories of physics seriously, I do not think they should be considered necessarily definitive in so fundamental or philosophical a question as the structure of time or causality.

Assume, as the meaning of cumulativeness cum creativity, that absolute knowledge of an event would necessarily include or entail absolute knowledge of its causal antecedents—but *not* vice versa. Let K stand for absolute knowledge (partially explicable as the unattainable limit of better and better human knowledge) of events preceding event E, and let K' stand for absolute knowledge of E itself. And suppose one had K but not K'. Then (because of creativity) K' could not be inferred; but still (because of cumulativeness) something about K' could be inferred; namely, it would have to entail K. This is significant, for not any and every proposition, or state of knowledge, can entail a given proposition or state of knowledge. Moreover, since K is here logically very "strong," being the absolute description or knowledge of certain concrete actualities, the limitations imposed upon K' are substantial.

It must be understood that K' is not a mere conjunction of K with additional propositions or bits of knowledge. Otherwise the point just made would be merely trivial. For, given any proposition q and any other proposition p, the compound proposition p and q will entail q. This is ruled out as an interpretation of process philosophy by its doctrine, found in all representatives, that concrete reality consists of unit-events each of which is genuinely singular, and not a mere conjunction of many events, though it intrinsically refers to many. Thus an experience in which various events of the past are remembered or perceived is not those past events plus some new features that themselves do not entail the events. Rather there is a felt qualitative unity such that the new quality intrinsically refers to the old qualities. "The many become one, and are increased by one."[1] This is the point of "creative synthesis." Peirce's theory of Firstness implies a similar doctrine. So does Bergson's theory of becoming or *duré*. To this point we shall return.

My suggestion now is: the causal limitations a present situation imposes upon its future are nothing but those that are logically implied by the principle that every future situation must strictly entail the present situation as belonging to its past. *Predictability is cumulativeness read backwards.* Thus my childhood, with its world, determined that either I, as adult, or else the world years later without me would be the kind of person or the kind of world that could refer back to just that childhood and that previous world.

The key to this reverse inference is found in deductive logic. Suppose X says to Y: "I am thinking of a class of propositions, call them the p's, each of which entails, but is not entailed by, the proposition q^*, which is, 'There is an animal in the room.' What can you infer from this about the p's?" Y: "I infer that the p's are all at least as specific or definite (logically strong) as q^*. Indeed, since they are stipulated to be nonequivalent to q^*, they must be *more* definite, as in 'There is a small animal in the room,' or 'There is a dog in the room.' Also any p must have a subject matter closely related to that of q^*; it cannot compare to q^* as would 'There is a rose or a pitcher of water in the room.'"

Suppose, instead of q^* we take a logically stronger proposition, e.g., "There is a small terrier in the room"; or even, "Our little terrier Fido is in the room." In this case the p's must be much more narrowly limited than in the other case. Thus: "Our little terrier Fido asleep (or scratching himself) is in the room." Entailment without equivalence is always a matter of dropping, in conclusion, some part of the logical strength, the information, contained in premises. The one-way view of causal necessity is the limiting and most concrete case of this, with the description of the later situation, the outcome or effect, being the logically stronger premise and the antecedent situation or cause the logically weaker conclusion. Becoming is enrichment of reality, adding definiteness but not subtracting any. The cause–effect relation is to be fully understood only from the standpoint of the effect, in which alone is the complete determinateness.

The traditional view was very different. The cause was the superior entity, or if not, cause and effect were "equal." Effects were to be known in their causes, as well as causes in their effects. And so, before an event existed to be known it was nevertheless completely defined and ready to be known. (Or else it existed before it happened.) This upside-down idea (I here begin a brief excursus from my main theme) was neatly embodied in the standard medieval theological view that God knows the world simply by knowing himself as its cause. Thus an effect was held to be implied by, logically contained in, though inferior to its cause, the cause minus something, and then what is the point to causal production? The only value production can have is to enrich reality. The cause-with-the-effect must be superior to the cause alone. Also, if causes do not annihilate themselves, effects with causes are the only effects there are. And surely God does not annihilate himself in producing the world, and so the world with its divine cause is more than the cause alone. Either this effect is superior to God, or it is God as enriched by the world he produces. Neither implication was acceptable to medieval thinkers.

Spinoza took the medieval scheme seriously and deduced the catastrophic consequence that the world must be in God, and in him taken merely as a necessary and eternal cause, i.e., the world in all details must be as necessary as God. Therewith, as Wolfson rightly says, Spinoza destroyed (one chief aspect of) "the medieval synthesis." For two centuries and more philosophers and theologians hesitated to try the remaining theistic possibility, which is to admit that effects as such are more than their causes, and hence supreme Reality must be the universal or inclusive contingent effect, as well as the universal or primordial necessary cause. It must be influenced by, as well as influential upon, all things. To avoid contradiction one must admit (as Whitehead and others have done) a real distinction in God between his nature as primordial and his nature as consequent, or as influenced by the creation. (End of theological *excursus*.)

In our logical training, attention to the "fallacy of affirming the consequent" (and deducing the antecedent) has been allowed to obscure the important truth that "A certain proposition q is entailed by every member of the class C of propositions" does tell us something about this class, and, moreover, that the more definite or logically strong q is the more we thus learn about the class of propositions entailing it. One important group of such classes of propositions is what is meant by "real possibilities" in the normal sense, i.e., possibilities for the future of some given present. Here q is very strong indeed. And this is one reason why the transition from cumulativeness to the possibility of implications for the future has been overlooked. Ordinary textbook cases of implication involve much weaker instances of q. Suppose q is: "I see something moving." Then "I see our dog Fido moving" is one of a fantastically wide variety of possible p's entailing q. Causal implication can start from an incomparably richer base than a mere visible moving something. So the reverse nonstrict inference to the class of p's can be incomparably more definite.

A full account would have to consider the distinction between lawlike statements and those specifying particular "initial conditions." It would also have to ask what, in "inanimate" nature, corresponds to memory and perception. I also happen to believe further (here comes a second theological digression) that the adequate understanding of lawlike statements requires the idea of a cosmic lawgiver. But still, all this would come under K, the knowledge or description of the antecedent situation from which the result, the effect, is to come. Even God's law-giving action must be antecedent to the effects it influences, not simultaneous with them (nor yet eternal). Thus the ultimate principle of "cause" or "condition" is univocal, even though there is also a "difference in principle" between divine and other causation. Thus God as causal influence *in* every event will (in one aspect of his being) be *antecedent* to every event, and as influenced *by* every event will be *subsequent* to every event. He alone is primordial and he alone is everlasting. That causes are logically independent of effects as, in normal cases of entailment, conclusions are independent of premises will be universally true. (End of second theological *excursus*.)

Obviously, one source of confusion is the metaphor that conclusions "follow" from premises. In our knowledge, drawing conclusions may temporally succeed positing of premises. But this is the reverse of the ontological relations. Thus "animal" follows logically from "human," but animals were there long before human beings. Events in their concreteness are never known in antecedent events, whereas they are habitually known in subsequent ones (more or less directly) by either memory or perception. The past is cognitively derived from the present by abstracting from that in the present which is novel. To realize today what yesterday was like we must drop out part of what we know about today's experiences. The full logical strength is in the present; it was in no sense in the past. Thus have multitudes of philosophers been misled, partly at least, by a metaphor. *Causal prediction is reading the deductive relations backward, from a conclusion to the class of premises capable of entailing it.* We are asking, in Whitehead's metaphor, what sort of future could "house" or accommodate what is now going on as *its* past?[2]

The chief mistake concerning causation has been acceptance of the false dilemma: either deductive logic cannot throw light upon the causal relations of events or each new event is to be viewed as a new premise for new entailed conclusions. On the contrary, each event is primarily a new premise for old conclusions. Only in a weakened sense, and purely derivatively from this, is it a premise for new conclusions. This is not particularly paradoxical. Each new experience of a grown man is a new premise from which that man's birth and childhood logically follows. Or, after the death, say, of Washington, each new stage of the writing of American history is a new premise from which the onetime existence of Washington logically follows (assuming, as we all do, that Washington can be and is denoted). The reverse inference, from the life of Washington to the future historians and their writings about Washington, is a weaker one, and merely gives us a class of possible or probable historians writing about him. And while the adult Washington presupposes the child Washington, the latter might have accidentally died before growing up. To assert the contrary is to leap into a "dark" whose degree of darkness cannot be exaggerated.

It is true that the laws of physics, as now known, do not suffice to validate all aspects of the foregoing scheme. But we should not forget, I think, that physics is the most abstract form of knowledge of nature. We know what it is like to be an animal, in a sense in which we can never know what it is like to be an atom (rather than a man experimenting with atoms). I cannot believe that physics goes as deeply into the nature of things as biology and psychology. It may be more accurate and more comprehensive than they, but at the price of not knowing what sorts of things it is dealing with, apart from human experiences of the things. Do we know what radiant energy or electricity are? We know some structural (mathematically expressible) truths about them, and we are familiar with certain human experiences partly traceable to them as causes, but this is all.

To the contention of some philosophers that the question "What is such and such, beyond its structural-causal status?" has no meaning, I reply, "It has a clear but in some cases not very definitely answerable meaning, which is: How does such and such differ from or resemble various aspects of our human experiences, and this in qualitative as well as merely structural respects?" We know what we are asking, but since qualities are not definitely knowable except by intuition, and our sharply definite intuitions are limited by the capacities of our sense organs, there is much that we cannot know about the qualities of reality.

Two mistakes in traditional reflections upon causality have been the arbitrary assumptions (a) that causal conditioning is symmetrical or biconditioning (events equally requiring their antecedent conditions and their subsequent results) and (b) that the way to understand effects is to consider what it means to be a cause. By (a) either creativity is wholly excluded (determinism) or else no strict cumulativeness is allowed (Mead). By (b) one is trying to understand causal deduction by asking how its conclusions imply its premises, thus taking the affirmation of the logical consequent as the primary deductive procedure! Not causes but effects are the premises, the logically stronger terms. The past is found in the present, not vice versa; and only because the past is in the present is the future also, though only partially, in the present, as that which, whatever else later becomes true of it, must contain the present as *its* past. When we know what it is to be an effect, then we can also, by logical principles, derive what it is to be a cause, for that is the simpler case. A cause defines a set of possible effects, a set that, though it may not yet have an actual member yet, is bound to acquire one.

As soon as we see that the key to causation is in the status of being an effect of antecedent conditions, we are ready to see also that both memory and perception are, by their very meaning, just such effects. And then we see what Hume overlooked. He sought causal connections between things perceived and/or remembered, rather than between perceivings or rememberings themselves and their data. More precisely, he sought connections between "impressions," taken either as not intrinsically referring to anything impressing itself *upon* experience, or else as things doing the impressing, while the results of this action, the real impressions, are dismissed from consideration. It was a strange error, repeated on a grandiose scale by Russell—and how many others!

That it was an error seems clear. If we can know that we know anything, we must be able to know what it is to experience, that is, to perceive or remember. And the time to look for relations between entities perceived or remembered but which perhaps, at least apparently, do not perceive or remember, is after we have done real justice to the internal relational structures of perceiving and remembering themselves. It is in this sense, and this only, that epistemology is prior to ontology. Our experiences are our privileged samples of reality. Humean positivism "misses the boat" at this landing as neatly as boats can be missed. To employ an old joke, the boat is missed by two, or rather three, jumps.

1. Humeans look for, and announce their failure to find, a symmetrical causal necessity, a biconditioning, whereas we know from propositional logic that the biconditional (equivalence) is a derivative and weakened relation, not the basic meaning of implication.
2. They look for necessity in the wrong place, in mere objects rather than in experiences as such.
3. Insofar as they take causality as a one-way (rather than symmetrical or directionless) requirement, they take the inference to be primarily from cause to effect.

Thus, in nearly all possible ways they beg the question against the most characteristic constructive metaphysical systems of recent times—Bergson, Peirce, Whitehead, also Montague, Parker, Hartshorne, and others. And some idealistic critics of Humeanism, e.g., Ewing, make some of the same mistakes. It is indeed a comedy of errors, or of failure in communication. For the creative-cumulative view of becoming is clearly implicit in doctrines that were held long before Hume (e.g., by the Socinians). Lequier held such a doctrine a hundred years ago.[3] It is much more widely held now. And partisans of Hume's view that causal relations are mere constant conjunctions have yet to tell us how they know that no such doctrine as the cumulative can be true.

Three admissions are in order. The process philosopher needs some solution of Kant's First Antinomy. He must either suppose a first moment of all becoming or admit an infinite or indefinite number of past events. My own view is that an actual infinity of already elapsed events is a tenable idea, and that mathematical finitism taken to exclude this is not obligatory. The second admission concerns a perhaps even greater difficulty. Granted, some will ask, that the past, insofar as remembered or perceived, is implied by the present, how far can this implication go, considering that much of the past is, so far as we can empirically know, neither remembered nor perceived? Here we confront the question of unconscious or faintly conscious memories and perceptions, also the question of various levels of nonhuman memory and perception, including for some of us divine memory and perception. I hold that a theist is here, as in other fundamental questions, in an advantageous position, provided he avoids certain mistakes in the idea of God, for example, the idea that God is universal cause but not universal effect, or that he is in every sense immutable. I also hold that a psychicalist, for whom all singular events (the momentary state of a stone is not one stony event but a vast number of molecular, atomic, or particulate events) involve memory or perception in at least some minimal sense, has the advantage over a materialist or dualist.

I believe that the difficulties mentioned in the previous paragraph are to be taken seriously, but are not insuperable. In contrast, the difficulties of Hume's view, as well as those of materialism and also "absolute idealism" (holding either that every event implicates every other, past, contemporary, or future, or that events and temporal relations are not real), seem to me incurable and sufficient to justify the rejection of these views. Some version of process philosophy seems therefore the only hope of understanding causality. It alone can show *how* events require their antecedents, from which, as I have tried to show, it is deducible that they entail an important part of the natures of their successors. More than this is not needed for the purposes of life; indeed, the more than this that is affirmed by determinism is pragmatically meaningless. It is intrinsic to the meaning of prediction that it be less than absolute. It is the very point of foreknowledge that it be qualified to allow for elements of choice between possible outcomes of present situations. Only the myth of the knower as mere spectator, outside the world of action and peering into it, as it were, through a metaphysical window, could ever have made determinism seem a sensible idea. The third admission is that there is certainly considerable obscurity in the requirement that the character of later events must *not* consist of a mere conjunction of that of past events plus some independent new character, so that the backward deduction would be of the form p and q entails q. Rather p, no less unitary (though more complex than q) entails q. I must admit that this unity is not to be explicated with the devices of deductive logic. It is, as Peirce and Whitehead agree, a unity of feeling. Its principles are aesthetic. The various data from the past must be embraced in a unity of feeling. If the data are not sufficiently homogeneous, no unity of feeling, no aesthetic harmony, can occur; if the data are excessively homogeneous, if there is insufficient contrast, aesthetic achievement will also be impossible. Aesthetic value is the mean between mere diversity and mere unity. Its twin evils are boredom and suffering. At the limit in either direction no experience can occur. A blow on the head may make human consciousness impossible because the requisite set of sufficiently unified but sufficiently contrasting data are no longer presented. What then happens, however, according to the process view, is not necessarily that there will be no aesthetic achievement at all in the bodily system but that it will no longer be on the human level but will be confined to that of the cells and their individual feelings, or (if death occurs) to still lower (molecular) levels. That the process of achieving unity on some level can and will always continue I regard (this is my third theological digression) as due to the immanence of divine power ordering the world with infallible wisdom and power. "Ordering" does not mean determining events in their details, for in every case the creatures must achieve their own syntheses of antecedent data, the directives from God being merely the supreme example of such data. Thus there is in this view no "problem of evil" in anything like the classical form. The world order is not a matter of detail, but of outlines. And it cannot be shown that the outlines are bad.

Some light may be thrown upon the unity requirement by considering concrete experiences. Suppose I remember having just offended a taxi driver by telling him rather sharply that he was not taking the most direct route, and I remember his having responded somewhat angrily. The memory is too immediate and its content too vivid to be simply dismissed. There are various aesthetically possible ways of synthesizing this memory with memories coming from my more remote past and with (at the moment only normally vivid) sensory contents coming (as I hold, with Whitehead) from the immediate past of my bodily organs). I can try to decide whether to apologize to the man, I can wonder why I spoke so sharply, and so on. We have only a vague understanding of how past experiences and present sensory conditions limit the possible ways in which a tolerable new state of feeling can be achieved. But do we not have reason to avoid two extremes: on the one hand, supposing that there are no limitations at all, and on the other, that there is but one univocal possibility exactly defining the state of feeling that in fact takes place? How can many, indeed a huge number, of conditions in millions or billions of cells, and in a similar number of past experiences of mine, all, in combination with any psychological laws you please, strictly define and dictate a single new unitary experience? And also, how can the definite set of data available from memory and perception for that moment of my experiencing fail to influence the experience that occurs? Between these extremes lies the limited creative freedom (it may be small) we are seeking.

My attempt to show by an analogy with deductive logic how there can be partial predictability of the future, assuming that earlier events are precisely implicated by their successors, will be misunderstood if it is taken to be one more effort to show that we can have certain knowledge of the future. I am willing to grant almost all the qualifications as to the possibility of induction that Karl Popper proposes. I am a fallibilist, with him and with Peirce. What I am trying to do is not to show how we can know, simply know, the future, but only how there can be truth about it. For if there is not truth about the future we cannot even err in our predictions. I hold that truth about the future while it is future can only be truth about those determining tendencies, or in Popper's word, propensities, which obtain when an assertion about the future is made. And Hume was, or should have been, asking if there are such tendencies, such limitations upon the real or causal possibility that is the referent of statements about the future. Our knowledge is as limited as Popper says it is, or something very like that, but the question of truth (here also Popper and I agree) is not at all the same as the question of human knowledge. What makes it true that the grass is green is the grass being green, no matter what we know of its greenness. Here I agree with Tarski and with Popper, but this does not tell us how to construe the truth of "the grass *will* be green." I take this to be made true by there being already a propensity, either in grass now existing or in something capable of producing grass, such that the grass being green later on is implied as the only still open possibility. A "will be" is a present causal situation implying the sort of future event specified. This is a theory about truth and reality, not about our knowledge.

It does follow from my view that ideally adequate knowledge of the past and present world would precisely delineate the propensities, the implications, of the causal situation. But only a modern Protagorean would suppose that this tells us much about our human knowledge. We shall never have anything close to the ideal knowledge I am talking about. We have the kind of knowledge we need to make reasonable, responsible decisions. If the solar system blows up tomorrow that will not be our fault, and our inability to know for certain that it will not need not trouble us. We shall have had our day and done our bit. And if I am right, we have our chance to know what it is that prevents us from knowing more definitely than we do the real possibilities and probabilities that constitute the future as such. We lack precise quantitative knowledge of the past, also of remote contemporaries who will influence our remote future, and we have only vague qualitative knowledge of either past or contemporary realities, including that decisive part of the past that is the already formed divine ideals and purposes for the world. But we have some glimmer of understanding of how this so partially known past and present can constitute truth about the future. We can in a general way know what we are missing. And for those who like such general understanding, that is, for philosophically inclined persons, this is a source of some satisfaction. With the vast scope of our modern knowledge, we should be able to bear the thought that the vastness of what we do not know is of a higher order of magnitude, if not in some genuine sense infinite. Where we do not know we can hope or trust. Presumably the sun will not blow up in our time.

CHAPTER EIGHT

The Meaning of 'Is Going to Be'

I begin with a simple summary of the point of this chapter. If truth is about reality, then if realities are created in the course of time, so are truths. "The grass will be green" is true, by the Tarski principle, *if* the grass will be green; but what is the force of the "will be?" Tarski's explication, as Carnap admitted to me, does not answer this question. Utilizing the concept of enabling or permitting but not determining conditions explained in Chapter Seven, we have three cases: (a) the conditions now obtaining permit the grass to have but one color, the color green, tomorrow; (b) the conditions permit the grass to be brown, say (or some color other than green), but do not permit it to be green tomorrow; (c) they permit the grass to be green, but also permit it to have some other color, tomorrow. Assuming that the grass will still exist at the future time in question, and will not be colorless, then one of these three cases must obtain or be true, and the other two must be false. Case (a) defines "the grass will be green"; (b) "the grass will not be green"; (c) "the grass may-or-may-not be green." Whichever of the three is true, the other two are false. Thus only two truth values are required, but how the predicate is related to the subject admits of three possibilities, determinately p, determinately not-p, and indeterminate with respect to p, according to the causal situation to which the assertion implicitly or explicitly refers. Predication can be trivalent even where propositions are only bivalent.

The justification for allotting the triadicity to the internal structure of the propositions, rather than to their truth values, is in the doctrine that reality is objectively or in itself indeterminate in its aspect of futurity. This is what Aristotle should have meant, whether he did so or not, in his famous sea fight passage. R. Montague[1] and R. D. Bradley[2] have defended the view that the untruth of "*A* will occur" is equivalent to the truth of "*A* will not occur." They are aware that this equivalence has sometimes been denied, but they argue that the reasons given for the denial are unsound and that no alternative position is tenable. What, however, is the most reasonable form of alterna-tive, and what are the strongest arguments in its favor? As Popper has so well insisted, unless the most promising opposing theories and the best arguments for them have been considered, one's own view has not been rationally justi-fied. Anyone can refute the more foolish forms of theory competitive with his own, no matter how foolish his own may be. I do not find in either of the authors mentioned a realization of what an intelligent opponent could urge against the equivalence referred to earlier.

The notion of "X doing act A at time t" may turn out to fit the facts when t becomes the present; but a prediction is not a timeless utterance like "X performing A at t." It is rather an assertion that at a certain time, future to the time when the assertion is made, events *will* exhibit such and such a character. Many writers appear to find nothing problematic here: "will" simply turns a verb into the future tense, enabling it to refer to later events. Yes, but in what sense are there events that have not yet happened?

Suppose a blind guess "comes true" (as we say); the question remains, was the guess true when made? X has done A, but it need not follow that X "was going to do it all along" (from the time of utterance). Note that "is going" (to do it) is the present progressive tense of the verb "to go," just as "I *will* do it" in the volitional sense means "I am even now resolved upon the deed." These linguistic hints can, I believe, be taken seriously. "X will do A" in the strict meaning (as will be seen presently, we often speak more loosely) implies "X's doing of A is already determined or settled upon," or "there is no longer another possibility for X at time t than doing A," or "all the real possibilities allowed by the present causal conditions include X's doing of A." Thus there is a formal analogy to volition, provided a present decision is taken as irre-vocable and invincible. "X will not do A" means, if intended in the strictest sense, "none of the now causally open possibilities include his doing the deed; it has been ruled out by the 'march of events.'" If this is the meaning, no law of excluded middle as between true and false can restrict us to the two cases, will and will not; for some of the real possibilities may include A while oth-ers do not. The march of events may neither have ruled it out nor ruled it in. (To reject this indeterminate case *a priori* is to assert complete determinism, a topic to which we shall return presently.) We may then say, "It is false that A will, also false that A will not, but true that A may-or-may-not occur, since the real possibilities are divided between those including and those excluding A." Whatever happens later will neither prove nor disprove this statement. The only way decisively to refute or establish a "may-or-may-not" assertion is to know all the relevant current conditions and causal laws and to see that they do, or do not, determine the choice between A and not-A. To accomplish this perhaps exceeds human powers; but it is not meaningless. A thing is not absolutely unknowable simply because knowing it with certainty is a humanly unattainable ideal.

"Will" and "will-not," like "may-or-may-not," statements are unprovable in any simple decisive way by subsequent events. That A happened cannot show that there was no other real possibility (unless determinism is an *a priori* truth); similarly, if A fails to happen, its happening may yet have been really possible. If anyone finds it paradoxical that a prediction can be "fulfilled" or "verified" and yet have been untrue, I ask him to recall that we use similarly paradoxical language when we say that a scientific law may be verified, that is, found to fit known cases, and still not be a valid law. For this reason, Popper rejects the term "verify" and prefers the weaker "corroborate." And just as he rightly insists that the decisive operation is the falsification of laws, so we may say that the decisive operation as to predictions is similarly the negative one. "A will occur" is decisively falsified if A does not occur; for the "will" here means that no causally open possibility fails to include A, and the subsequent nonoccurrence of A shows that at least one possibility did fail to include it. By contrast, the prediction is only indecisively corroborated if A does occur; for we thus learn only that some possibility included the A feature, not that all did. We have then a genuine analogy to the corroboration of laws.

In the foregoing, we have shown how the causal conception of predictive truth may be embraced in the general theory of scientific reasoning, without assuming strict determinism. To suppose determinism absolutely true is to imply that the "may-or-may-not" form is always vacuous, or a mere profession of ignorance. Certainly if there is but a single real possibility in each case, this possibility either does or does not involve A, and hence either A will or A will not happen. Accordingly, the semantic analysis of truth with reference to future events should not be so formulated as to make "will" and "will not" the sole possibilities. For to accept this dichotomy is to decide by definition, or from semantic considerations alone, that there cannot be a plurality of real possibilities for a given future date. It is to make determinism in the maximal sense logically true. (I shall mention later a supposed escape from this consequence of the dichotomous view.) One of the rules of philosophizing should be, first seek the completely general or necessary principle, then define special or contingent forms by restriction. But we should also bear in mind that certain forms may, in some sorts of problem, be mere limiting conceptions that could not be actualized but, at most, approximated to. Determinism is, I believe, precisely such a limiting conception, the infinitely special case in which indeterminacy or creativity would shrink universally to zero. Absolute zeros are hard to establish, and in some contexts may be nonsensical.

How can an absolute prescription for a later event be in its conditioning predecessors? Everything of the future event would thus become present except a featureless, diaphanous "reality." And if the principle is generalized, the whole of becoming is in effect being viewed as though mapped, with infinite exactitude, in each of its states. If people had more imagination, I question if there would be so many determinists.

Our analysis leaves the principle of excluded middle intact as to propositions. Any will, will-not, or may-or-may-not statement, if not true, is definitely false; it can only be right or wrong to say that all, or that only some, or that no possibilities at a specified present or past time for a later time include *A*. But whichever of the three statements is true, the others are both false. We have here simply one more instance of the familiar exclusive and exhaustive triad: all, some only, or none. The third "value" is thus in the statement forms, not in their truth status. And since, by hypothesis, we are not dealing with an empty class (there *are* possibilities for the future), and "all" and "none" are contraries, they can both be false, but cannot both be true.

It is worth noting that the volitional meaning of "will" behaves in the same way, formally regarded. "It is untrue that he wills or intends to do it" fails to imply "he wills not to do it," for he may be irresolute or neutral as to the deed. If we abstract from the volitional tinge, we have in this third case simply that he may or may not do it. The outcome has yet to be "decided." The all, some, or none pattern is involved here, too; for there are possible actions one is opposed to taking, those one wills to take, and those about which one is indifferent or irresolute. To translate these subjective meanings into objective characteristics of the future one must abstract from the fallibility of human decision, which may be overruled either by the subject himself or by factors beyond his control. But the triadic structure remains in spite of this abstraction. There might be an irrevocable decision for or against, or no decision. All this has nothing to do with the law of excluded middle as to propositional truth values, but much to do with how the propositions whose truth is in question are to be interpreted or formulated.

Concerning "changes in truth value," a basic principle for interpreting this ambiguous phrase is the irreversibly *increasing* definiteness of truth. That which today, Monday, is settled for the day after tomorrow, Wednesday, will still be settled on Tuesday, and ever after, for that Wednesday; but some of what are now open possibilities for Wednesday will become closed, one way or the other, on Tuesday. Thus a will (or will-not) statement changes status only from false to true; and may-or-may-nots change only from true to false. In either case, however, what changes is not really the truth value of a certain proposition, but the status of some quasi proposition; a "statement schema," rather than a well-defined statement. Thus consider '*X* doing *A* at *t*'; if we do not know what actual world state includes its assertion we do not know what evidence is relevant to its truth and how, and hence we do not know what the statement commits us to. If *t* is understood to be in the past of the assertion, then indeed it does not matter at all when, more particularly, the assertion was made. But if the assertion is a prediction, then it does matter. For the closer the time of utterance approaches *t*, the more numerous must the true will (and will-not) statements become, and the less numerous the true may-or-may-nots. If, however, the time of utterance is fixed, then one of the three forms of futuristic statements must have been and must ever after remain true, since the possibilities for *t* must at that earlier time have been: all positive as to *A*, all negative, or divided. If the last, no subsequent happening can alter this retrospectively dated modal feature of reality: it can never in future be false that *A* was among the things that might (or might not) have followed the utterance after the specified interval.

"Truth changes," then, not in random fashion, but according to a necessary general rule. The vague and highly indefinite real possibilities for the remote future become step-by-step replaced, or rather supplemented, by more and more definite possibilities, as that future becomes imminent. Predictive truths, properly specified as to time of utterance, are never subsequently falsified; the only change is the addition of new truths for new times of utterance, new real states of nature, as these come into being. The very propositions themselves are new, for the "now" to which they refer is no mere date, but an actual situation, which as such could not be referred to beforehand, still less timelessly, or "in eternity."

Should any persistent reader argue that it must be true in advance or timelessly that a certain statement is to become true at a certain time, the answer of course is that, on the contrary, from a timeless, or remotely past, point of view, we should have at most "the statement may-or-may-not become true." This statement itself will suffer from indefiniteness. For it cannot identify anything concrete or particular, such as John's intentions at such and such a time. A semantic theory that contradicts this doctrine is trying to settle ontological questions by fiat, or, at best, according to logical convenience. I believe convenience at this level has little if any weight. The possible truth of blind guesses has value for science or common sense only if there is some connection, known or unknown, with causal laws; and so far as such laws obtain there is, according to our theory, definite truth about the future. What more do we need? Scientific corroboration can be achieved in the usual way, by eliminating the falsified claims to predictive understanding, and trying thus to narrow down the predictive and lawlike assertions among which the true ones must be found.

A year ago it may have been settled that today roughly so and so many suicides would occur; a week ago, the inevitable number of suicides for today must have been considerably more precisely defined; a half minute ago nearly every suicide occurring during the past ten seconds may have become already inevitable, a settled fact. All these degrees of determinateness will remain valid for all the future, with respect to their dates of assertion and the events of today or the last ten seconds. Such, on the theory we are explaining, is the modal structure of time, or if you prefer, of happenings. Definiteness is progressively made; it is never unmade. There is becoming, but no unbecoming or de-becoming of facts.

If "it will happen" means it is now already settled that "it" cannot fail to happen, then that a statement schema of this sort should change its truth is no more odd than that "it is now raining" should do so. In both cases the assertion is incomplete until the time reference is fixed. Moreover, the notion that dates can be assigned from eternity is one of the fairy tales—or controversial assumptions—that haunt this subject. Dating requires actual events and experiences somewhere. So far from "now" being dispensable, in favor of mere values on a time coordinate, it is the other way; all dating derives from "token-reflexive" demonstratives whose meaning varies with the contexts of their utterance. It is no mere date that makes an "it is now and henceforth settled that" determinately true or false, but an actual event or event sequence, which cannot be referred to except retrospectively, as the process that has just been going on or that went on in the less immediate past.

The crux of the matter is the theory of denotation. If this is a simple relation between language and things, then it is difficult to avoid the timeless theory of truth.[3] But if, as seems evident to me, denotation is a triadic affair, which for some purposes may be collapsed into a dyadic one, between language, experience, and things experienced, then it is another matter. For experiences occur; they have no status in eternity, hence neither do denotations. But without denotation, there is no factual truth. Actual experiences are either now or they are past; the future of experience, like all things future, is merely the limited real potentiality whose indeterminacy must be resolved somehow, but need not be resolved this way instead of that, rather than that way instead of this. Since the more concrete or definite the denotation, the more we must know about the experiences that embody it, the utterly abstract standpoint that surveys all time from the vantage point of no time can contain only completely abstract truths such as those of arithmetic or metaphysics. That all factual truth is time-dependent is itself a timeless truth; for it is utterly abstract and affirms no fact, but only a universal necessity of any and every fact, wholly neutral to factual alternatives.

Suppose W_1 means that at time t_1 all the possibilities for time t_3 include A, so that, as of t_1, A "will" happen; and W_2 means that at time t_2 all the possibilities for t_3 include A; then there is no contradiction in $W_2 \cdot \sim W_1$. For the possibilities not including A may have been ruled out by the further becoming of the world's definiteness between t_1 and t_2. There would, however, be contradiction if the conjunction held timelessly, for then the said possibilities would *always* be excluded for t_3, and W_1 would never be false. (I owe this symbolism and some other suggestions utilized in this chapter to my former colleague John Wilcox.) Nor can $W_2 \cdot \sim W_1$ have obtained at t_1, for then both statements in the conjunction could only refer to the same possibilities. Possibilities already ruled out at t_1 for t_3 cannot be reinstated at t_2: process is always a narrowing of the "openness" of a given moment of the future, never its widening. On the other hand, if M_1 means possibilities for A at t_3 are at t_1 divided, and M_2 that they are divided at t_2, then $M_1 \cdot \sim M_2$ may obtain, even at t_1, for it may then be already settled that the indeterminacy concerning A

at t_3 cannot last beyond t_2. The status of other combinations can readily be worked out.

Besides attacks from formal logicians we have to expect objections in the name of ordinary uses of words. Do people always and consistently mean by "*A* will be" that nothing else is any longer really possible, and by "*A* will not be" that *A* has become really impossible? Or by "may or may not" a division of real possibilities? Hardly, and if ordinary speech had this degree and kind of clarity and consistency, the history of philosophy must have run very differently. People commonly hesitate, in this and many other matters, between two or more meanings, and only if the requirements of their situation are very exacting with respect to the distinction do they attempt to resolve the ambiguity. How exacting are the requirements with respect to our issue? We deal with the future largely in terms of probabilities, scarcely in terms of absolute inevitabilities and impossibilities. Yet only the latter can be distinguished from situations of divided possibilities. Thus our ordinary practical predictions are, strictly speaking, qualified may or may nots, whose correlates are divided possibilities, though they may often be so strongly weighted toward one side or another of the division in terms of probability as to be not worth distinguishing from the strict will or will-not forms. Also we cannot ordinarily undertake to contrast possibility and impossibility in the subjective sense (the possible, for instance, being taken as what is not known to be false) with objective possibility and impossibility. After we have summoned available knowledge, "possible" and "probable" as bases for our decisions have to mean what that knowledge seems to exhibit as possible or probable. The question what perfect knowledge would make of these categories is a highly theoretical one, and it is not surprising that common sense and common speech avoid it so far as possible.

We have philosophy in order to encourage more careful consideration of just such neglected subtleties. The notion that only science is concerned with them is a position that may have its plausibility, but is not self-evident. Even ordinary speech does get into situations in which distinctions between probable and inevitable, and improbable and impossible, become relevant. Thus if it be argued that "what will be will be," and hence the future is fixed in advance and our choices must have been fixed in advance, the reply is that "what will be" and "the future" need not be identical; we must consider the may or may not be, the unsettled. Again, it is an easy step from ordinary ways of speaking to the at least verbal notion of a divine or perfect knower for whom everything is simply thus and thus, or not thus and thus, and nothing is merely possible or probable. This gives us a familiar theological idea, whose familiarity does nothing to mitigate the extreme and only less familiar paradoxes it entails. Centuries ago another idea was proposed in Socinian theology, the idea that perfect knowledge would exhibit all things as they are, the definite or settled as settled, and the indeterminate, unsettled, but open to further decisions as precisely that. Many superior minds have elaborated the consequences of this view, which are, in important respects, much less painful or intellectually frustrating than those of the other view. Is ordinary language supposed to adjudicate this issue? I think it is, on the whole, on the side of real indeterminacy, but clearly, consistently, and obviously on this side? . . . Why should it or must it be? It is merely usual language for usual purposes. There is one apparently serious difficulty. If we say, "it is possible that it will, but also possible that it will not occur," "will" cannot in this use be interpreted as "I have recommended that it be." But this difficulty is like that posed by the various meanings of "or," and many another term logicians have found cannot be simply adopted from ordinary use, but must be limited somewhat artificially. One could simply say, "A at t possible or probable now, at time t_{-1}"; there is no necessity to say, "possibly or probably A will happen at t." But since ordinarily we are not trying to make explicit the distinction between reality as relative to our knowledge and as absolute (or as relative to complete knowledge), there is no particular harm, or philosophical significance, in the usage "probably it will occur." It is merely a verbal way of doing a certain job well enough for the usual purpose. Philosophical purposes are not very usual. It is somewhat exasperating to have to emphasize this point so often nowadays.

An analysis that in part duplicates the one I have given is offered by Colin Strang, who, if he does not enter the promised land, is just outside the gate.[4] The sense of "will be" that implies something about the present state of reality Strang terms the "loaded" sense, and he shows as I have done that there are three cases—will, will not, and may or may not—one of which is in any given case true and the other two false. He also admits that ordinarily when we refer to the future the loaded sense is what we have in mind. But in rare cases, he thinks, we do mean "will" or "will not" in a "straight" or unloaded sense to which the present state of affairs is irrelevant. The only case he suggests, however, is that of a wager. One can wager only that something will or that it will not take place, and one of these is bound to win and so be proved true. My proposition here is timeless or "straight" truth is irrelevant to a wager. The wager when made is more or less likely, or not likely, to win, and hence reasonable or unreasonable, according to the causal probabilities; eventually, it has won or not won. Suppose it has won; this does not show it to have been true when made (any more than a successful prediction from a law establishes the law), still less that it is timelessly true. Truth is some sort of correspondence, and the temporal status of the truth is the same as that of the correspondence. There can be no timeless relation to something whose mode of being is temporal, for relation to X includes X, and if X comes into being, so does the relation.

Thus my difference from Strang is simply that I reject his "straight sense" of truth altogether, so far as factual propositions are concerned. He makes no effort to show how from the ultimate success of a wager one passes either to its antecedent or its timeless correctness. Note also that the reason we do not treat "may or may not" as subject to wagering is that we lack the resources to ascertain with certainty that the nonoccurrence of an event that has, or the occurrence of an event that has not, in due time, occurred was nevertheless causally possible. Hence, if we were unable to agree about the scope of the causal conditioning at the time the wager was made, we shall probably not agree even when the event has taken place. Betting on the point is thus impracticable. Yet the causal conditioning at any given time does go as far as it goes and no farther; and if two men differ about this, one of them is correct and the other in error.

How clear Aristotle was about these things I am not prepared to say. I do think that in some passages, particularly in the discussion (*Metaphysics E3*) of what will be as also necessary, and the illustration of the inevitable, contrasted to the fortuitous, aspects of a man's death, he was closer to the truth than many a contemporary philosopher.

Some will ask, if the antecedent conditions of an event do not uniquely determine the event, for instance, a human choice, what does determine it? The answer is simple: precisely that freedom that the whole argument is about. The chooser, in the present, selects or makes his act; the antecedent conditions, including the chooser's previous "character," do not select or make it. They select or settle the range of possibilities any one of which he can choose; but only he, then and there, determines the precise action itself. This is the creative element in life, the actual making of definiteness where before was the indefinite, the possible. An explication of "truth" that rules this out is employing an ontological argument to settle a metaphysical issue. Predictions are made true or false by the real world they describe; "future events," as fully determinate already, are not a part of this or any world.

How there can be an objective distinction between past and future that is compatible with the principles of relativity and quantum physics is one of the really hard questions, now being avoided by most writers partly because of its difficulty, and partly because it is somewhat unfashionable for physicists and philosophers to try to connect their two subjects.

Because future events are incompletely defined particulars, they are not past events; because, nevertheless, they are to some extent defined, this advance definiteness including the necessity that the residual indefiniteness be resolved *somehow* as the events become present, the events in question are not mere logical possibilities, but characterize the future. This is what it is to be future, on our theory. One may reject the theory; but have sufficient grounds for the rejection been given? Precognition is cited as at least a logical possibility, and hence an objection to the theory. This, however, is the question at issue. One must presuppose that "future" in "awareness of the future" has some other meaning than the one proposed. Since I see no other meaning that will stand analysis, I regard precognition of wholly definite particulars as logically impossible.

We are told (Waismann had said it before) that if will, or will-not, statements about events "become true," we can have no idea when. But, of course, in principle we can: they become true when the real possibilities have been causally narrowed down to the point required by the statements. Naturally, having once been closed for a specified feature and date, they can never afterwards be reopened. "The moving finger writes. . . ." One knows the quotation. But it is a *non sequitur* and an example of the "prejudice of symmetry" that the future events must be written down beforehand or eternally in similar detail.[5]

Mr. Montague suggests that the crucial question is: what must eventually be the case for a prediction to be true? He can see nothing else than the occurrence of the predicted event. This is, I have argued, a form of the verificatory fallacy that Popper never wearies of attacking. Just as for a law to obtain it is not enough for there to be an instance in conformity with the law, but in addition contrary instances must be universally excluded; so with a prediction, contrary real possibilities must all be excluded. With this substitution, the analogy is exact. Indeed, is it a mere substitution? Recall that laws tell us not only what does and what does not occur, but also what would and would not occur under *counterfactual* conditions, and does this not involve the idea of real potentialities? On this point, Peirce seems to me to have seen more clearly than most students since his day. The only way to render single verifications of predictions decisive is to reject the concept of real possibilities, that is, to make determinism logically true.

One may indeed deny that the determinateness of the future must be one of law, of repetitive pattern, or of any kind of causal necessity. Thus Mr. Bradley seems to think that there might be a random sequence of unconnected yet determinate events, and that propositions might be timelessly true of members of this sequence. This implies two time series: the actual one we experience, with a settled past and a future that we take, pragmatically at least, as partly settled and partly unsettled but open to settlement, beginning now; and another one, laid up in heaven, so to speak, and complete once for all, thanks to which propositions have their timeless truth. (For propositions are not true simply in themselves, unless perhaps when they are analytic, but only thanks to some reality other than the propositions.) If either of our authors is acquainted with this second series of mutually independent events, or anything remotely like it, he has the advantage of me. I have no access to it and fail to see how he has. I find no serious attempt to explain how the trick is done. Access is always to the present or past, and the causally conditioned but not fully determined future. Should we not leave the second series, complete once for all, and whether causal or not, to the timeless vision of the Schoolmen's God, of which it is a sort of ghost, and content ourselves with the only time we can genuinely deal with, the ever-unfinished series whose prospective members are merely advance outlines drawn by causality, members that, when more than outlined, when fully detailed or actual, will be past and not future? This actual series is a partly new series each moment, a totality enriched by new members.

Events, on this view, are not mere constituents of the universe, but steps in its very making, a making that cannot ever be complete and properly final. The creative becoming is inexhaustibly potent, and can and will always add to any actual whole of definite actualities. Thus truth is genuinely protean, and only in very abstract forms, as in metaphysics or mathematics, is it timeless, or statable entirely without regard to the time of its utterance.

CHAPTER NINE

Theism and Dual Transcendence

The idea of God is a metaphysical idea. By this I mean that its definition employs only categories, concepts of strictly universal significance, claiming application to any and every conceivable existence. The defining characteristics distinguishing God from any other being, actual or conceivable, can be specified by such concepts. This is not true of any other individual being. God is individual, but not what is properly called a particular individual, although some nontheists I could name and some theists are not aware of this distinction. Theism, affirming the divine existence, is a universal, not a particular proposition. Proof: to say that God exists is to imply that everything there is or could be is divinely known as something that is or could be, also that its actuality or possibility is conditioned by divine creativity. Among existential statements asserting an individual existent, theism is uniquely universal. Argument about its validity is metaphysical argument.

In metaphysics, because of the unique generality of its propositions, truth is necessary truth and falsity is necessary falsity—in a broad sense, logical impossibility. To err in metaphysics is to fail to make coherent sense. To be right in it is simply to make coherent sense, while using strictly universal categories. In all this I am Aristotelian, and even, up to a point, Kantian. Kant defined metaphysics as seeking universal and necessary truths. I am also closer to "that Gothic metaphysician" Carnap than he perhaps realized, but less close to Quine, to whom the quoted characterization of Carnap has been attributed.

By 'God' philosophers, including many famous theologians who were also philosophers, have meant a being radically superior to all other beings. Let us call this superiority *Transcendence*. To explicate Transcendence certain technical terms have been used, including absolute, independent, infinite, uncaused, unchangeable, eternal. These terms are all metaphysical categories or are definable through such categories. This is as it should be since, as we have seen, the idea of God is metaphysical. The terms are also all negative;

hence, if we use them exclusively we fail to distinguish God from mere or absolute nothing, which also is not relative or dependent, nor is it finite, caused, changeable, or temporal. How then does God differ from mere nothing, and why worship a mere negative?

The superiority of God to us, for example, is not a relation of infinity to a mere nothing, nor is it a relation of a mere nothing to something finite. We are positive somethings and so must God be positive. I am far from alone in holding that our chief theistic tradition, which I call classical theism, dismally failed to meet this requirement without contradiction. The only alternative, on the same level of generality, to absolute or independent is relative or dependent, and so with the other negative terms mentioned. The positive correlative for infinite is finite, for unchangeable is changeable, for eternal (as meaning nontemporal) is temporal. Unless there can be a dependent, finite, changeable aspect of God, God must be a mere nothing and atheism correct. David Hume says something like this through his character Cleanthes, but at the time few got the point. My book *The Divine Relativity* came 170 years later.[1] Twenty years before that book came Whitehead's statements that all actuality is finite and relative, and that, although the primordial nature of God is absolute, infinite, and deficient in actuality, God's consequent nature is actual and finite, and is "in flux" and "always moving on." It is also said to depend in a definite way upon the world.

Independently of and before Whitehead's publishing his idea of God or lecturing about it at Harvard, I believed, with one of my first Harvard teachers, that God has a changing and insofar temporal aspect, and yet exists eternally and so is not temporal in a merely usual sense.

Dual Transcendence, a formula I invented, although Whitehead's "God is dipolar" comes close to it, names and partly clarifies and generalizes what a number of thinkers have been implying for nearly four centuries, but especially since Hegel, and most of all in or close to this century. Transcendent independence, infinity, unchangeability, and the other negative categories are indeed necessary aspects of deity; but so also are transcendent dependence, finitude, and capacity for change. Transcendence applies to both sides of the polar contraries that have been used to distinguish God from other beings, not to one side alone. There need be no contradiction because, as is clear in Whitehead's talk of two natures, the contradictory properties are not asserted of God in the same respect.

Transcendence or divine superiority is not identical with absoluteness or infinity, or with any mere negation. How could it be? No one-sided abstraction, least of all a negative one, is to be worshipped as God.

Of course classical theists did say some positive things about God. They used terms like goodness, knowledge, power, existence, and love. What they did not do is give us anything like an adequate discussion of the relation of these positive terms to the categorial negatives they also employed. Yet Aristotle already saw that knowledge of something depends on that something.

Even God cannot know to exist something that does not exist. Very logically Aristotle concluded that God, whom he defined as totally independent, the unmoved mover of all, does not know other individuals. Aquinas gave what I, and not only I, see as a flatly contradictory solution of this problem. Some of his disciples say that human understanding is unable to avoid paradox in these mysterious matters. In fact, as Berdyaev says, by dogmatically denying finitude and relativity to God, classical theism gives genuine understanding little chance to function. The mystery is man-made! In our one-sided definition of God we have worshipped abstractions, not God. It is a form of intellectual idolatry. I show in my book on the subject that we can conceive a transcendent or divine relativity making God superior to any conceivable other being.

Among the technical, one-sided alleged synonyms for Transcendence is necessity. God was called the necessary being, while all others were considered contingent. It is as close to self-evident as anything in metaphysics can be that knowledge of a contingent truth must be contingent in the same sense. I have given a proof of this that satisfied Carnap.[2] Aristotle saw the conceptual relations here and concluded that God, defined as wholly free from contingency, cannot know contingent aspects of the world, including of course Aristotle himself as mere chance existent. Aristotle also said that individual animals are not worth knowing, but only species, which are eternal and so, on his principles, necessary.

The polarity, necessary–contingent, comes under the principle of dual Transcendence. It is advantageous to focus the entire issue on this modal contrast. For the logic of modality, though scorned by some logicians, especially Quine and R. M. Martin, is taken seriously and has been worked on extensively by others. So (see Table 9.1) let us explore the mathematically possible combinations of the four concepts: divine Necessity, symbolized by a capital letter N, divine Contingency by a capital C, nondivine or worldly necessity by a small letter n, and worldly contingency by small letter c. We then have sixteen combinations, using zeros for the total absence of modal status, whether necessary or contingent. Nine of these combinations could be called theistic, and the remaining seven *non*theistic, in three cases definitely atheistic. As for agnosticism, it is, I think, sufficiently covered by the zero case, plus some doctrine about the limitations of human understanding or confession of personal inability to judge.

Table 9.1[3]

I	II	III	IV	V	VI
1. N.c	4. C.c	7. NC.c	10. c	13. N	16. 0.0
2. N.n	5. C.n	8. NC.n	11. n	14. C	
3. N.cn	6. C. cn	9. NC.cn	12.cn	15. NC	

This table is an example of what I mean by mathematically exhausting the possible combinations of concepts used in stating an issue. Long ago in Asia Nagarjuna, the great Buddhist, did something of this kind, as did Plato still earlier in his classification of kinds of motion. But neither achieved, in my modest opinion, the clarity of Table 9.1.

The first three columns are theistic, especially the first and third. Column IV is the atheisms, column V the forms of acosmism, and column VI the zero, nihilistic, or agnostic case.

In column III are the forms of Dual Transcendence. Numbers 7 and 8 are open to logical objections. Number 9 is my view and it can be attributed, I think, to Whitehead and some others, but to no one I know of before about 1600—with one exception, Plato. It is possible to interpret the great father of Western philosophy in this sense. We shall come back to his view. But otherwise the doctrine is essentially modern, not ancient or medieval. In India it can be read into the Vedas, but was not defended clearly until rather recent times.

Column II, taken as theistic, is marginal, though Wm. James, John Stuart Mill, and John Hick could be so classified. By supposing God to exist non-necessarily, we make theism, if true, a fact that might not have been, yet can have no explanation in terms of causal conditions. (For Hick, at least, does not suppose God to have been brought into existence, as all contingent things, for all we can ever know, have been.) And a truth of which neither a necessary nor a causal account can be given is a logical monstrosity. That 2 and 3 are 5 needs no explanation, other than our insight that it could not be otherwise. But an existence that could have failed to obtain but has nothing behind it to explain its possibility is indeed an anomaly. It would be an eternal accident. I hold with Aristotle that there can be no accidents in pure eternity, but only necessity. What eternally is could not have failed to be. This for me excludes column II entirely. What comes to be is contingent; what never came to be but eternally is, is necessary. Here I regard Aristotle, followed by Anselm, as simply right and Hume, Kant, and a host of others as simply mistaken.

Having found the views that could be held, the next step is to consider principles or rules that can justify eliminating some of the options as illogical, as not making coherent sense, with the hope that only one option of the sixteen will be left as the one that must be true, since the others are not even possible.

One rule of elimination already suggested is: extremes are always wrong. At first sight this rule does not seem to help in this case. Item 9 seems to be the positive extreme, all concepts affirmed, item 16 the negative extreme, all denied. Yet Leibniz held that metaphysicians have erred only in what they have denied, not in what they have affirmed. Moreover, I agree with him in this. However, as we shall see presently, although the negative extreme in the table, item 16, is indeed wrong, the positive extreme, item 9, is not its absolute opposite, and is not vicious. However, there are in the table several extremes that are vicious. Item 2 and 4 are one-sided in favor of necessity or contingency respectively. Neither necessity nor contingency is *merely* negative, as is easily shown. What is most positive, however, is the contrast between the two modalities; without this contrast both lose their meaning. This in an instance of Wittgenstein's Principle of Contrast. Not only does it eliminate items 2, 4, 10, 11, 13, and 14, but it favors item 9 over all the others. For it has all the contrasts.

Another rule is a corollary of the modal rule: If a conjunction of propositions is contingent, then so is each of the propositions. Thus $N(p \cdot q) \equiv (Np \cdot Nq)$. This eliminates items 1 and 3, that is, classical theism and Aristotelian theism, unless one accepts Aristotle's denial of divine knowledge of contingent things. Eight of the sixteen items, including four of the theistic, are disposed of so far.

We have argued against column II that it posits an eternal yet contingent fact, ruling out any conceivable explanation of the fact, whether in terms of conceptual necessity or of causal production. So we are left only with the choice between a nontheistic view and the three options in column III. Item 7 implies that the supreme creative power is capable of not creating at all. Such a freedom to make no positive use of freedom seems nonsense. Item 8 is the bizarre idea that, although God has contingent qualities and can accept the free, hence contingent acts of creatures as contributions to the divine awareness, the creatures have no such capacity, no such freedom. And how could these creatures have the *idea* of freedom if there were nothing of the kind in themselves or their fellows? So we seem left with item 9 against the seven forms of nontheistic thought. Items 13–15 posit a solitary supreme reality whose supremacy is not superiority over others, for there would be no others. It cannot know unless mere self-knowledge is something. Or perhaps the three persons of the Trinity solve the problem? Each is equal it seems to the other two, yet somehow they are not simply identical. In India many people seem to find some credibility in a solitary supreme reality, but few in the West do so.

Column VI brings us back to the question of extremes. I deny that it makes sense to simply dismiss modal conceptions. All reasoning depends on there being necessary connections somewhere, and it also depends on their being nonnecessary connections. A logic in which there were only necessary connections would make anything follow from anything else. No distinction between fallacies and valid deductions would obtain. With only nonnecessary connections all deductions would be invalid.

Is item 9 a vicious extreme? Rather, it is an extreme of good sense. It does not make God the absolute opposite of nothing at all. Classical theism (item 1) did that by defining God as an absolute maximum of value, called perfection, as incapable of increase as of decrease. This assumed that the notion of all possible values coactualized in one being is a coherent idea. We have good reason to reject this assumption. As Leibniz held (or should have held) but forgot when he came to God, there are incompatible yet positive values. Item 9 is not the extreme assertion of positivity; it is the extreme *coherent* assertion of it, avoiding the pseudo-concept of perfection. There is a genuine concept of perfection, but it is a corollary of item 9.

In still another sense, item 9 is not an extreme. It does not assign to God what many have meant by *omnipotence*, from which it followed that divine wisdom and power simply determined details of the world, implying that creaturely freedom determined nothing or was not freedom at all. God has optimal or best possible power, surpassing that of any conceivable other; so that the divine power is the greatest conceivable. However, genuine power is power over those who have some power of their own. *Power cannot be monopolized*, even in the best form of power. Something is left undecided for others to decide. The classical problem of evil was in this way a pseudo-problem, employing a pseudo-concept of divine power. Not simply *human* freedom has to be taken into account; any creature simply as such must be an above-zero form of less-than-divine freedom. What I call the "formula of immanence and Transcendence" is as follows: properties optimal in deity are less than optimal but still positively present in all creatures. Thus if love is optimal in God no creature is totally without love in that word's most general meaning. Similarly if freedom is optimal in God no creature is wholly without it. I take the new physics to make this compatible with our knowledge. It alters the problem of evil radically. Without the problem of evil, what is left of the atheist's case?

We have so far not faced the traditional problem of theistic *analogy*. To relate abstractions like infinite, absolute, or transcendent to concrete experiences, from which their meaning must somehow be derived, we must either give literal examples from direct observation or use analogy to extend our interpretation of things we do literally experience. Only extreme mystics claim to directly and distinctly experience God. Hence only by analogy can most of us give meaning to the divine infinity, or divine finitude. Transcendently infinite what, transcendently finite what? Mind, matter, goodness, beauty? These get meaning from examples.

Traditional theistic analogies have been chiefly of one basic kind. God is like a ruler, in contrast to the ruled subjects, or like a superior human person, in contrast to lesser persons or things, for instance, children. So God is called Lord or Father. To eliminate male chauvinism I prefer to substitute parent, in contrast to a child of either sex. I call this the interpersonal analogy, also the simple or non-dual analogy.

The dual analogy is this: a person has two aspects, soul and body, or the psychical and the physiological; God is the supreme form of the mind–body distinction. This was Plato's stroke of genius, found also both earlier and later in India. For Plato (I here follow Cornford and Levinson) the divine was the World Soul, related to all else as a human consciousness is to its human body, with whatever differences between human and divine cases of mind and body as are implied by dual Transcendence. Plato's *Timaeus* is supremely great here; alas, Aristotle and the Middle Ages made no real use of Plato's analogy. Whitehead also missed the boat here.

Let capital S stand for soul or the psychical in its divine form and B for body in the divine form of the entire cosmos of creatures throughout all the past of the creative process (in which the big bang was at most an incident); let small s stand for soul in such as we are and small b for body in such as we are. We have again nine combinations expressive of theism.

Table 9.2

1. S.b	4. B.b	7. SB.b
2. S.s	5. B.s	8. SB.s
3. S.bs	6. B.bs	9. SB.bs

Item 1 has scarcely been held. Item 2 is Bishop Berkeley. Item 3 is both Aristotle and medieval or classical theism. Item 4 has scarcely been held, but a materialist might perhaps hold it. Items in column II in this table, as in the previous table, have had few great defenders. Item 9 is Plato and is, I think, implied by Tertullian and Hobbes, both of whom attributed body to God and surely also soul or mind! A few minor philosophical theologians of recent times have used the Platonic analogy, including W. P. Montague. These theologians also in general imply the dual form of Transcendence.

Objections to the mind–body analogy are easy to think of, but must be balanced against three considerations: first, it is equally easy to find objections against the interpersonal or simple analogy; second, where the latter is weak or unhelpful, the other analogy is strong or helpful, and vice versa; third, apart from these two analogies we have no good way of giving positive meaning to our theistic concepts. To neglect either one is to do a poor job in construing these concepts.

The admission of a mind–body duality is not the same as a mind–matter dualism. For the body of a given soul can be viewed as a society of lesser forms of mind subordinated to the human or divine mind. The cells of the human or any animal body are not dead and are highly organized; there seems no way to prove that they have no feelings of their own. In abstraction from its body, what is a mind?

I am deeply convinced of two things about God. If there is a true description of deity, it must affirm the duality of Transcendence and give up the one-sided idea that the merely absolute, infinite, or immutable is the God of religion. It must also give up one-sided trust in the Biblical interpersonal analogy for the divine nature, and accept also the mind–body analogy of

Plato, understanding this analogy in its dual aspects of the influence of mind on body and body on mind. The interactionist view of the mind–body relation is the only one that will work here. And I believe it is the only one that makes sense. We do things to our bodily cells and they do things to us—*we* and *us* here mean our experiences. Psychophysiological interaction there must be. I trust you will see that the dualities in dual Transcendence are somewhat parallel to those in mind–body interaction. The one-sided, all too simple view in both cases was a natural first step in grasping the truth. As Whitehead says, we must "seek simplicity—and then mistrust it."[4] You may object that a World Soul would not be creator, since we do not create our bodies. Ah, but take care! The Platonic poet Edmund Spenser thought otherwise. He wrote, "For the body from the soul its form doth take/for soul is form and doth the body make."[5] The neurophysiologist Sperry holds that an infant's experiences influence the development of its brain cells; we thus (and in further ways) have a creative role in our psychophysiological system. Deity may be the eminent form of this duality.

Remember that the body is not simply one individual, but a vast society of cells, each an organized individual. It is our consciousness at a given moment that is a single reality, not our body. A person as an integrated awareness has incomparably more power over any one of its nerve cells than any one cell has over the person. An adult body is in substantial part what the person's thoughts and feelings have made it. This comes much closer in some respects to the creative power attributed to God than the power of parents over offspring.

Recall that the divine side of the analogy is the side that is transcendent in both categorial aspects, as absolute, independent, or infinite, *and* as relative, dependent, and finite. God's dependence or finitude surpasses all others in principle. The control of the cosmic body is uniquely excellent and adequate. It has no limitations, provided that what it controls is a society of free creatures. And what else could it be? No ruler simply makes the decisions of subjects; no good parent even wants to do this for offspring, and there is no evidence that any of us simply decides what our cells shall do.

For our scheme to work we must also give up the traditional dualism of mind and mere body. Cells need not be supposed absolutely mindless or insentient. There is direct evidence they have their own feelings. How otherwise can they give us intense pains and pleasures, if they are mere bits of mindless matter? Hurt certain of our cells and you hurt us. We care about our cells with a truly innate care. Unconsciously but truly we love them, share in their weal and woe. This is the final aspect of our analogy. So God loves us. Whitehead's feeling of (others') feeling is the key. Before Whitehead no one so clearly and neatly captured the principle of interaction in nature. Peirce and Bergson were fairly close but less clear. And most of the rest were not even close, and are still not close.

Dual analogy, protected from vicious anthropomorphism by dual Transcendence, furnishes all the contrasts needed for the significance of our universal categories. Above all, it preserves the contrasts between necessity and contingency, and between ordinary or particular individuals and the individual with universal functions—among these functions, that of ordering the others into a cosmos in which, though the many individuals determine worldly details, they form a coherent universe in which a vast variety of forms of life can coexist in symbiotic harmony, the future can be minimally foreseeable, and life can have a meaning. Rejecting this idea is eliminating a supreme contrast that illuminates all contrasts. We are fallible, God is all-wise and all-good; we are born and die, God precedes and outlasts us, and gives us the ultimate context that gives value to all lesser contexts.

What really credible rule justifies eliminating the contrast that assigns to all our basic concepts their appropriate functions? Transcendent, unsurpassable freedom and its contrary pole, ordinary, surpassable freedom, can supply all the contrasts life involves or needs. Creator–creature, these ideas in their full generality necessarily acquire endlessly new exemplifications. God as such, world as such—both are necessary; but whereas God is the universally functioning individual, world is only the system of localized, nondivine individuals, each of which is contingent in its very existence. Necessary is only that there be some world or other, and some appropriate divine knowledge of whatever world there is. All the rest is contingent.

I have heard a very great natural scientist say, "There is nothing but freedom." In spite of Robinson Jeffers, there is no "iron consistency" simply determining all. That divine and some lesser forms of freedom necessarily exist only means that, since freedom is the basis of contingency, the very ground of alternative possibilities, to freedom as such there is no alternative. Freedom limited only by past acts of freedom, including acts of the supreme freedom, is reality as such. Or, as Whitehead puts it, creativity is "the category of the ultimate."[6] Bergson says, though less clearly, much the same, and so does Peirce. Twentieth-century metaphysics, like twentieth-century science, poses questions scarcely conceived by the ancient Greeks or Jews, or the medieval, Islamic, or Hindu thinkers. Nor did Kant have much idea of them. This is a new ball game. However, understanding it is scarcely possible without some awareness of the earlier games and the earlier players.

CHAPTER TEN

The Ontological Argument and the Meaning of Modal Terms

Since Norman Malcolm, John Findlay, and I, largely independently, proposed certain new ways of viewing the ontological argument for the existence of God various criticisms have been made of these new formulations.[1] I think a basic defect in some of the criticisms is that they fail to do justice to the logical truth that no philosophical argument can be convincing apart from some suitable conceptual framework, and that convincingness is finally relative to what premises of reasoning one finds acceptable. For me, at least, the ontological argument belongs in a systematic examination of the modal terms contingent, possible, and necessary. In various writings I have made such an examination.[2] It is essentially that of Charles Peirce, when certain implications are made explicit and certain loose ends tidied up.[3] There is a similar relation to Whitehead's view of modality. But neither of these writers ever applied the doctrine to the question of the ontological argument.

A favorite charge against ontological arguments is that they confuse linguistic necessity, *necessite de dictu*, with ontological necessity, *necessite de re*. There are, however, philosophers of note, including Aristotle and Peirce, who question if the two kinds of necessity are so readily and entirely separable as is often implied.

If I sincerely say, "I am aware of just having felt a twinge of pain" I cannot rationally deny that the pain occurred. The pain *must* have occurred, given the awareness. Is this merely because we use "aware of" or "remember" as successful achievement words?

In that case, our confidence in memory, even the most immediate, is mere postulate or stipulation. We "call spirits from the vasty deep" of the past, but do they come when we do call?[4] I hold that a certain element of retrospective reliability-in-principle is not merely a stipulative but a built-in feature of what we call remembering (and also perceiving). And I think that the sheer denial of this is incoherent and indefensible. An epistemology that fails to see that experience is an effect that intrinsically implicates, renders conditionally necessary, its own antecedents must remain a tour de force. Granted memory in a certain basic Bergsonian sense (a form of Whitehead's "prehension"), it is a conditional, extralinguistic necessity that the remembered did occur. Only "conscious" (verbally or symbolically formulated) or at least somehow *interpreted* memory "deceives," not memory pure and simple. It is the same with the element of givenness in perception. Abstracting from aspects of interpretation and verbalization, perception guarantees, renders conditionally necessary, the perceived. (And here, too, some of us think, the data are temporarily antecedent, are causes.) This is no mere matter of language at all. Animal perceptions have their data or causes that (in spite of Hume) logically *must* have been physically there, even if only in the animals' own bodily organs.

I hold with Peirce that linguistic necessities, the better they are employed and understood, tend to express ontological ones. If the necessities are conditional they express intrinsic relationships, the "necessary connections" Hume failed to find—partly because he thought of them as symmetrical whereas they are one-way, and partly because he looked for them everywhere except in the right places. Not only does "fox" linguistically entail "animal," but there *could not* have been foxes without there having previously been animals of other kinds. And the first animal had its strictly necessary (but not strictly sufficient) conditions.

I have argued in Chapter Seven that there are modal terms with a good meaning in that there are genuinely open though definitely limited choices in every present about *its* future. Causal indeterminacy, real (not merely linguistic) possibility, which in certain abstract limits is necessity—probably it is now necessary that the sun should continue to exist for millions of years longer—is what modal terms are finally about. Possibility is futurity. Hence nothing that has never been exclusively future can have been or be contingent. And I see no consequence of this principle that can properly be taken as a *reductio ad absurdum*. Moreover, in my methodology the ultimate test of metaphysical truth is precisely coherent meaning, free from intrinsic absurdity. (Scientific truth, truth not about the eternal but about the purely temporal, is another matter. Its negative tests are, of course, partly empirical.)

It follows from the preceding that the existence of an eternal being, one that could never have been a mere possibility for future realization, cannot be contingent, not even logically so in a suitable language. This central point of Anselm (also Aristotle) I hold to be validated by a proper theory of the locus of possibility in experience. If we think of the unreal but possible existence of a being defined as unproducible (James Ross's apt term) we are thinking incoherently. The only remaining question is: can we form a coherent idea of an unproducible being at all, whether as existent or otherwise, and if so how? Anselm's argument gives an affirmative answer much too easily at this point.

Because the ontological argument assumes a coherence of the "idea of God" that it cannot, of itself, justify, it is not in isolation a cogent proof of the divine existence. I have not said that it was. It is, however, a disproof of what Charlesworth well terms "empirical atheism," and equally of "empirical theism." The residual issue is between Carnapian (or Comtean) positivism (*a priori* or "logical" atheism) and "logical theism." This is the real issue, and it is difficult enough.

Another way to identify the ontologically contingent is by the principle of *positive exclusion*. A fox here-now excludes a wolf in the same portion of space-time. But what does "God-here-now" exclude? I say nothing, except the merely negative "absence of God-here-now." But to exclude nothing, or the merely negative, is no more an exclusion than to eat nothing is an eating. No positive contingent entity excludes merely its own negation.

Some empirical theists suggest that what the divine existence excludes is "absolutely unredeemed evil." If this means evil that in no way whatever contributes to any good, I deny that such evil is conceivable. (Any actuality or fact must have some positive aspect. Every tragedy has some good effects.) If it means simply evil to which a better alternative was conceivable and possible, then its occurrence does not contradict the existence of God, who on my view has no choice but to grant some measure of creativity to every creature, that being what a creature is, a nondivine instance—or sequence of instances—of creativity. It follows that the exact goods and evils of the world could not be matters of unilateral divine decision. The classical problem of evil derives from a pseudo-conception of divine power, or of creaturely powerlessness, or both.

Before we ask what could make an alternative to an existent *not* possible we need to ask what could make such an alternative possible. Answer: alternative existential possibilities exist in that creativity, *becoming* as in principle partially free from antecedent determination exists and is the ground of possibility and necessity. Creative freedom is the very principle of alternativeness. To this principle itself there is, of course, no possible alternative. If, then, God is necessary, it must be as the essential or universal factor in creativity, common to all the positive possibilities that coherent thought could be about, or (the same thing) that becoming could produce. I do not find that my critics have refuted this idea; they seem not to have noticed it.

There are a number of marks of what could equally well exist or fail to exist. Thus, what is not identifiable *a priori*, or by pure concepts, cannot have existence *a priori*, certifiable by mere concepts. One must point to the actual experienced world to denote ordinary individuals. But deity is identified by the property "in all possible states of reality surpassing all other beings." No localized being can be so described, but only a reality cosmic (or supercosmic). And no being that could be produced or destroyed can be so described without incoherence.

Again, the contingent always involves an arbitrary degree, somewhere between zero and the maximum, of some property. There is no purely conceptual way to identify such a degree. As Leibniz pointed out, only absolute maxima and minima are definable *a priori*. An adult person is "more knowledgeable" than a fox or an infant; however, concepts alone do not suffice to define what the person knows that distinguishes him from other creatures. But God knows whatever is so—period. This identifies God without further ado. No empirical content need be specified, for whatever it may be, God knows it. And were the content otherwise God would know *that*. The divine being is the one who could and would know whatever might be the case. All differences between possible worlds are indifferent to the mere existence and cognitive perfection of God. They are not indifferent to God's actual knowledge, the concrete divine actuality. But this, as I have argued at length elsewhere, is contingent and not part of what is proved (granted that we can conceive God coherently) by an ontological, or other metaphysical, argument.[5] What is proved is only that there is some divine actuality or other, not what one there is. And any possible one will surpass in excellence all other actualities coexisting with it.

On one condition I would renounce any sort of ontological argument: if it could be shown that "there might have been, or might be, nothing at all" makes coherent sense. For me it does not. The alternative to something is something else, not nothing. On this axiom I take my stand. Hence I reject the supposed axiom that all existential affirmations are logically contingent. The question is not can we go from thought to reality *a priori*. Of course we can; the act of thought itself is real, and it is never merely the thinking of that very thinking, but (if coherent) of a realized or unrealized possibility for the future of some present or past time—unless it is about what is neither an unrealized nor a realized contingent possibility, but rather an eternal necessity, the common element realized in no matter what possibility. These are all that coherent thoughtful experience can have as immanent objects, but one or the other of these it cannot fail to have. Thinking is a mode of experiencing and there is always an experienced reality. If what is experienced or thought is concrete, then it is contingent, temporal, and knowable only empirically.

This includes the concrete actuality of God (though *that* there is *some* such actuality is—if deity is conceivable at all—abstract and necessary *a priori*). If the experience or thought is sufficiently abstract to qualify creativity itself, and hence any possible state of reality, its being *somehow* instantiated is necessary. God's identifying characteristics, I argue, are of this degree of abstractness. "Something" in general means, theistically, some product, content, or aspect of the divine life. Either this or "divine life" lacks coherent sense.

The central religious question is thus one of meaning, not of empirical fact. Here I agree with Carnap. The philosophical problem is to think coherently. Buddhists renounce conceptual approaches to the deepest truth about life. I do not scorn this mystical position. But I am less impressed by the Western idea of a religious faith that is wholly empirical, and hence implies a deity whose existence is a conceptually arbitrary fact, yet one totally beyond possibility of causal-genetic explanation. Is it not more reasonable to suppose that truths are exhaustively divisible into two kinds, contingent truths for which we seek a genetic explanation, and necessary truths for which the explanation is in terms of meanings, *a priori* necessities? Empiricistic theists ask us to admit a third kind, one for which there can be no explanation at all.

Consider the following argument.

p^* for: deity, defined in such and such a way (for example, as unsurpassable by any other conceivable being) exists.

1. $\Diamond\, p^*$ [(logically) possible p^*]

2. $\Diamond\, p^* \rightarrow\, \sim \Diamond \sim p^*$ [if p^* is possible, then (strict implication) it is necessary]

∴ 3. $\sim \Diamond \sim p^*$ [p^* is true by logical necessity; a priori theism]

Suppose the critic rejects number 1, taking p^* to be either necessarily false or else an ill-formed statement, incapable of truth or falsity. This is the *positivist* position (Carneades, Comte, Carnap). Against it the theist is powerless, unless he has arguments other than the ontological. Assuming positivism, number 2 and number 3 should be rejected as absurd. But then also the theistic question must be regarded as *nonempirical*, a question of meaning not of fact.

Suppose the critic accepts number 1 but rejects number 2. Then he affirms that p^* is a logically possible proposition whose contradictory is also logically possible. In short, he takes p^* to be contingent. This is the *empirical* position.

Against empiricism the ontologist argues as follows: p^*, if taken as a contingent proposition, violates the basic semantic rules for such propositions:[6]

a) It affirms a state of affairs, the uncaused and everlasting, yet logically contingent existence of God, for which existence, therefore, neither a genetic nor a conceptual explanation is possible.

b) It affirms a state of affairs that excludes no positive form of existence whatsoever.

c) It does not affirm any arbitrary, conceptually uncertifiable degree of properties or excellences.

d) It does not affirm an individual or species of individual identifiable only empirically, rather than by pure universal conceptions.

e) It does not affirm a being (or beings) subject to mortality or degeneration, or dependent for existence upon a suitable environment that might escape its control.

f) It does not affirm a being dependent upon a special set or kind of constituent parts, whose possible nonexistence or poor combination would threaten its own existence.

g) It does not affirm a being localized in space-time (even our entire known universe is localized in time, though not in space).

From these considerations I conclude: if p* is taken as logically contingent, either it does not really refer to deity or it is a logical anomaly in comparison with which the alleged anomaly of inferring existence from concepts sinks into insignificance.

It is true that by "logically necessary" I have to mean more than "deducible from logical constants alone," in other words, more than "analytic" by the narrow formalist definition of that term. But I do not mean more than analytic in the broader sense mentioned by Hick of "following from meanings alone."[7] In other words, the denial of a logically necessary truth in my sense does imply contradiction when implicit definitions of terms are made explicit. I believe that thought that tries to combine "could be false" with "excludes no positive possibility but only a purely negative one" is incoherent because it is in violation of any relevant meaning of "could." And so with the other rules of contingency. But none of this is analytic in the narrow formal sense. Since Gödel showed that mathematics is not completely formalizable, it seems too late to demand that all nonempirical, noncontingent truth should be formally analytic. It is time to reckon candidly with the failure of efforts to establish this dichotomy. Metaphysical truths are *informally analytic*. Moreover, the concept of the bare existence (not the entire reality) of deity is metaphysical, whether "deity exists" is necessary truth or illogical absurdity.

A logician (David Braine) in his review urges against me that the two modalities (*de re, de dictu*) "cannot be the same, although they may be conjoined."[8] But have I not shown that in the case of theism the conjunction is correct, and does this not suffice to refute monolithic empiricism? As for the nonempirical issue—*a priori* theism versus *a priori* nontheism—I have elsewhere proposed five ways for deciding it.[9] They are my real arguments for belief.

In regarding theism as either necessarily true or else lacking in consistency and definiteness, I am treating it as I do other metaphysical proposals. If they miss necessary truth, they do so only by defects in clarity or internal coherence that make them necessarily untrue. Here, indeed, Braine has an objection I confess I have trouble meeting. In mathematics there are propositions that are nonempirical although we have, it seems, no *a priori* means of establishing their truth or falsity. Might not theism be of this kind?

Perhaps, however, the mathematical undecidables are in a class by themselves just because they are mathematical. Yet they do seem to show that Peirce was mistaken when he said: concerning the "ideal world," the world of pure possibility, "we are virtually omniscient."[10]

One might argue pragmatically that whereas we have no need to live by an answer to the mathematical questions mentioned, since they seem to make no difference to our basic conceptions of existence and value, the theistic issue seems not to be neutral in this pragmatic sense. Thus, for example, the belief that we are contributing to an immortal divine life, if we can conceive such contribution and such life, enables us to see abiding significance for our otherwise apparently ephemeral achievements. Again, the idea of an eminent Freedom giving directives to lesser forms of freedom makes intelligible how there can be objective order, real laws of nature (statistical or approximate though these laws may, and I think must, be). In such ways, possibly, we can justify the supposition that some though not all nonempirical truths are within our grasp, and that for those we cannot attain we have no essential need. The latter do not follow in a finite number of steps from concepts we are bound, more or less explicitly, to employ, while the former—so the theistic proofs claim—do follow from such concepts. Thus I accept the verdict of Hume and Kant that there can be no cogent *empirical* theistic proofs (or disproofs). All are *a priori*: however, the ontological is but one, and not by itself the most important, of the *a priori* arguments.

It is the logic of the term *God* that *everything* must, in any possible state of affairs, be known to him. As Findlay magnificently put it, God must be "lord of possibility" as well as of actuality.[11] But God's own "nonexistence" could not be known by anyone, divine or otherwise. (For the divine existence excludes, and would be excluded by, no positive experience whatever.) An absolutely unknowable possible truth is another anomaly of empirical theism or atheism.

Does not *a priori* theism have its purely logical advantage?

In this difficult matter, prejudices are strong, and they are not solely religious—or antireligious. There is also the bias, in our culture and especially in English-speaking countries, in favor of uncritically extended empiricism. Because of these obstacles to communication I may be excused for offering several additional versions of my reasoning.

Over and over we are told that the divine existential independence from antecedent and environmental conditions the idea of God implies is one thing and the necessity of the judgment *deity exists* is quite another. My reply is (a) you are not playing my language game, and (b) I suspect that you are playing not a language but a pseudolanguage game. You are not using words to mean anything clear and consistent. Consider, "there are foxes"; is it compatible with the meaning of "fox" to admit, as an open alternative, that there might always have been foxes, or must the kind of thing we call fox have had a genesis? I say that this alternative is closed *a priori*. We mean by fox a kind of thing (wholly dependent upon alterable conditions) that could not have existed through a beginningless past, and that exists, if it does, because of prior conditions that were capable of producing something else instead.

Substitute for fox anything you please; either it is (in my language) an unspe-
cialized abstract metaphysical necessity, as in *something exists*, or it is a special
and by its very meaning conditioned and contingent sort of thing that must
have had a genesis.Judgments of existence, if they are serious, not mere pre-
tence, imply a pattern of meanings. But the usual contingent cases all conform
to a pattern that is inapplicable to *something exists*, or to *deity exists*. Here we
must start over again and look for an unusual pattern. I have proposed such
a pattern. Have my critics a different and better proposal to make? It is true
that, if I am right, any steady-state cosmology that assumes a beginningless
past career of hydrogen or helium atoms is inadmissible. Yet how can empirical science establish such a career? As Bridgeman held, cosmology in this
sense of infinite extrapolation in time is hardly empirical at all. This was the
basic error of Aristotle's anti-evolutionism.

Wittgenstein's Principle of Contrast, which he thinks metaphysicians tend
to violate, as according to him they violate the proper distinction between factual and conceptual questions, is a guiding idea in sound metaphysics. "Such
and such exists" usually implies, as contrasting possibility, the conceivable
nonexistence of such and such. But, in all noncontroversial cases the contrasting nonexistence is, at least for all we could know, to be found in the cosmic
past. What "might not have existed" once did not, and its contingency consists
in the creative freedom at work in those antecedent phases before its genesis,
as well as in the freedom still at work that might and presumably eventually
will put an end to its existence. "Deity exists" cannot derive its contrast in this
way. How then? My contention is that here the purely contradictory judgment
is ill-formed. It would have to mean always-everywhere there is the nonbeing
of deity. But whereas we know what it means for a fox to be absent everywhere, everywhere being occupied by something other than a fox in a fashion
that would be impossible were a fox to be there, we have yet to be told what
it would mean for God to be absent everywhere. He (she) alone can be where
anything else also is as *his* (*her*) creature. I maintain that Anselm was literally
correct; the "nonexistence of God" is a phrase with no corresponding coherent
thought or possible reference.

Does this deprive the judgment "deity exists" of meaning? If it does, then
"something exists" is equally meaningless, for its negation also expresses no
genuine thought. But in fact contrast is not lacking in either case. "Deity
(or something) exists always, everywhere, and without possibility of failure"
contrasts with "specific forms of reality exist not always, not everywhere, and
with possible failure." We are not saying that everything exists necessarily, as
Spinoza did say (or at least did not make clear what else he was saying). He
did violate the Principle of Contrast.

Does the ontological argument blur the distinction between conceptual and factual questions? It makes the divine existence a conceptual matter, in contrast to all ordinary forms of existence. But then, if "fact" means

contingent truth, the point just is that neither the divine existence nor the divine nonexistence could be such a truth; rather, whichever of the contrasting verbal possibilities is true it is true by conceptual necessity. Moreover, if "contingently instantiatable property" is a concept, and why not, then "necessarily instantiated property" (e.g., the property of being something) is its contrasting form. Being divine is a necessarily instantiated property for the same reason as being something, and this reason is that the possible variety of instantiations is *infinitely* various, in a sense in which the variety of possible ways of being a fox are not. God as incapable of not knowing whatever is true must be able to take on a form of knowing corresponding to *any* possible existent or kind of existent. The divine actual knowing of an actual contingent existent is a contingent knowing, and is not entailed by God's mere existence. God's actuality is not merely conceptual and is incomparably more than bare existence, somewhat as my present actuality is vastly more than my bare existence as "myself," for that was already there when I was a child.

So long as the failure or refusal to distinguish existence and actuality persists, clarity concerning the ontological argument cannot be attained. The ontological argument really does blur the fact–concept distinction if it is used by those who identify God with "pure actuality." Indeed, "pure actuality" is an ill-formed expression, a poor way of trying to express the necessary divine existence, which is quite compatible with the contingent divine actuality. As I like to put it, existing is being *somehow* actualized, as my "identity" is somehow actualized each moment of my life; actuality is the de facto *how* of this actualization, and this, granting the reality of freedom and with it contingency, is always accidental. Ordinary individuals are doubly contingent, (a) they might not have existed at all, and (b) they might (after some identifying early state) have existed otherwise, in other actual states. Deity is noncontingent with respect to the *somehow* and contingent only with respect to the *how* of actualization. I submit that there is here sufficient contrast to give meaning, and that the distinction between contingent fact and conceptual truth is not blurred.

The insistence that every existential affirmation must have an equally conceivable denial is merely the dogma that there are no existential necessities. Against the ontological argument (and metaphysical arguments generally) it is question-begging. The true principle is: an affirmation either admits of a conceivable denial, and then it asserts a possible but not inevitable product of the creative process that pervades thought and whatever thought can be about, or it does not admit of a conceivable denial, and then it asserts a truth about the creative process itself, for instance, that it could not fail to produce something, or that it essentially has an aspect of divine or eminent process or creativity. If this latter affirmation is false then it could not have been true— as it could not have been true that there was nothing, or that 2 and 3 made other than 5. Falsity here means a misconception of that without which there could be neither meaning nor anything meant; it reveals a failure to understand what one is saying about the freedom of reality to take this course or that course (but not no course), the freedom that is implied in all talk about alternative possibilities for thought or reality.

Between "foxes (or human beings) exist" and "deity exists" there is an infinite gulf. Anselm discovered this gulf, Aristotle and Philo were virtually aware of it; perhaps in time it will become normal for philosophers in general to be aware of it.

CHAPTER ELEVEN

Categories, Transcendentals, and Creative Experiencing

Philosophy . . . the criticism of categories.
—J. E. Creighton[1]

I begin—because I take the history of philosophy seriously—with the Scholastic distinction between categories and transcendentals. A category is a concept applicable to every being except God. A transcendental is a concept applicable to every being including God. Every being, it was thought, can be said to be *one*, *good*, and *true*—the last word meaning that the being can be known, and, at least by God, is known. Sometimes *beauty* was added to unity, goodness, and truth; sometimes also *power*, ability to influence others. I accept all five transcendentals. But I think the Scholastics, like the ancient Greeks, somewhat misconceived the relation of being—also substance—to other fundamental concepts. Being seems to contrast with becoming, which applies to every concrete reality other than God as classically conceived; yet nothing in the five transcendentals explicitly involves becoming, even as a possibility. God was for two millennia defined as immutable perfection; other realities were by comparison imperfect as well as mutable. What in any sense becomes was supposed less than what simply is without becoming—as though the idea of changeable entities was arrived at by subtracting from the idea of immutable perfection!

I think this view was seriously mistaken. Subtracting from the idea, or pseudo-idea, of a perfect and changeless whole might give the idea of an imperfect, changeless part, or an inferior analogy to the changeless whole, but not the idea of becoming or generation. When Hegel made a dialectical passage from "being" *and* "not-being" to becoming he did not show, and no one has ever shown, how the combination defines becoming. As McTaggart pointed out, from "pure," "complete," or unqualified being plus negation one arrives at best only at the idea of limited, determinate, partial being. The derivation of becoming is a fake. Yet becoming is indeed, as Hegel says, the more inclusive notion, and does (though without contradiction) imply (some) affirmation and (some) negation of (some aspect or instance of) being. But this is not all that it implies.

We do not in fact encounter actualities, or the concrete, as simply imperfect beings, but rather as processes, instances of becoming. Vision, with its apparent exhibition of static entities, is deceptive. With hearing of sounds (also with feeling of pleasures and pains) it is more obvious, but even with vision it is true, that perceiving is a process, and so is each instance of the perceived. Becoming is what we start with, not being. It is being, not process, that needs to be derived. Peirce and Bergson were among the first in the West after Heraclitus to realize this clearly; but Whitehead has articulated the point most fully. The notion of a being such as an animal is a complex idea involving a series of bodily events and also (as we normally interpret these events in others and directly intuit them in ourselves) a series of psychical events when the animal is awake or dreaming. To reduce these events to a succession of properties of a simply identical substance is an extreme abstraction. It does not give us the concrete level of reality. To me it seems clear that there is no sheer identity that has my present experience and had my infant experiences. The actual subject that experienced in infantile fashion and the subject that experiences as an elderly philosopher are vastly different and in some genuine sense numerically distinct. The infant self is one of the causes of the adult self. Causes are not identical with their effects. Further arguments for the pluralistic view of genetic identity will be presented later.

According to a view two thousand years old in the Orient and increasingly favored in the West by scientists and philosophers, the world consists not of changing yet identical things or persons, except in rough, provisional analysis, but of instances of becoming—or, to use Bergson's, Whitehead's, and Berdyaev's term, of *creativity*. Alone among these three writers, and in contrast also to Peirce, Whitehead posits real *units* of becoming, momentary actualities that become but "do not change."[2] Being a mathematician, used (as Peirce also was) to careful reasoning about continuity, and living (as Peirce did not) in an age in which discontinuity had been introduced into physics, Whitehead arrived at the old insight of Buddhism: becoming is not continuous change in a single actuality, but a series of unitary actualities each of which is somehow produced or created out of its predecessors. The Buddhist phrase "dependent origination," taken a bit vaguely, now unites East and West more closely than hitherto. In my view Whitehead is superior to the Buddhists in analyzing the "dependent" aspect as well as the "originative" or creative aspect.

In another way, too, Whitehead and the Buddhists have common ground. "Mind only," a Buddhist slogan, could be vaguely identified with Whitehead's "reformed subjectivism," or my "psychicalism." I make these comparisons partly because I suspect that many cherish the idea that process metaphysics will go away if only one ignores it. It is, however, a late Western parallel to an ancient, widely influential, long-lasting Eastern tradition, some of whose central doctrines are now acquiring global relevance. The new-old metaphysics will not go away—unless human culture goes away. Alas that, this, because of horrible new explosives or poisons, and horrible, though not so new, human weaknesses, now seems all too possible.

By rejecting strictly continuous (though accepting dependent) originating or becoming, Whitehead is able, as Bergson and Peirce were not, to acknowledge definite units of actuality. True, our self-awareness is not distinct enough to exhibit clearly such units in our successive experiences. But we come close to intuiting them. We can experience at least a dozen musical tones in a second (but not a hundred or a thousand) and so it seems reasonable to think that this is about the number of successive experiences on the human level. There is no reason for supposing that the number on other levels, say, in the experiences of birds (with their higher temperatures), is the same, and there are good reasons for supposing otherwise. On microlevels the tempo of succession must be very different indeed. This alone explains why, apart from our own experiences, we cannot observe the units even approximately. Epicurus, Leibniz, Peirce, Whitehead, and Bergson tend to agree that human perception gives only relatively distinct intuitions of reality.

The substitution of 'actual entity,' or 'actuality,' for 'being,' as label for the most concrete instances of reality, serves two purposes. It avoids begging the question about the status of being in relation to becoming, and it also shows the relation of concrete actuality to universals or possibilities. "Actual" contrasts to "possible," rather than to nonentity. If real possibilities are anything, they are certainly involved in actual instances of becoming, as Aristotle saw so well. A normal experience is preceded for us by a given situation in which we were deciding among what we took to be possibilities. An experience as actual contrasts with earlier experiences in which the future was a partly indeterminate potentiality. Fully *definite* entities, or—the same thing—actualities, are encountered only as past, not as future. Immediate memory, which, when used in a certain way (Ryle, Whitehead), we sometimes call introspection (really retrospection) is the closest we come to definitely intuiting the concrete units of reality. And these units are instances of becoming or creativity. After they have become we can treat them, or their ordered sequences, as beings. Self-identity is an abstract view of the manner in which earlier members of a "personally ordered" series of units are given, and insofar are integral, to later members.

Are all actualities unitary, good, true (knowable and divinely known), also beautiful and influential upon other actualities? Yes, according to my neoclassical process metaphysics. Of course there are enormous differences of kind and degree in the goodness, beauty, influence. Reformed subjectivism denies "vacuous actuality," devoid of sentience and intrinsic value, and in this way can literally accept the *bonum* or good that Aquinas more ambiguously credited to inanimate entities. And since (according to Bergson, Whitehead, and the writer of this sentence) every actuality is intuited, however indistinctly, by its successors, every actuality has some *power*, however slight. It even has some power over God, who "physically prehends" or directly intuits, and therefore is influenced by, actualities once they have become.

It was the very late Scholastics, e.g., Campanella, who most clearly related the divine attributes to categories of nondivine beings. Believing that God has perfect power, knowledge, and love, they thought that all other actualities must have imperfect forms, however minimal in some cases, of these qualities. I agree with them. Leibniz, with certain partly unfortunate qualifications, took up the idea, and some process philosophers in some respects come even closer to Campanella on this topic. Whitehead's explication of "prehension" as "feeling of [others'] feeling," thus a form of sympathy (as he also says), encapsulates the point. Reality is an "ocean of feelings," and each feeling influences, elicits some sympathy or love from, later feelings.[3] It even influences God, who feels all actual feelings, being the One "to whom all hearts are open" (Anglican *Book of Common Prayer*). It does not make sense, as Campanella saw, to compare God as unsurpassably powerful, loving, or wise to creatures as in zero-degree powerful, loving, or wise, but only as surpassably so. I have sometimes called this "the logic of immanence and Transcendence." Whitehead, in attributing at least minimal creativity or genuine freedom and feeling to *every* creature, conforms to the principle, and by doing so furnishes the only reasonable way of dealing with the alleged problem of evil, which, in its classical form, is a pseudo-problem, misinterpreting unsurpassable power and attributing a zero of genuine, decision-making power to at least some of the creatures.

Instead of 'being,' *creative experiencing* should be taken as the inclusive transcendental. Concrete actuality, as we can know it, is experiencing as prehending a determinate past and, with each new total prehensive act, constituting a new determinate actuality that itself will be prehended by subsequent actualities. All this is what Whitehead means by creativity as "category of the ultimate." "The many become one, and are increased by one."[4] Seldom has a philosopher said so much with so few words. Becoming is increase in multiplicity of the real. With Peirce and Bergson, Whitehead rejects the notion of becoming as at once addition and subtraction, gain and loss. For us human beings with our imperfect prehensions there is loss, but not ultimately, not for God's uniquely adequate prehending. Divine creativity is the unsurpassably adequate prehending by which every actuality, once it has created itself, utilizing past actualities [including God] as its data, is everlastingly preserved. Hence "the truth itself is the way all things are together in the Consequent Nature of God."[5]

Whitehead is aware, with Heraclitus and Hegel, that philosophic truth is the *unity of contraries*. But none of these three writers tells us, I think, sufficiently clearly how this unity is to be understood.

Many concepts are categorically universal besides unity, power, goodness, beauty. Thus always there is *diversity* as well as unity, *being influenced* as well as influencing (effects and causes), *novelty* as well as *repetition or permanence*, *chance* (Epicurus) or *contingency* as well as *necessity* or law, *later* as well as *earlier*, *subject* as well as *object* (or experience and its data), *dependence* as well as *independence*, *concrete* as well as *abstract*. Always reality is both particular and universal, actual and possible, finite and infinite. The question obviously arises, which side describes the togetherness of the polar contraries? Or is there a third concept that describes this togetherness and is the whole truth? Whitehead's "ontological" (or "Aristotelian") principle says that the abstract is in the concrete, not vice versa. Two is in two apples, also in the mathematician's thoughtful experiences, or in divine experiences, not in some realm of essence all by itself. Whitehead also implies that temporal objects are *in* (later) subjects as their data, and eternal objects (of these more later) are said to be in some manner in all subjects, primordially and supremely so in deity as subject.

Since prehension is, in this philosophy, the key to causality, and all prehension of actualities is retrospective, unit experiences (or actualities) are the single effects whose causal conditions are previous experiences. Thus subjects include objects, effects, causes. The inclusion is qualified by the indistinctness of nondivine prehending but is unqualified in divine prehending. The consequent aspect of God is the inclusive and supreme effect, partly new with each new creature, as the primordial aspect is the exclusive and everidentical (but abstract) universal cause of all things. It is no less true that God is universal effect than that God is universal cause. But God as universal ever-identical cause is an extreme abstraction and the concrete residence of this abstraction is in God as universal, but ever partly new, effect. Whitehead hesitates concerning the relation of deity to time, usually referring to God as "nontemporal," but in one passage he rightly qualifies this by "and in a sense temporal." I prefer Berdyaev's forthright saying that there is a kind of divine time. And Whitehead describes the consequent nature as "always moving on."[6]

In my book *Creative Synthesis and Philosophic Method* (recently reprinted in America) I give a long list of categorial contraries such that the polarities in the left-hand column are related to those in the right-hand column as the concrete is to the abstract, the inclusive to the included.[7] The concrete or inclusive poles depend on the abstract or included as later effects on previous causes, and—more concretely—subjects on given objects.

Two great formal logicians, Aristotle and Peirce, saw in logic a key to ontology. Peirce looked also to direct intuition, consultation of concrete experience, to exhibit the ultimate variables of reality. Insofar he was like Husserl. Both said that phenomenology (or Peirce's phaneroscopy) was prior to metaphysics. Whitehead to some extent agrees in practice with both points, but is less explicit. He thinks also that we must consult the wisdom embodied in language. Peirce and James held that concepts should be defined in relation to behavior and that no concept without intelligible relation to our potential action has cognitive meaning. I accept these four aspects of philosophic method. All can be seen in Whitehead's thinking. A metaphysician or ontologist should be a logician, phenomenologist, linguistic analyst, and pragmatist, and I can put my categorial commitments in all of these ways. But I cannot make all this clear in a brief article.

In a previous issue of *The Monist* (vol. 63, no. 3 [July 1980]: 277–89)[8] I have argued that Peirce's categories of Firstness, Secondness, and Thirdness, revised to eliminate certain defects, largely coincide with Whitehead's idea of actual entity as (a) a unity of feeling quite independent of particular later actualities but (b) prehensive of and hence dependent upon earlier ones, also (c) anticipatory of, implying, and dependent upon the future, not in its particulars but in its probabilities or approximate characters. Probability, or partly limited and real possibility, is the third relation over and above sheer (but one-way) dependence and independence. Peirce was absolutely right about the importance of these three kinds of relatedness, but mistaken in supposing that the number of entities on which something depends is the key to the categories. It is true that being second is asymmetrically dependent upon something else being first, and being third on something else being second. However, this is just as true of being fourth and something else being third, and so on with all higher numbers. It is the asymmetry of the dependence, not the numbers of the items involved, that is crucial. Peirce seems to have erred here. Yet there are three basic modes of dependence and its negation.

In all process philosophy, though only in mine with complete explicitness and (I hope) consistency, a basic asymmetry is central. Extreme pluralists (Hume, Russell, perhaps, Theravada Buddhists) assert *mutual* independence between things or events, extreme monists (Blanshard, some Mahayana Buddhists) assert mutual dependence (so far as things in the plural are real at all); moderate pluralism or moderate monism asserts dependence *and* independence as, without contradiction, united in one-way relations such that Y depends on X, which is independent of Y. Time's arrow is one aspect of this: we depend on our ancestors who did not depend on us, except in the general sense of the probability of there later being descendants who would, they hoped, make good use of their achievements. Subjects depend on their particular objects or data, which do not depend on but temporally precede and causally condition them. Things *must* become objects for subsequent subjects, but not necessarily for the subjects that happen to become their successors and fulfill the requirement.

In formal logic the basic relation is of p entailing q, which (normally) does not entail p. Biconditioning or equivalence is a special and indeed degenerate case where p and q state one and the same fact.

A logic in which all propositions were equivalent (as Brand Blanshard's or any necessitarian position implies) would be a useless logic. A logic in which all propositions were mutually independent, the formal analogy for Hume's and Russell's theory of events, would be equally and even more obviously useless. Abstract from the history of metaphysics the doctrines that clearly avoid both of these errors and you have some approach to the doctrines most worth discussing today.

Classical determinism is the symmetrical version of causality. The totality of the necessary conditions is taken to provide a sufficient condition, which means that it necessitates the effect. This is the negation of time's arrow. The asymmetrical view is that for concrete actualities there are no strictly sufficient conditions. Not their predecessors but they themselves "make" them occur. This is why Jules Lequier, Sartre, and, probably independently, Whitehead write of "self-creation."[9] This is the real freedom, coming to be as determinate out of a situation that did not causally necessitate this determinateness. Indeterminism is piecemeal or retail contingentism, whereas determinism is either complete necessitarianism (Spinoza, Blanshard) or else it admits only wholesale contingency of a created totality whose parts necessarily imply one another. Peirce saw sharply that these are the options. Granting determinism, either all is necessary and there is no contingency or, although the world system as a whole exists by chance (with no sufficient reason), each item in the world is sufficient reason for every other.

I hold that the most reasonable view is this: necessity and contingency must both (Principle of Contrast) be applicable to reality, the former in the way temporally antecedent events are necessary conditions for an event, the latter in the way events are less than sufficient conditions for their successors. Something like what happens has sufficient conditions, but not any concrete happening in its full definiteness. Furthermore, the question of determinism is not an empirical one, but a matter of categorial coherence. The asymmetrical view is also the only one that has pragmatic meaning. It helps us not at all, in "making up our minds" or deciding among options, to be told that any decision we make will have been determined by the past. Decision-making is one thing, deducing the concrete future from the past is another, and there is no way to harmonize them, even in principle. "Compatibilism" is pragmatically null. As Peirce said, determinism is mere talk. It cannot be lived by and hence cannot be genuinely believed. The probabilistic view can and must be lived by. Probability is not only "the guide of life," it should be seen, and many physicists now do see it, as the guiding idea in science also. Peirce and Bergson were among the first to say this. Still earlier the great Clerk Maxwell said that determinism is theological rather than scientific. I add, it is bad theology.

Russell wrote: "asymmetrical relations are the most relational of relations."[10] Given a one-way relationship, one can always define the two-way or symmetrical one. The latter is a special case, not the general principle. X and Y are equal if "more" or "better" apply to them in relation to some third entity Z but not in relation to one another. S and Y are simultaneous, or at least contemporary, if both have temporal status but neither temporally follows the other; p and q "condition each other" if p conditions q and q conditions p. The symmetrical case is complex and derivative, and is arrived at by treating as zero some distinction between the two items compared. It conveys a lesser amount of information. Suppose A and B "love each other." Obviously A's love for B is not simply B's love for A read in reverse. In relativity physics contemporary events are those neither of which influences the other (in the ordinary message-sending sense, or apart from Bell's Theorem in quantum physics and certain very subtle and for most purposes entirely negligible kinds of influence). If this symmetrical negation were all that was involved, the events would not even be in the same universe together. They have this relation because of the one-way influences coming to each from a past that partly overlaps the past of the other, and because of a similar overlapping of influences they exert on the future. Thus the basic concept used in explaining the total situation is that of one-way relatedness. Alas, that Russell forgot the primacy of asymmetry in making *mutual* independence of events his basic ontological principle. A symmetrical negation is doubly unfit for this role. Hume was half right in making "separability" or independence essential for "distinguishability" or genuine plurality. He missed the truth that one-way independence suffices for plurality. If Y prehends and hence depends on X, which did not and does not depend on Y, Y is distinguishable from X as a whole is inclusive of, dependent on, but not identical with, its constituents. A subject X remembering, or otherwise prehending, Y is not identical with Y. Indeed concrete subjects prehend not themselves but subjects preceding themselves. If the preceding subjects are in the same personally ordered series, we call the prehension memory. Otherwise, it is perception.

One-way dependence or inclusion is modeled not only by entailment but by another truth of formal logic, which is that the contingent includes the necessary, not vice versa. If p is necessary and q is contingent, then the conjunction "p · q" is contingent in the same sense. $N (p \cdot q) \equiv (Np \cdot Nq)$—necessary truth includes only necessary truth. Even the necessary truth that there must be some contingent truths entails no definite contingent truth. It follows that if God is, as classically conceived (Aristotle, Aquinas) wholly necessary, then there cannot in God be anything that entails or strictly implies any contingent truth. But "X infallibly knows that p" entails "p." Therefore, in God as classically conceived there could be no knowledge of contingent truths. For this reason Aristotle denied that God knows the contingent aspects of the world and Spinoza denied that there are any contingent aspects. Faustus

Socinus, facing the same problem and convinced of human freedom as implying contingent decisions, asserted contingent aspects of the divine knowledge. This brave and perspicacious step anticipated process theology by more than three centuries. Historians have yet to tell us this. They have been too prejudiced or too busy to notice Socinus's theology.

Hegel's idea that "the real is the rational" seems to mean that the contingent is unreal. Or is he merely hopelessly unclear? I have yet to meet a Hegelian who answers this question convincingly. Those who look down, as Hegel did, on formal logic as a tool in philosophy are not likely to be very clear on very much. Bergson and Heidegger are examples.

One source of error in the theory of categories is the failure to distinguish carefully between levels of abstractness. Otherwise the primacy of asymmetry may be overlooked. Thus 'concreteness' makes sense only because 'abstractness' does; so that the two ideas are interdependent. The dependence is symmetrical. There could not be either a purely universal (or abstract) universe or a purely particular (or concrete) universe. (As Peirce sagaciously said, these are two forms of nominalism; each tries to select one side of a logical polarity as alone applicable, whereas realism asserts both sides.) But this conceptual symmetry (which is part at least of what Buchler means by "ontological parity") is compatible with, and made intelligible by, the consideration that concrete*ness* is (as Russell says) itself abstract, and only its instances are concrete. When the latter are taken into account, the symmetry vanishes. Particular instances of a universal are not possible without the universal; but the universal exists if there are any instances, no matter which out of possible ones. If (were this possible) there were no actual pairs and no one thought of pairedness, then pairedness would have no existence. But pairedness did not require for its reality my twin brothers. Particular instances require what they are instances of, the universal; but the latter requires only that there be some instances or other. This asymmetry is ultimate. Moreover, there is a basic temporality in it. Thus animality existed long before you or I as animals did. Becoming is the creation of *new instances of old universals* (also creation of more specific new universals, e.g., human). Particularization and becoming are one. Hence there are no particulars or individuals in purely possible worlds. They are really only possible *sorts* of world containing only general *kinds* of particulars or individuals. Leibniz and Ross (and those logicians who follow him) have been mistaken here. "Possible world" is a dangerously misleading formula, essentially nominalistic in the Peircean sense. If I am not mistaken, Peirce, who believed deeply in the reality of universals and possibilities, never seriously employed this expression, certainly not in the Leibnizian sense.

Philosophies that lump abstract and concrete entities together and look for relations holding within this miscellaneous class of entities, will not find and lucidly, economically, state much truth. This is how (without having carefully studied them) I incline to regard Justus Buchler's "ontological parity"

(that universals and particulars, possibilities and actualities, are equally necessary to each other) and Archie Bahm's doctrine of universal interdependence.
(I may misunderstand what these writers [especially Buchler] are trying to
do.) I have similar misgivings, based on greater effort to understand it, concerning Weiss's doctrine of Finalities as coordinate to and mutually interact-
ing with each other. Weiss does accept from Aristotle, Peirce, and Whitehead
the asymmetry of settled past and partly unsettled future; but what he says
about Finalities seems to confuse levels of abstractness and to rule out any
really intelligible integration of his various abstractions. For this, a minimum
requirement would be that "ideality" be seen as in actualities, not vice versa.
Yet Weiss is one of the few writers who seem to be doing very much with the
metaphysical problems today.

R. G. Collingwood, who thought with care and learning about metaphysical problems, argued that the study of being-as-being is sterile, since
there is little to be said that is applicable to everything that in any sense is. But
metaphysical generality is not confined to a definition or explication of 'being.'
A truth is metaphysical if it applies to actuality as such, or potentiality as
such, or existence as such. (As I shall explain presently, I distinguish this last
from actuality as well as from being.) No such truth can be merely contingent
or merely empirical but must be necessary and *a priori*, i.e., metaphysical in
Aristotle's sense. A metaphysical generality is universal *on its appropriate logical level* or level of abstractness.

As for being, Whitehead was first of all in defining the concept in terms
of becoming. Being is whatever is a "potential for every [later] becoming."[11]
Abstract entities, as well as concrete entities already actualized, are potential
data for all future experience. God's being also fits the definition. Any further
actualities will (at least unconsciously) prehend God as God now already is,
whatever else they may prehend.

Collingwood was also, I think, forgetting that any concept must have
its meaning from experience; so that being cannot be defined except in terms
of some form of experience or awareness. In view of his familiarity with the
idealistic tradition, I wonder why this was not apparent to Collingwood.

The reason metaphysics must be systematic is that all concepts of metaphysical generality express aspects of the essence of reality as such and can
only be understood through the interrelations of these concepts. Ryle shocked
some of his fellow linguistic analysts by writing about this interconnectedness
of philosophical problems.

On the other hand, it is quite erroneous to take the interrelatedness
of metaphysical categories to imply that a philosophy must be a system of
all knowledge, contingent as well as necessary. This is "synoptic philosophy" or cosmology, a blend of metaphysics and science. It is a bold and
ever-unfinished and tentative undertaking, not metaphysics in Aristotle's or
my sense. Contingent truths are additions to metaphysical (i.e., necessary)

truths, and, as we have seen, the conjunction of necessary and contingent truth is itself contingent.

Metaphysics, as Collingwood saw but overstated, is very limited in its content. In this it resembles formal logic. Indeed, there is some question how far the two subjects are distinguishable. If logicians want to consider with care what is meant by the variables in quantification, by the lowest logical level, or by modalities in their extralinguistic reference, and the like, they will have to be metaphysicians. But they need not be biologists, chemists, or physicists. Nor need a metaphysician be these things. I maintain, for example, that simply as metaphysician Aristotle had no good ground for asserting, and ground enough for denying, the immutability of heavenly bodies, animal and plant species, and God. It does, of course, help that empirical science has discovered the baselessness of all but the last of these assumptions. Still it is a logical truth that absolutes like immutability could not be established by observation. And it is a metaphysico-logical truth that arbitrary constants (like those implicitly used to describe atoms in Greek and early modern science) are not reasonable candidates for the unconditional necessity Aristotle rightly attributed to eternal entities as such. In some respects Whitehead is more Aristotelian than Aristotle, as (consciously so) was Peirce.

A basic question about entities, abstract or concrete, is how the idea of continuity or its negation applies to them. Peirce (following Aristotle) holds that a continuum is not a definite multitude of distinct or definite items, such as points. Whitehead agrees as to space not being a collection of points. Yet in his eternal-objects doctrine he seems to forget this. For he does not deny, and once in conversation asserted, that his eternal entities or "pure potentials" form continua. "Blue is an eternal object"—this Whiteheadian saying forces upon us the question, "Is each shade and hue of blue a definite and eternal point–like item in the continuity of possible colors?" To this query, which I once put to him late in his life, he replied, "That's a very subtle argument. Perhaps I've missed something."

Peirce holds that the eternal is a continuum of possibilities, a "multitude beyond all multitude," lacking, as eternal, in definiteness.[12] Whitehead's "forms of definiteness," if taken as themselves fully definite, would have been rejected by Peirce. On this point I side with the earlier thinker. The parts of possibility are only possible parts, lacking distinct "identity." But, strangely enough, Peirce views actuality also as continuous. Thus, when we experience first blue and then yellow, we pass (he holds) through an infinite number of actually experienced intermediate qualities in no matter how short a time. This notion that experiencing is continuous prevented Peirce from finding any definite units of actuality, and also from making much of his wise assertion of "immediate memory," or of direct intuition of the past.

It seems absurd to stress, as Peirce does, the truth that continuity is the order of possibilities and yet add that it is also the order of actualities. Surely actualities are discrete. Half a cell is not a smaller cell; every offspring differs *finitely* from its parents; nature *always* "makes leaps," though mostly small ones. There is no evidence that we have infinitely many successive experiences in a second. Discreteness simply means that some possibilities are *not* actualized, and what is actualization if not the emergence of definite multitude out of an indefinite continuum? Peirce once suggested (thinking perhaps of James's "drops or buds of experience") that there may be finite units of experience but added that we have no knowledge of these. Yet it is Peirce who emphatically denies any easy access to introspective facts.

I hold, with Leibniz and Whitehead, that actuality is a definite multitude of definitely singular actualities. 'Singular' does not mean in every sense simple, far from it—and insofar as Buchler's term "complex" for the constituents of reality is justified—since each actuality prehends its predecessors. Against Leibniz, Whiteheadians hold that the final singularities or "monads" are not enduring, changing individuals but, as the Buddhists and a few Islamic thinkers first said, momentary items, created (and then in a sense superseded) rather than changed. "Prehension" is the Whiteheadian analysis of supersession.

The analysis of an enduring individual into (in some cases) millions of successive "socially ordered" momentary actualities seems to some philosophers excessively pluralistic. However, extremes of monism and pluralism are not determined numerically. Extreme monism holds that what seems many distinct actualities are so universally dependent upon one another as to constitute but a single identical actuality, one subject with many predicates. Extreme pluralism (Hume, Russell) holds that the many actualities are so universally independent of one another that they in no sense constitute an essentially ordered cosmos. Leibniz was a strict monist in his theory of the successive states of a monad; each state implicates every other, past or future. The opposite extreme holds that no state implicates any other. Theravada Buddhism seems almost interpretable in this sense (at least according to Stcherbatsky).

Whitehead's view is equally far from either extreme; only past states are integrated into and condition a given state. Aristotle is less clear but, according to Bochenski (in conversation), is approximately interpretable in this sense. Whitehead rejects both the radical denial and the unqualified assertion of genetic identity. I today am *partly* identical with my yesterday's self since I prehend and in a manner include that self. Weiss and many others seem not to understand this. But many think they do understand it. Peirce disagrees here only because of his misapplication of absolute continuity, his Synechism. This was really an extreme cosmic monism of a sort, except for the admission of an open future and time's asymmetry. Peirce depreciated individuality; the self is "only a vicinity" (what is going on here).[13]

Whitehead's view best avoids all extremes in this matter and is close to the "middle way," which Buddhism perhaps never quite found. There is partial identity, not only between me now and me yesterday but also, in a somewhat different way and degree, between me now and you yesterday. In all this Whitehead agrees with Mahayana Buddhism except with respect to the future and to space. The problem of contemporaries separated spatially, as to which relativity and quantum theory are still not quite reconciled, is unfinished business in process metaphysics, and probably in any metaphysics, past or present, East or West. The neatest solution so far proposed is by a physicist[14] influenced by Whitehead.

The category of *existence*, as I, but apparently no one else, interpret it, is distinct from but definable through the categories of actuality and of "defining characteristics" of societies of actualities. Jimmy Carter exists if, and so long as, his defining characteristic (including being born of a certain mother) gets concretized somehow in actualities; God exists eternally and necessarily in that the divine essence or defining characteristic (unsurpassability by others, or all-excelling greatness and goodness) is necessarily and always concretized in some suitable actual phases (whose distinguishing is a moot point in process theology) of the concrete divine life. Divine genetic identity is the unsurpassable form under this transcendental.

Individual *existence* is universally contingent except for God, but concrete *actualities* in which an essence is embodied are always contingent, even in the divine case. Not that God might have been merely abstract, but that just what concrete form the divine essence takes is contingent, though necessarily (as we shall see) it takes some form or other.

"Deity exists" is necessarily true, unless there is no coherent idea of the divine essence, in which case the proposition is necessarily false. But just how the essence exists, in just what concrete form, is contingent. I seem to have been the first to analyze the matter in this way.

If "God exists" is necessarily true, "something exists" is so also, and "there might have been nothing" is absurd or contradictory. I am not alone in believing it is just that (Jonathan Edwards, Milton Munitz, Bergson). I hold also that "something nondivine exists" is likewise necessarily true (for similar reasons of generality, abstractness, and nonspecificity). But all specific forms of nondivine life (and divine knowing of these forms) are contingent and noneternal.

Contingent individuals or species lack essences in the strict sense in which God has an essence. The divine essence alone is individual, yet definable purely conceptually, without use of empirical references. Thus "cognitively infallible" identifies God, but no comparably abstract description identifies any other individual. Tillich is right, God is not *a* being.[15] But God is *the* being, the only one identifiable *a priori*, the sole individual with universal functions. This is one form of ontological argument: what is identifiable *a priori* is knowable *a priori* (though only in its most abstract aspect, its mere identity, not in its internal differences). No actuality, nothing concrete, even God as concrete and actual, is identifiable unless empirically.

Empirical individualities (or species of such) have no wholly definite essences. The "pro-life" question, "When does a human life begin?" is indeterminate and can never be answered by observation alone but only by fiat. Was "I" there in the fertilized egg? Yes, by some criteria, no, by others. To base laws, especially those with dire penalties, on such semantic puzzles is both tyranny and folly. But God must always and in any case be definitely God, all-surpassing and beyond all rivalry in power, wisdom, love.

Peirce was right about the superiority of triadic to dyadic divisions. Essence, actuality, and existence are all distinguishable; but the last is definable through the first two. And actuality includes all that there is; all-surpassing actuality includes all lesser actuality (by prehending it with full adequacy), but even divine actuality perpetually acquires new content through its and the nondivine forms of creativity. All such content is everlasting but not eternal. Thus the divine reality is indeed that in which we "live and move and have our being," and by which "the sting of death" is overcome; but it is not in all respects immutable or impassible, nor does it actualize all possible value—this being an ill-formed formula, along with "pure actuality" and various other fragments of the one-sidedly negative theology.

Divine potentiality is the all-inclusive potentiality, as the divine actuality is the all-inclusive actuality. To be actual is to be actual for God; to be possible is to be possible for God. In this sense God is "being itself." What could be content for God is the same as what could be at all. Not that God could have anything that could be simply by fiat, "let it be so," for that, too, is ill-formed if the "anything" involves freedom or creativity in what is to be had. Any nothing worth having, indeed nothing at all, is apart from all freedom, which essentially has the dual form, divine–nondivine. For a Buddhist this is dualism in an unacceptable sense. For me, to deny this duality is unacceptable. It is not really a dualism; for one pole includes the other, not by determining, or unilaterally creating, but by adequately prehending it.

Thus far I have not distinguished between causal dependence or necessity and logical dependence or necessity, or between modality *de re* and modality *de dictu*. Somewhat as Aristotle and Peirce did, I conceive these two aspects as more intimately related than most philosophers have supposed. Logical modalities express relations between cases of knowledge. If p entails q, then at least ideal or perfectly clear knowledge of p would include knowledge of q. But our knowledge is, at most, ideal only about abstractions, as in elementary arithmetic, simple syllogisms, or other algorithms. It is never anything like ideal of particulars or individuals, actualities or societies. As Hume found, but interpreted anthropocentrically or skeptically, we cannot know events clearly enough to see what ideal knowledge of them would include. If we distinctly remember certain events as having happened, then we know that something like what we remember did happen and that our remembering experience depends on this fact and would appear to ideal knowledge as thus dependent.

But what we call "remembering that p" is always a mixture of genuine mnemonic prehension, or intuitive grasp, and verbal interpretation; the latter is a human and highly fallible function. Always there is a mixture of given data and theorizing in our reports of what we remember. The same is true of our reports of what we perceive. As prehending we have the real past indistinctly intuited; but for practical reasons we cannot limit ourselves to this indistinct information, nor does language encourage us to do so. Error arises (as Descartes came close to seeing aright) from the unavoidable process of trying to *guess* what it is that the lack of clarity in our intuitions conceals from us. Causal dependence and logical dependence (or modality) are one for God, but not for us. Leibniz had a partly similar doctrine, limited by his symmetrical view of causal dependence and other now-antiquated features of his system.

Those who insist on the difference between logical and real modalities often fail to distinguish adequately between necessary and (allegedly) sufficient conditions for events. In short, they have usually been determinists. This was true of Hume. And those who have affirmed that the necessary conditions are logically necessary have supposed that they are also sufficient conditions. In short, they, too, and with fewer exceptions, have been determinists. Thus two questions have been jumbled together, as so often happens in philosophy. It is important to see that the theory of time's asymmetry, of a "closed" past and an "open" future, would, for ideal knowledge, mean logically closed and logically open. It would not mean the block universe or absolute monism that James feared (and falsely attributed to Fechner), and it would not imply that relations, time, and space were unreal, or any of the consequences by which "absolute idealism" discredited itself at the turn of the century.

Because the process view of genetic identity (as genuine but highly relative and partial) is so important and so much disputed, I will make one more attempt to show its reasonableness. Consider:

1.0 "John believing and not believing that q." Every John changes some of his beliefs. So, in a sense, 1.0 cannot be contradictory. But there are two logically distinct ways of removing the apparent contradiction:

1.1 "John now-believing and not then-believing that q." Here the predicates are different, so the negation introduces no contradiction. This is the Leibnizian doctrine. Its logical structure as noncontradictory is lucid. But there are obvious flaws. One is this: predicates, such as "believing that q," are abstract and applicable to an indefinite number of subjects. There seems no reason why they should be strongly time-bound in their meanings. In contrast, most thinkers will admit that becoming, at least often, produces new subjects.

The only other comparably clear solution is:

1.2 John-now believing, and John-then not believing, that q. Here the subjects are different entities, and again there is no contradiction. But here, and not in 1.1, we respect the abstractness of predicates and concreteness of subjects (the subject, not its predicates, is the ground of definite assertions). If John's father was also called John, John-now and John-then could be two different persons. Is the distinction between John as fertilized egg, embryo, or infant and John as adult so much less than, or so absolutely different from, that between John and his father?

I submit that if this reasoning is not a cogent philosophical argument there are few such arguments. I find the reasoning conclusive. Something like it was suggested by a historian of logic, Heinrich Scholz, one of the noblest and wisest persons I have known.[16]

The Whiteheadian view that change is to be finally analyzed as successive becoming or creation of actualities, prehended by their successors, rather than that becoming is to be analyzed as change of a single actuality, is given strong support by another argument from logical laws (excluded middle rather than of noncontradiction) used by another logician, von Wright, to refute the idea (Bergson, Peirce, and many others) that becoming is continuous.[17] Von Wright does not mention Whitehead in this context, but his reasoning helps to confirm one of Whitehead's most important ideas, that only possibilities are continuous.

Standing on the shoulders of the giants mentioned in this chapter, and those of some dozens of others that could be mentioned, we may be able in some respects to see further and more clearly than they in the theory of categories.

CHAPTER TWELVE

The Higher Levels of Creativity: Wieman's Theory

In ordinary use "creative" has a laudatory meaning. In metaphysical use, the value aspect is attenuated though not simply eliminated. The theory (in process philosophy) is that neither creative novelty nor value can be totally lacking, or at zero, in any concrete actuality. But how far above zero the novelty or the value may be is left open. Any singular actuality is an experience, and no experience fails to achieve at least a minimum of "satisfaction" (Whitehead). It has some value, and also some novelty, in every case. The novelty is that of a synthesis of temporally prior data, themselves actualities. The value is that of felt harmony. (Even in intense suffering there is something of this value. Mere discord does not produce an experience, a synthesis, at all.)

On very low levels of actuality, as in atoms or light rays, there is extremely slight novelty (hence the relatively sharp predictions of physics, especially when dealing with large collections of similar actualities) and there is presumably equally slight value. In plant cells and the lower animals there is more novelty and more value. In our species, and (possibly to a more nearly comparable degree than we have been assuming in the past) in other primates and in whales, there is immensely greater creative power and greater value. The felt harmonies are more complex and rich. The value of harmonious feelings is proportional to their intensity, and this seems to depend upon the depth and variety of the contrasts in the data. Novelty is contrast in time, compared to variety in space. Both contribute, via memory and perception, to intensity and hence to value. The higher animals, especially humans, enjoy a rich life of thought that adds new dimensions to the contrasting factors of experience.

There is no reason to suppose that experience becomes more habitually harmonious (rather than relatively discordant) on the higher animal levels than on the lower. We do not surpass other creatures by being less capable of suffering; if anything we suffer more intensely and more frequently. But this does not cancel out our advantage. Just to be a complex viable organism is an immense harmony in itself. On all levels nature is primarily harmonious and only secondarily in a state of conflict or discord. Optimism in this sense is sober truth. Here I am in agreement with Peirce, and with the classical tradition, which held that being as such is good. The belief that nature is sick is itself a sick view. It is health, organic harmony, that makes the world go round, not disease. As has been said, the pessimist Schopenhauer enjoyed his life; he "smoked good cigars" and appreciated good music. He enjoyed the harmonious functionings of his bodily members. So does every animal.

To experience at all is to create value. The optimism of this statement is minimal only. A suffering animal achieves some value; otherwise the will to live would lapse. But the animal does not, while suffering, achieve the optimal value possible for its kind of creature. Also a creature may achieve the value it does enjoy in such a way as to limit disproportionately and tragically the value opportunities of other creatures.

When we speak of someone as a creative person we are saying much more than that this person produces novel values simply by continuing to exist as an animal. We are thinking of the scope and intensity of the novel experiences, especially relatively harmonious ones, or those in which useful plans for action arise.

Individuals are creative in the laudatory sense chiefly through fortunate modes of interaction with their fellows. In our species, mere instinct—though it remains powerful, make no mistake about that—furnishes nothing like definite designs for living, its members must learn from others in infancy and childhood suitable patterns of action; accordingly for them, culture, psychological inheritance, thinking the thoughts of others, and feeling their feelings have enormously increased importance, compared to the modest role such inheritance plays in the life of other animals. Thus many birds do to some extent learn what songs to sing by listening in early life to their elders' singing. But we human beings, if left without culture, are worse off by far than any other kind of creature. We are created, as genuinely human, by internalizing the thoughts and feelings of others. Human living is a process of self-creation, radically influenced by the creativity of others. In every conversation we create something of one another's personalities.

At least two writers have addressed themselves to the question "What is the ethical ideal that fits the self-creative, other-creative nature of our species?" Berdyaev's moral imperative was, "Be creative and foster creativity in others."[1] And Berdyaev has worthwhile things to say about specific ways in which the principle can be applied. The other writer is Henry Nelson Wieman, usually classified as a theologian, but, during the latter part of his long career, a teacher in departments of philosophy, notably at the University of Southern Illinois. Wieman stresses the point that how creative we can be depends radically upon the extent to which we open ourselves to the influence of others. Being creative is a social phenomenon, something we do together, in large part. Wieman sums up his point in the phrase "creative interchange." He developed a carefully elaborated doctrine about the structure of such interchange and the conditions favoring it.

By *creative* Wieman does not mean merely productive of novelty. He is trying to conceive the optimal form of such production, that mode of exchanging thoughts and feelings that produces rich experience and tends to increase the capacities of the participants for being creative in this optimal sense. Wieman's many descriptions of creative interchange, or of "the creative event," and of the contrast between created and creative value, are worthy of careful attention. Whatever defects there may be in these accounts, there are also without doubt considerable merits, and the importance of the subject justifies patience with what may seem rather glaring faults in some aspects of the doctrine. Human life at its best certainly owes much to, perhaps even consists in, the process Wieman is describing.

It might be said, and Wieman did not, so far as I know, reject this way of looking at the matter, that creative interchange is not far from what at least ought to have been meant by "loving one's neighbor as oneself." But there are advantages in Wieman's way of putting the idea. If we understand the social nature of our species, and the way in which shared experiences, shared thoughts, and shared perceptions, literally create us as truly human, we shall see that the way effectively and optimally to love our fellows is indeed to engage in the process Wieman describes.

Wieman was in the Judeo-Christian tradition of humbleness before God, and he did not exempt himself from the need to continue learning from others. He thought, too, that there are in human nature many sources of difficulty in bringing about conditions favorable to optimally creative interaction between persons. He was deeply convinced that, to effectively serve our human fellows, we must have as our final motivation neither self-love nor love of others but love of God, as above and beyond all of us, as "source" of our values, as surviving our deaths, and as alone worthy of unqualified reverence and dedication. So far Wieman was like theists of other ages. The aim of life should be the glory of God, not of self or even of humanity.

However, Wieman felt that in this age of science and of pervasive doubt or denial of the possibility of metaphysics, one could no longer mean by "God" a cosmic creator whose creativity is not the process of cultural interchange we can observe in human life but something unobservable and cosmic in scope. So Wieman was led to take a remarkable and daring step: he declared that creative interchange as we observe it in human life *is* God. For this identification a variety of ingenious arguments are offered.

God traditionally was the cause or source to which all valuable things are to be attributed, and, says Wieman, creative interchange, optimal interaction among persons, is the "source of human good." (Wieman even, in one passage, suggests that a lesser form of creative interaction on the cellular level explains the very origin of multicellular animals.) To the obvious objection that the process Wieman calls God is really a quite human process of personal interaction Wieman replies that this process is really superhuman, and he denies that his theology is a form of humanism. By a human activity, he maintains, we ought to mean one the results of which are humanly conceived in advance and deliberately aimed at, whereas (by definition) the outcome of a creative process cannot be foreseen. What you or I can do to serve God is to act in ways favorable to creative interaction among persons, but since the point of the interaction is to transform us and lead us to insights we could not have had in advance, it is not for us to claim credit for such transformation. We are changed and exalted by an other and greater being than ourselves.

Above all, Wieman claims that his deity is observable and that in this era of triumphant empiricism only observable phenomena can be taken into account as relevant to human decisions. He is vividly (and rightly) impressed with the gap between traditional religious ideas and the rapidly changing world brought about by science and technology. Like Dewey, he seeks to generalize scientific method to cover values as well as facts. This understanding is bound to appeal to many. And, with qualifications, it is on the right track. The human species is a contingent phenomenon, and only disciplined observation can tell us the truth about its nature and potentialities. In our ethical doctrines it is this truth about our species that must be expressed.

There is, however, one aspect of our humanity that a monolithic empiricism seems unable to take adequately into account. This is the human capacity to raise metaphysical questions. The enormous vogue of astrology is one of many empirical evidences that empirical science does not meet all our needs. In this age sober metaphysical reasoning is not widely appreciated. But its place is not taken by sober scientific reasoning. When good metaphysics goes, bad metaphysics tends to take over. "When the gods depart the half gods arrive."[2] The alternative to proper worship is idolatry. Perhaps never have so many forms of idolatry flourished as now.

Wieman has tried to give us sober scientific reasoning about religion. In doing this he has said some true and important things. But has he succeeded in the central point; has he justified his identification of the worshipful deity with creative interchange among human beings? Consider the following quotation:

No man causes to come into his mind an idea he has never glimpsed nor extends good will where he feels ill will and his sense of justice forbids such an extension. Neither can anyone achieve a higher ideal when it contradicts the one he thinks highest. Yet new ideas, extended brotherhood, and higher ideals do enter human life from time to time. So also do experiences of love and beauty which the individual could not have imagined before they occurred. Creativity is the name we give to this process of emerging idea, wider brotherhood, higher ideals, richer forms of beauty, and love more profound. Therefore this creativity is more than human in the sense of doing what man can do *when human doing is defined* as producing what man intends and imagines before it occurs.[3] (Italics mine.)

What is going on in this passage? I submit that we have here what linguistic analysts (e.g., Lazerowitz) characterize as a proposal to alter language, offered however as a theory about the world. What dictionary, and who but Wieman, ever defined "human" as is here done? Unless the participants in a dialogue anticipate the course of the intercommunication and what it will do for them it is not they that are doing the mutual influencing, it is not human but superhuman, or nonhuman action! It seems quite clear that Wieman is confusing a semantic change with a discovery of truth. By all ordinary criteria of "human action" creative interchange is such action. And Wieman's theology is a form of humanism. By dictionary meanings and standard criteria it is a form, an enlightened form if you will, of the deification of humanity.

In creative living together we do not imagine beforehand just how things will come out; therefore, says Wieman, we do not do what is done. If a hen lays an egg but, at least the first time, does not imagine the egg in advance, then not it, but some other power, lays the egg. To be sure human beings have more foresight in their doings than the other animals, but of course this advance imagining or conceiving always has its limits. What has this to do with the dictionary meaning of "do"?

Does God, according to Wieman, imagine beforehand the results of creative interchange? No, for Wieman denies that God imagines anything or is a conscious being. So by the criterion proposed God does not do what is done either. By what other criterion does God do it? None is provided that will show both that we do not do it and that another power or agent does it. Of course, and tautologically, no single human being does what is done in intercommunication. It is a collective human achievement, but surely not less human for all that? Of course we need our fellows to accomplish anything much. And of course we do not foresee the concrete outcomes of human interactions. Others have said these things before Wieman. What is new is denying that the interactive process is "human" and terming it "God."

The reason Wieman and some of his disciples could overlook the semantic nature of the proposal about God, and be so convinced of its importance, is that very real human needs are at stake here. The generic process of sharing experiences and thoughts with ideal generosity and freedom, of taking our fellows as seriously as we take ourselves, wanting to appreciate them as we want to be appreciated, and opening ourselves to the spiritual and intellectual growth thus made possible for all parties willing and able to participate in the process is indeed the way human beings accomplish the most good they have it in them to accomplish. Any one of us is as nothing compared to the process as a whole throughout the human species. And so there is a certain plausibility in the idea that the power we should reverence, whose cause we should promote as divine, to whose service we should utterly dedicate ourselves, is this very process. If this is idolatry, as I fear it really is, there are many less noble forms of idolatry about, or in history.

The "power" in question is "observable," not as a single agent, but only as a *kind* of activity or doing, the identifiable doers of which are human persons, using standard criteria for "doers" and "human persons." Wieman is telling us how optimally to create value in one another. Only verbally is anything nonhuman identified by the language Wieman uses.

If it is true, as Wieman believes, that the ultimate devotion should be to something transcendent of human and animal life, then we must either close our eyes to the confusion just pointed out between semantic maneuvering and genuine assertion or else find another definition of deity, or of the highest form of reality, than Wieman's. To gain the avoidance of metaphysical speculation only at the price of an elementary philosophical error seems no solution for the problem of religion in an age of science.

"Interchange" means a symmetrical relation. As I have argued elsewhere, any such relation presupposes a nonsymmetrical one. We all receive emotional and intellectual stimulation from many who died before we were born and who, therefore, while they give to us, can receive nothing in return. We might ask the proponents of Wiemanism: If the symmetrical form of intrahuman stimulation, so far as optimally beneficial, is divine, what is the one-way form? Is it human? No, for certainly our ancestors did not foresee what we would make of their work. Is it divine, or is it something between human and divine? (And how nearly optimal must creativity be to count as divine. Are there many degrees of being God?)

Looked at closely, interchange is really a complex tissue of one-way influences. I now influence you a second or more later, and the you of the moment thus influenced can never influence me as I am now. A philosophy that takes a symmetrical relation as ultimate is one that stops short of the full analysis of its problems. This applies to Dewey's doctrine, worked out with Bentley, that our knowledge essentially refers to *transactions* between organism and environment. It applies, it seems to me, to Weiss's doctrine of four Modes or five Finalities of Being, each coordinate with the others. It would apply to Whitehead if we had to take seriously passages in which he speaks of everything as being in everything else, or if his rejection of "simple location" meant that every actuality inheres not only in all its successors but also in its contemporaries and predecessors. We do better to avoid such interpretations and to take seriously the asymmetry inherent in the technical explications Whitehead gives of creativity and prehension, concepts without which Whitehead's system is either nothing very new or a maze of inconsistencies.[4]

To the traditional query, "What importance can human life have in view of our mortality, and the mortality, for all we can ever know, of the species itself?" Wieman has only such answers as ordinary humanists can have. They boil down to social immortality, and to a trust that creative interchange will always find a way to keep the species going, or somehow enable our lives to make a contribution to some surviving form of life. Process theology, with its doctrine of objective immortality of all experience in the Consequent Nature of God, has a clearly different and, some would say, a more adequate answer. This answer easily includes social immortality in the ordinary sense and whatever hope it is reasonable to have for the future of our species.

Another value jeopardized by Wieman is the value of seeing in nature large manifestations of deity, so that our admiration for nature and love for other forms of life on the earth can be definitely included in our love for God. The present ecological crisis is relevant here. Wieman's view seems excessively anthropomorphic. Asian religions may have something to teach us in this respect.

Whatever the difficulties of justifying a metaphysical idea of deity, the orderliness we must attribute to nature, which inhabitants of any conceivable world would have to attribute to it to exist at all, furnishes the basis of a rather simple argument for the idea. Granted that all becoming and causality is of the nonclassical or creative type (a belief Wieman seems to share, as did Dewey and Peirce, as well as Bergson and Whitehead), we face a dilemma: Either the instances of creative action throughout the universe merely happen to fit together sufficiently to maintain a viable world system or there is a supreme or eminent form of creative decision-making that, because of its unique intrinsic worth, is accepted by all lesser forms sufficiently to enable it to set tolerable limits to the conflicts, frustrations, and aspects of disorder inherent in the idea of a multiplicity of free or self-determining actualities.

Order is either an affair of each entity adapting to the many others or it is an affair of each entity adapting, not only to the many others, but to one supreme entity, the same for all, and thus able to give guidance to all. The objection to the first alternative is that one cannot adapt to a chaos, and therefore the explanation begs the question. If the others are sufficiently ordered, I can adapt to them, otherwise not. But a single radically superior reality could furnish a common directive to the lesser realities. If all adapt to the One, they will *ipso facto* have some measure of adaptation to one another. In this way one can explain how, in spite of elements of disorder and change, things are nevertheless basically harmonious and sufficiently predictable. (That there are secondary aspects of evil and misfortune is explained by the partial self-determination or creativity attributed to each actuality.) Like humanists in general, Wieman must take the laws of nature as sheer mysteries, simply inexplicable. Another value of genuine theism lacking in Wieman's doctrine is furnished by the belief that beyond any human appreciation for an individual there is an all-cherishing, all-comprehending appreciation that enfolds us all, and with us all creatures whatsoever. Then we do not need to have our courage or self-respect rise and fall with every wind of human sentiment toward us, since there is always one who knows what we do or do not amount to. To be loved by human beings thus becomes a beautiful luxury rather than a sometimes bitterly frustrated necessity. What, by the way, would Robinson Crusoe do with Wiemanism?

To return to the question of symmetry: mutual creativity, spiritual exchange, is not a self-sufficient power. The one-way absorption of thought and feeling from our ancestors, from history, literature, art, in a word culture, is what makes human interchange a far different thing from the exchange (which is definitely creative in some degree in all animals) found among the subhuman creatures.

Finally, there is a need to be alone. Jesus in the wilderness was exchanging with no human persons, and every creative artist, philosopher, scientist, statesman, knows that solitude has a role to play in the creative life. A psychiatrist has diagnosed our time as disastrously productive of the psychopathic personality, quite incapable of the sort of process Wieman wishes to favor, and he relates this to the idea of teachers, sociologists, parents, and others in authority that the great thing is to get people to conform, "adapt," or "adjust" to society. His view is that there is in human individuals a deep need to rebel, precisely not to conform but to surpass and progress beyond the given modes of life, with its threefold limitation: nature, instinct, and death.

I should prefer to say, the need is to create, and create on the level worthy of human beings, not as angels but as animals with unique symbolic powers by which they can escape, not indeed from nature, death, or the instinctual bases of life, but from mere reiteration of already created values (trivially varied), and by which they can appreciate and pursue ever partly new goals that retain their meaning even in the light of "all time and all existence" and in spite of death and genetic limitations.

CHAPTER THIRTEEN

Politics and the Metaphysics of Freedom

Political freedom is a highly special case of a very general category. It is quite possible to discuss the special case without explicit clarification of the general principle. But there are advantages in seeing the special against the background of the universal. The universal principle of freedom is that of "self-determination," as contrasted to "determination by others." Political freedom means that the behavior of citizens is in some important respects protected against determination by the rulers. (Of course, one may hold that in complete democracy the rulers are the citizens so that self-determination coincides with political determination. However, there can be no such complete democracy, and in any case the citizen as political agent—voter and the like—is an abstraction from the concrete man, who has also private functions.) It is obvious that in all societies men have some political freedom, if relatively unimportant aspects of behavior are considered. Thus indeterminism (positing limits to determination by others) rather than determinism is true, politically speaking. The practical question then is one of degree: how much self-determination (rather than determination by rulers) is there, in what important respects of behavior, and—perhaps above all—how much definite assurance is there in advance as to the boundaries of freedom, that is, are there recognized limits to governmental interference, guaranteed "rights" to make one's own decisions? This is the political question of liberty.

More general is the question of social freedom. How much can I determine as to my own life, and how much do others decide for me, not simply as rulers, but as relatives, neighbors, employers, and so on? Here, too, nobody can really suppose that the total absence of freedom is possible. If anyone ever decides anything for others, surely we all decide something for ourselves. If there is "decision" at all, there is decision as to one's own life. Once more we find that relative indeterminism, not strict determinism, is valid. Determination by others is never complete. And here again, the practical question is the question of degree. The slave has some powers of self-determination, but they are not proportionate to his human capacities of thought and imagination. The person who is morbidly dependent upon a mother or father, is still in some degree a free agent, only not as free as a person should be.

Our conclusion so far is that in the relations of human beings to others of their kind there is always a mixture of self-determination and determination by others. Freedom does not mean self-determination in the absence of determination by others; and, equally, determination by others does not mean the total absence of self-determination. A man with a gun can shoot me, and I may therefore decide to do his bidding rather than to die. I may even be unable to decide otherwise, being in the grip of ungovernable fear. But there are always ways and degrees of doing the man's bidding; he cannot possibly forestall every nuance of my decisions in all matters. Always there is self-decision, and always in human life there are elements of one's own decision that come from the decisions of others. Action is social in essence, it is freedom influenced or partially limited by the freedom of others. We are rendered partly indeterminate by our social situation, but the final residuum of definition must come from ourselves. The social situation itself, after all, is the impingement of the spontaneity of others upon our own. The limitation of freedom is thus, it seems, other freedom, not some principle contrary to freedom. The contrast is between self and other, not between freedom and necessity, or freedom and causality. If self were unrelated to others, if individuals had no social character, if love, sympathy, awareness of others, were not intrinsic to consciousness, then indeed might freedom be unlimited—but then it would also be empty and meaningless. For it would not be freedom to do anything worth doing, since there would be no significant sphere of interaction, or possibility of knowing anything worth knowing, for what is worth knowing if there is no one to share in the knowledge? The social limitation upon freedom is what gives it positive content and value.

Here I believe is the general principle that requires only to be divested of arbitrary specifications in order to become the ultimate metaphysical category of freedom and its limitations. These arbitrary specifications are three.

1. It is usually supposed that the "social" conception of freedom must be restricted to relations of human beings. Animals, one imagines, have no freedom, since instinct is the absolute regulator of their actions, at least on the lower levels of animal life. And as for inanimate things, their movements are, if possible, even more "automatic," being controlled entirely by natural laws. It follows that insofar as our decisions are influenced by the lower orders of creature, our freedom is limited not by freedom but by something else, by mere force or necessity or causal law. If I am coerced by a man with a gun, it is really the gun,

not just the man in himself, which determines my decision. Here, it seems, freedom is limited by what is simply other than freedom. Here freedom is apparently not entirely a social phenomenon.

2. It is often supposed that my present decision is fully determined by the present external situation together with my own past, in other words, by present stimuli and the habits or associations set up in my mind and body by past responses to stimuli. In this case, no freedom is *ultimately* "social" in the sense in which we have defined social freedom. For, according to this defined sense, social freedom is a determination of self partly by self and partly by others, and if the present act is precisely determined by external stimuli and by events in the past, then the present act as such has no self-determination at all. Causality, or the relation of a present event to its antecedent conditions, is on this view not an instance of social freedom.

3. The third way in which the full scope of the principle of social freedom is obscured is by supposing that God—or the dialectical process—limits our action in a nonsocial way. If God in eternity assigns the details of our behavior, then our "self-determination" is only a label for one portion of the divine determination of all things. Even if this is not assumed, and God is believed to be not entirely determinative of our volitions, the religious idea is fully expressive of the social principle only if it implies that our decisions and God's mutually qualify without fully determining each other, that we influence without fully determining divine responses to us, and deity similarly influences our responses to it. Most of the older theologies denied such mutuality of influence in the religious sphere.

These are the three obstacles to a metaphysics of social freedom. It may be suggested that they are not insuperable, and that some benefit would ensue to the cause of political freedom if the possibility of such a metaphysics could be more generally understood.

Since "instinct" is merely a word for innate aspects of behavior, and since obviously no one can form any distinct conception of innate patterns capable of determining precisely all the details of behavior, the assertion that animals are merely instinctual automatons is arbitrary and has no scientific status. There are innate patterns *more or less* determinative of animal behavior, that we know, but how much room is left for spontaneous or free determination from moment to moment we do not know. Out of this ignorance no legitimacy can accrue to the denial of animal freedom. But it may be legitimate to experiment conceptually with the idea that while animals have no conscious freedom of our human sort, no abstract notions of alternative courses of action, they may nonetheless act in a manner never wholly determined in advance. And present-day physics at least allows us to entertain the hypothesis that the humblest entities in nature are not wholly without a range of open alternatives of behavior, however slight or trivial these may be.

It may be well to complete the picture by remarking that so far as physiological conditions of behavior are concerned, the cells of one's own body are living organisms, animals within an animal, and if these are endowed with any residual spontaneity, then their influence upon us may in the general sense be social, that is, freedom-limiting freedom.

The deterministic theory of causality is incapable of any kind of proof, and has been rejected by many leading philosophers of recent times, e.g., Lequier, Fechner, Boutroux, Peirce, James, Dewey, Whitehead, Varisco, Bergson, Popper, as well as by many leading scientists, e.g., Clerk Maxwell, Heisenberg, Bohr. There is thus no necessity to allow this theory to inhibit our development of a metaphysics of freedom. It is often said that causal determination is compatible with freedom because an act may be regarded as "self-determined" if it flows from the past character of the given individual. But on the same principle, any past act however remote was rendered fully determinate in advance by still earlier states of character and still earlier acts. Thus no act of self-determination *of what is otherwise indeterminate*—the very definition of freedom, according to some of us—can ever be located. What freedom is there in having one's decisions made for one by the "self" as it was in the newborn infant to which one's character can be traced back? This infant self is "another," so far as the now actually deciding present self is concerned. After a violent revolution of character, "one's" previous self may be not only other, but alien and distasteful. Thus I suggest it is essentially erroneous to try to soften the edge of causal determinism by baptizing it with the label of self-determination. No free act can be located unless some present act removes an indetermination that the totality of antecedent acts and external conditions failed to remove. Does this mean that there can be no causality, that process is a mere chaos? No more than the denial that other men fully determine my decisions amounts to anarchism. Other men do not *fully* determine my decisions, but they do partially determine them. They influence my decisions, but only I fully and finally determine or make them. Now just the same can be said about the totality of causal antecedents. My past experiences enter into my present spontaneous acts; they largely—but still, not completely—determine the character of these acts. Moreover, it is no very deep secret that the same ultimate social principle is operating in both cases. I am influenced by my past for the same reason that I am influenced by other people, because the richness of experience is constituted by its participation in other experiences. The present act would be empty if it inhibited all reference to antecedent acts. It is a secondary matter whether these antecedent acts are "my own" or those of other persons. In either case they furnish the given act with content. The present act selects, from among the other acts accessible to it, those which conform to its emotional requirements, these it emphasizes and puts into the focus of attention.

The past three hundred years have seen a vast international effort to remove from the philosophy of religion those features that prevent a social interpretation of the relations of God to the world. Schelling, Fechner, Pfleiderer, Lequier, Bergson, James, Brightman, Macintosh, Whitehead, Berdyaev, Niebuhr, and many other names could be mentioned. The details of the results cannot concern us here. But the general consequence for the philosophy of freedom is that there need be no religious barrier to the recognition of social freedom as a metaphysical ultimate. Such freedom can be attributed even to deity and to us in relation to deity.

What results from these considerations? That there is at least no logical necessity, no scientific fact, and (if some of us are right) no fundamental religious value to compel us to suppose that social freedom is a mere special case of some more ultimate principle of causality or power. The limitations upon freedom can be construed as consisting entirely of freedom in other forms. Causes are past acts of freedom that furnish present acts with content and so partially determine them. The reason freedom is limited by freedom is that all action and all existence is social, participatory. Sympathy and love, as religion for thousands of years and (with certain reservations) psychiatry for some decades have been telling us, are primary and not secondary phenomena.

Has this doctrine any practical bearings? It may seem indeed that no such metaphysics of social freedom is needed in order to justify political or social freedom. Certainly men can desire reasonable autonomy in relation to other men without asking metaphysical questions. The frustrations inherent in being treated as subhuman instruments of certain men's purposes are apparent enough, in any philosophy. However, a reflecting creature fully possesses life only when it sees consciously how the special case contrasts with and expresses general principles, and how, essentially, he is related to the cosmos. Now my contention is that deterministic philosophies fail to achieve this consciousness. They do not give a coherent account of how human freedom and natural causality are blended in the one reality of life.

There is every advantage of clarity and coherence on the side of a generalized social indeterminism. The various levels of specialization of freedom can then be interpreted according to a single set of basic ideas. Freedom is self-determination, implying partial but only partial determination by others. Suppose this to be a general, ultimate category. Now the point, never perhaps fully seen prior to Whitehead, is that this social conception of freedom contains in principle all that is needed to explain the interrelations of freedom and causality. Causality is the social aspect of freedom, neither more nor less. All causes are stimuli, and all stimuli are social. They are "influences" to which we have to respond, but that never completely and uniquely define the response. The response defines itself as it comes into being, prior to which event it is only a *more or less* determinate "real potentiality."

If this formula can be justified, then the social case of freedom is special only in the sense that human society is special among societies in general. From the special traits of human society arise the special kinds of freedom or liberty we rightly cherish as our human prerogatives. Here we recall once more the principle that the content of freedom comes from participation. A man can participate in the horse's desire for water or grass, but the horse cannot participate in the man's desire to sow fields to be harvested months later. The man cannot, indeed, participate in certain small details of the horse's desire for food and water, and he must allow the horse to determine these details. But the horse cannot participate in any essentially human purpose at all. The situation thus is that horses can realize their own essential values while being made to contribute to human values utterly beyond their ken. But when we try to use other human beings in this fashion, we find, or they find, that the relations of participation are much more ambiguous, and the dangers of radical frustration incomparably greater. Slaves can understand their masters often all too well, and masters often understand slaves all too little. Yet it is generally possible for the master to explain his purpose to the slave, or for the slave to explain his to the master; there is some mutuality of participation between them as human beings. The essential sign of this mutuality is language. The master may refuse to explain his purposes, or the slave his, but if they really share a common language, then indefinite mutual participation is open to them.

It is true that some people have a more limited language than others and have less power of participation than others. When we are dealing with actually feebleminded or insane persons, or with infants, we are for some practical purposes not dealing with human beings at all. Essential mutuality is lacking. But apart from these extreme cases, any inequalities in participatory power that exist are too uncertain, fluctuating, and equivocal to justify the supposition that some men are in relation to other men as men are to lower animals. Even supposing that a man is vastly my superior in understanding of other men's needs and purposes, there is a common limitation of all men that for some purposes nullifies any such superiority. This limitation is the attention span. No one can at any one time think of the concrete emotions and circumstances of very many other persons. Indeed, he can scarcely do it with one other person. We are all almost stone-blind to the lives of others, even those close to us, if we compare our awareness of their lives with their own awareness. And in this respect there is no vast difference between superior people and most people. The endless complexity in even seemingly very simple people and the simplicity at any one moment of even very complex people has for consequence that each man must in good part look to himself, simply because no one else could have time and energy, even had he the ability, to do it for him. But were this not so, it would still be true that each individual, according to the metaphysics of freedom, is essentially self-determining, and a new self-determining actuality each moment. This is the very nature of process and becoming according to thinkers like Berdyaev, Bergson, and Whitehead. The scope of the self-determination (by which in Bergson's fine conception we are all artists of reality) depends upon the level of complexity, the range of diversity, in the participations open to the individual. The outstanding measure is language, including the arts as languages. Now by this measure it becomes obvious that such differences as those of skin color are essentially irrelevant. For any language and any degree of linguistic or artistic subtlety or lack of it may be found associated with almost any shade of color. Color differences are irrelevant to political freedom. But the same may also be said for certain other differences, such as those between the members of the politburo and ordinary Russians, or those whose independence of mind caused them to be banished to the prison labor camps. The former are not more than human beings, the latter not less. And if the rulers of Russia were really superhuman, they would understand the need for greater autonomy and for the honest expression of differences of thought and feeling that are the natural modes of human mutuality.

Turning to ourselves, in the Western world, it may be that we need to put more emphasis upon the aspect of participation that is essential to social freedom. It would be simpler for us not to try to understand the peoples of Asia. Our color feeling is partly just the wish to evade a complex task. But, alas, we cannot evade it! We begin to see that our merest safety depends upon our learning more of what it is like to be Chinese or Hindu or Korean. (And I think the safety of Frenchmen depends upon their understanding better than they do what it is like to be a citizen of the United States. If our power and wealth humiliate the less fortunate, this is not wholly our fault. And if we and the French alike face a terrible danger, shall pride or bad manners take precedence over the mutual will to surmount the danger?) We must achieve some minimum of mutuality with larger portions of the world's populations, or we are lost. We must, I suspect, even look toward ways of increasing relations of mutuality with Russians themselves. I do not mean that we must become pro-communist, or even "anti-anti-communist." I mean that we must learn to make it a permanent assumption that Russians too are people. They cannot wholly like the extremely severe restrictions to which their liberty is subjected; and they would surely like them much less if they had more understanding of any alternative. We must never forget the basic mutuality of participation that unites human beings with human beings and divides them (relatively speaking) from the rest of known creation.

We need in such ways as this to cultivate our sense for the ultimate roots of freedom in the nature of things. Communists through their theory of dialectic have their own way of relating their practical doctrines to the nature of things. The dialectic is in my opinion ambiguous at best in regard to the factors of freedom and of participation. We have open to us a better metaphysics.

I should say, even, a better religion. For there is scarcely a notable theologian of recent times who could not in my opinion be shown to have moved at least some of the way from medieval theology to a religion of social freedom. My suggestion is that we become more aware of this movement and derive from it encouragement in our effort to lift the participating-freedom of humankind to a higher level.

Notes

EDITORS' PREFACE

1. There are other tables of contents for books that Hartshorne planned or intended to write but only the table of contents of *Creative Experiencing* is accompanied by a manuscript. Of interest to scholars is the fact that the table of contents for *The Universal Orthodoxy*, a book that Hartshorne announced would follow *Man's Vision of God* (Chicago: Willett, Clark and Company, 1941) and was to complete the trilogy that began with *Beyond Humanism* (Chicago: Willett, Clark and Company, 1937), is among Hartshorne's papers. See *Man's Vision of God*, xviii, 133, 155, 220, 240, and 288.

2. *Hartshorne and Brightman on God, Process, and Persons: The Correspondence, 1922–1945*, ed. Randall E. Auxier and Mark Y. A. Davies (Nashville: Vanderbilt University Press, 2001), 3.

3. *Philosophical Review* 38 (1929): 284–93; Hartshorne incorporated the review into Chapter XVII of *Beyond Humanism* (1937).

4. See Hartshorne's use of language in *Omnipotence and Other Theological Mistakes* (Albany: State University of New York Press, 1984) and the discussion of male bias in theology, pages 56–58. See also Audience Discussion of "God as Composer-Director, Enjoyer, and in a Sense, Player of the Cosmic Drama (April 7, 1987)," *Process Studies* 30, no. 2 (2001): 258.

5. For an assessment of Hartshorne's importance to philosophy, see Donald Wayne Viney, "Philosophy after Hartshorne," *Process Studies* 30, no. 2 (Fall–Winter 2001): 211–36.

6. For example: John B. Cobb, Jr., and Clark H. Pinnock, eds., *Searching for an Adequate God: A Dialogue Between Process and Free Will Theists* (Grand Rapids, MI: William B. Eerdmans, 2000); David Ray Griffin, *Reenchantment without Supernaturalism: A Process Philosophy of Religion* (Ithaca, NY, and London: Cornell University Press, 2001); Douglass Pratt, *Relational Deity: Hartshorne and Macquarrie on God* (Lanham, MD: University Press of America, 2002); George W. Shields, ed., *Process and Analysis: Whitehead, Hartshorne, and the Analytic Tradition* (Albany: State University of New York Press, 2003); Carol P. Christ, *She Who Changes: Re-Imagining the*

Divine in the World (New York: Palgrave Macmillan, 2003); Jay Wesley Richards, *The Untamed God: A Philosophical Exploration of Divine Perfection, Simplicity and Immutability* (Downers Grove, IL: InterVarsity Press, 2003); Santiago Sia, *Religion, Reason and God: Essays in the Philosophies of Charles Hartshorne and Alfred North Whitehead* (Frankfurt am Main: Peter Lang, 2004). Daniel A. Dombrowski has done more than any other single person to bring attention to Hartshorne's philosophical importance. His recent books include: *A Brief, Liberal, Catholic Defense of Abortion*, authored with Robert Deltete (Urbana and Chicago: University of Illinois Press, 2000); *Divine Beauty: The Aesthetics of Charles Hartshorne* (Nashville: Vanderbilt University Press, 2004); *A Platonic Philosophy of Religion: A Process Perspective* (Albany: State University of New York Press, 2005); *Rethinking the Ontological Argument: A Neoclassical Theistic Response* (New York: Cambridge University Press, 2006). Finally, it should be noted that Hartshorne's theory of birdsong has received favorable treatment by David Rothenberg in *Why Birds Sing: A Journey into the Mystery of Bird Song* (New York: Basic Books, 2005).

HARTSHORNE'S PREFACE

1. Editors' note: *Wisdom as Moderation: A Philosophy of the Middle Way* (Albany: State University of New York Press, 1987).

2. Editors' note: Hartshorne included Chapter Nine as having been unpublished. Chapter Nine was published in 1986, which indicates that the preface was completed before that time.

CHAPTER ONE. SOME FORMAL CRITERIA OF GOOD METAPHYSICS

1. Editor's note: Hartshorne prefaced his dissertation with three quotations, one of which was from "R. N." (sic) Whitehead's *Concept of Nature* (1920). See Hartshorne's *The Unity of Being*, edited by Randall E. Auxier and Hyatt Carter (La Salle, Illinois: Open Court, 2011).

2. Editors' note: See David Hume, *A Treatise of Human Nature*, Analytical Index by L. A. Selby-Bigge, Second Edition with text revised and notes by P. H. Nidditch (London: Oxford University Press, 1978), 233 and 634.

3. Editors' note: For the reference to Whitehead's concept of "feeling of feeling" see *Process and Reality: An Essay in Cosmology*, ed. David Ray Griffin and Donald Sherburne, corrected ed. (New York: Free Press, 1978), 211.

4. Editors' note: Peirce writes, "In short, the idea of a general involves the idea of possible variations which no multitude of existent things could exhaust but leave between any two not merely many possibilities, but possibilities absolutely beyond all multitude." *Collected Papers of Charles Sanders Peirce*, ed. Charles Hartshorne and Paul Weiss (Cambridge, MA: Harvard University Press, 1934), 5:67–68. Elsewhere, Peirce writes, "The evolutionary process is, therefore, not a mere evolution of the *existing universe*, but rather a process by which the very Platonic forms themselves have become or are becoming developed." *Collected Papers* (Cambridge, MA: Harvard University Press, 1935), 6:135, paragraph 194.

5. Editors' note: Whitehead writes, "In the present, the future occasions, as individual realities with their measure of absolute completeness, are non-existent." *Adventures of Ideas* (New York: Free Press, 1967), 192.

6. Editors' note: Peirce writes, "That Time is a particular variety of objective Modality is too obvious for argumentation. The Past consists of the sum of *faits accomplis*, and this Accomplishment is the Existential Mode of Time." See "Issues of Pragmaticism," reprinted in *Charles S. Peirce: Selected Writings (Values in a Universe of Chance)*, ed. Philip P. Wiener (New York: Dover, 1958), 220.

7. Editors' note: Whitehead, *Process and Reality*, 351.

8. Editors' note: Whitehead, *Science and Modern World* (New York: Free Press, 1967), 192, chap. XII.

9. Editors' note: See "Six Theistic Proofs," in *Creative Synthesis and Philosophic Method* (La Salle, IL: Open Court, 1970), 275–97. For discussion of Hartshorne's theistic arguments, see Donald Wayne Viney, *Charles Hartshorne and the Existence of God* (Albany: State University of New York Press, 1985).

10. Editors' note: For Whitehead's rejection of Plato's World Soul analogy, see *Adventures of Ideas*, 130.

11. Editors' note: See "Merleau-Ponty from an Anglo-American Perspective," in *Insights & Oversights of Great Thinkers* (Albany: State University of New York Press, 1983), 339–63.

CHAPTER TWO. MY ECLECTIC APPROACH TO PHENOMENOLOGY

1. Editors' note: For a discussion of metaphysics as a descriptive science see Whitehead's *Religion in the Making* (New York: Fordham University Press, 1996), 84–88. Whitehead introduces the concept of philosophy as the "critic of abstractions" and the related idea of the "fallacy of misplaced concreteness" in *Science and the Modern World*, (New York: Free Press, 1967), 51–59.

2. Editors' note: Richard Rorty was Hartshorne's student at Chicago. See Hartshorne's "Rorty's Pragmatism and Farewell to the Age of Faith and Enlightenment" and Rorty's "Response to Hartshorne" in *Rorty and Pragmatism: The Philosopher Responds to His Critics*, ed. Herman J. Saatkamp, Jr. (Nashville: Vanderbilt University Press, 1995), 16–36. Hartshorne's article on Rorty also appears as Chapter 24 of Hartshorne's *Creativity in American Philosophy* (Albany: State University of New York Press, 1984), 252–64.

3. Editors' note: "Perhaps this is only an ideal."

4. Editors' note: Elias Canetti (1905–1994) uses *Massenphänomen* in his work, but not in the sense that Hartshorne intends here. The closest parallel to what Hartshorne says that we found is this: "The atoms in Democrites have the character of a crowd conception. It is remarkable that the Greek theory of nature, which has proved to be the most fruitful, owes its origin to an obsession with an invisible crowd consisting of the smallest units" (Canetti, *The Human Province* [New York: Continuum, 1978], 189. The expression here translated "crowd conception" is *MassenVorstellung*. It may be, as J. R. Hustwit suggested to us, that Hartshorne might have used *Massenphänomen* in place of *MassenVorstellung*.

5. Editors' note: For the two quotes from Peirce, see "Some Consequences of Four Incapacities" and "The Essentials of Pragmatism" in *Philosophical Writings of Peirce*, ed. Justus Buchler (New York: Dover, 1955), 229, 256.

6. Editors' note: For this quote, see the section labeled "The Principles of Phenomenology" in *Philosophical Writings of Peirce*, 76–77.

7. Editors' note: Hartshorne's most historical books are *Insights and Oversights of Great Thinkers: An Evaluation of Western Philosophy* (1983) and *Creativity in American Philosophy* (1984).

8. Editors' note: The book by Royce to which Hartshorne refers is *The Problem of Christianity* (1913).

9. Editors' note: *The Philosophy and Psychology of Sensation* (Chicago: University of Chicago Press, 1934).

10. Editors' note: Karl Popper (1902–1994).

11. Editors' note: For Whitehead's discussion of order and disorder as fundamental characterizations of experience, see *Modes of Thought* (New York: Free Press, 1968), 50–51 and 75–85. See also *Adventures of Ideas*, 227–28 and *Interpretation of Science*, ed. A. H. Johnson (Indianapolis: Bobbs-Merrill, 1961), 213, 219–20.

CHAPTER THREE. NEGATIVE FACTS AND THE
ANALOGICAL INFERENCE TO OTHER MIND

1. Editors' note: For further elaboration, see Chapter Ten of this book.

2. See my *The Logic of Perfection* (La Salle, IL: Open Court, 1962), 92–93.

3. Editors' note: According to Hartshorne, God is the one individual identifiable *a priori* or by concepts alone (*The Logic of Perfection*, 62). There can be only one all-inclusive individual, an individual that influences all others and is in turn influenced by all others. For other discussions of these ideas, see "God as Absolute, Yet Related to All," *Review of Metaphysics* 1, no. 1 (1947): 24–51; *A Natural Theology for Our Time* (La Salle, IL: Open Court, 1967), 34–43; and *Creative Synthesis and Philosophic Method*, 252–53.

4. See Morris Lazerowitz, *The Structure of Metaphysics* (London: Routledge and Kegan Paul, 1955), 181, 183, for an illustration of the trivializing of the question of negative facts that result when the preceding distinction is not made. Editors' note: Hartshorne's review of Lazerowitz's book appeared in *Philosophy and Phenomenological Research* 19, no. 2 (December 1958): 226–40, and is reprinted with slight changes in Hartshorne's *Wisdom as Moderation: A Philosophy of the Middle Way*, chap. 5.

5. R. Wolheim, in "Privacy," *Mind* 51 (1950–1951): see especially 92–94, seems to show how neglect of the question of negative facts can be connected with depreciation of the argument by analogy.

CHAPTER FOUR. PERCEPTION AND THE
CONCRETE ABSTRACTNESS OF SCIENCE

1. Editors' note: Whitehead, *The Concept of Nature* (1920; repr., Cambridge: Cambridge University Press, 1971), 40.

2. See *The Philosophy of G. E. Moore*, ed. P. A. Schilpp (Evanston and Chicago: Northwestern University Press, 1942), 660–63.

3. Ibid., 223–51.

CHAPTER FIVE. METAPHYSICAL TRUTH BY
SYSTEMATIC ELIMINATION OF ABSURDITIES

1. Editors' note: See, for example, Hartshorne, "Could There Have Been Nothing? A Reply [to Houston Craighead]," *Process Studies* 1, no. 1 (Spring 1971): 25–28.

2. Editors' note: See Hartshorne's *Creative Synthesis and Philosophic Method*, chap. XVI, "The Aesthetic Matrix of Value." For further discussion of Hartshorne's aesthetic theory, see Daniel A. Dombrowski, *Divine Beauty: The Aesthetics of Charles Hartshorne*.

3. Editors' note: See, for example, Hartshorne's *Insights and Oversights of Great Thinkers: An Evaluation of Western Philosophy*, chap. 14, "The Neglect of Relative Predicates in Modern Philosophy."

4. Editors' note: Hartshorne is referring to Jacques Monod (1910–1976), the Nobel Prize–winning biologist. His *Le Hasard et la Necessité* (Paris: Éditions de Seuil, 1970) was translated by Austryn Wainhouse as *Chance and Necessity: An Essay on the Natural Philosophy of Biology* (New York: Alfred A. Knopf, 1971).

5. Editors' note: Hartshorne closed an earlier draft of this chapter with these sentences: "Freedom is the universal of universals. I have written an essay defending this belief, simply called Freedom as Universal. Since this completes the story I end this essay." Hartshorne's essay "Freedom as Universal" is published in *Process Studies* 25 (1996): 1–9.

CHAPTER SIX. THE CASE FOR METAPHYSICAL IDEALISM

1. See A. C. Ewing's *The Idealistic Tradition* (Glencoe, IL: Free Press, 1957), 25.

2. Editors' note: See Chapter One, note 2.

CHAPTER SEVEN. CREATIVITY AND THE
DEDUCTIVE LOGIC OF CAUSALITY

1. Editors' note: Whitehead, *Process and Reality*, 21.

2. Editors' note: Whitehead says, "Causation is nothing else than one outcome of the principle that every actual entity has to house *its* actual world" (*Process and Reality*, 80).

3. Editors' note: See, for example, Jules Lequier *Œuvres complètes*, ed. Jean Grenier (Neuchatel, Switzerland: Éditions de la Baconnière, 1952), 473.

CHAPTER EIGHT. THE MEANING OF 'IS GOING TO BE'

1. "Mr. Bradley on the Future," *Mind* (October 1960): 550–54.

2. "Must the Future Be What It Is Going to Be?" *Mind* (April 1959): 193–208.

3. See R. M. Martin, *Truth and Denotation* (Chicago: University of Chicago Press, 1958), chap. IV.

4. "Aristotle and the Sea Battle," *Mind* (October 1960): 447–65.

5. Editors' note: "The Prejudice in Favor of Symmetry" is the title of Chapter X of *Creative Synthesis and Philosophic Method*. See also the section in *Insights and Oversight of Great Thinkers: An Evaluation of Western Philosophy* titled "The Prejudice of Symmetry," 164–67.

CHAPTER NINE. THEISM AND DUAL TRANSCENDENCE

1. *The Divine Relativity: A Social Conception of God* (New Haven and London: Yale University Press, 1948).

2. Editors' note: Hartshorne argues that it is impossible for a God with no contingent aspects to know a contingent event. If any event is contingent then it could be otherwise (e.g., this bird at this place and time singing rather than sleeping). If the event could be otherwise, then God's knowledge of the event could be otherwise (i.e., God knowing this bird at this place and time as sleeping rather than singing). The contingency is not that God might have been ignorant but that what God knows might have been different. Therefore, if God knows a contingent event then there must be a contingent aspect of God. The only non-atheistic alternatives, says Hartshorne, are to follow Aristotle and deny that God knows the world or to follow Spinoza and deny that nothing in God or in the world could be other than it is. See Hartshorne's *Aquinas to Whitehead: Seven Centuries of Metaphysics of Religion* (Milwaukee, WI: Marquette University Publications, 1976), 13–14. Hartshorne gives this argument in a variety of places. For other examples, see *The Divine Relativity*, 13–14, and *The Darkness and the Light: A Philosopher Reflects upon His Fortunate Career and Those Who Made It Possible* (Albany: State University of New York Press, 1990), 232–33, 247.

3. Editors' note: In the margins of the manuscript for this chapter, Hartshorne wrote: "Poor arrangement. Should be 4 rows and 4 columns. At 89 I still had not done it right. A friend told me how to do that, as a nonagenarian." The 4 X 4 arrangement appears in a number of Hartshorne's articles but in only one of his books. See *The Zero Fallacy and Other Essays in Neoclassical Philosophy*, ed. Mohammad Valady (La Salle, IL: Open Court, 1997), 83. The friend who helped Hartshorne with the table was Joseph Pickle. The 4 X 4 arrangement looks like this:

N.n	C.n	NC.n	O.n
N.c	C.c	NC.c	O.c
N.cn	C.cn	NC.cn	O.cn
N.o	C.o	NC.o	O.o

4. Editors' note: Whitehead's precise words are: "The guiding motto in the life of every natural philosopher should be, Seek simplicity and distrust it," *The Concept of Nature*, 163.

5. Editors' note: Edmund Spenser wrote, in his poem "A Hymn in Honour of Beauty": So every spirit, as it is most pure, / And hath in it the more of heavenly light, / So it the fairer body doth procure / To habit in, and if more fairly dight / With

cheerful grace and amiable sight. / For of the soul the body form doth taek: / For soul is form, and doth the body make.

6. Editors' note: Whitehead states, "'Creativity,' 'many,' 'one' are the ultimate notions involved in the meaning of the synonymous terms 'thing,' 'being,' 'entity.' These three notions complete the Category of the Ultimate and are presupposed in all the more special categories," *Process and Reality*, 21.

CHAPTER TEN. THE ONTOLOGICAL ARGUMENT AND THE MEANING OF MODAL TERMS

1. Malcolm's famous essay, "Anselm's Ontological Arguments," was in *The Philosophical Review* 69 (1960): 41–62. Various writers criticized this in *Philosophical Review* 70 (1960): 56–103.

Findlay's "Can God's Existence be Disproved?" was in *Mind* LVII (1948): 176–83, reprinted in Antony Flew and Alasdair MacIntyre, eds., *New Essays in Philosophical Theology* (London: SCM Press, 1955), 47–56. For his mature view, see "Some Reflections on Necessary Existence," in *Process and Divinity*, ed. William L. Reese and Eugene Freeman, 515–27 (La Salle, IL: Open Court, 1964); also *Language, Mind and Value* (London: Allen and Unwin, 1963), 8–9.

My first reference to the point of Anselm's Proslogion III upon which Malcolm's preferred argument is based was in "The Formal Validity and Real Significance of the Ontological Argument," *Philosophical Review* 53 (1944): 234n. The idea was elaborated in the discussion of Anselm in the anthology *Philosophers Speak of God*, by Hartshorne and William L. Reese (Chicago: Chicago University Press, 1953), 96–98. A recent account is in Chapters XII and XIV of *Creative Synthesis and Philosophic Method*; other versions are in *Anselm's Discovery* and Chapter II of *The Logic of Perfection* (all Lasalle, IL: Open Court, 1970, 1965, 1962, respectively).

For a partly similar and partly very different approach, see James Ross, *Philosophical Theology* (Indianapolis and New York: The Bobbs-Merrill Company, Inc., 1969).

2. Editors' note: In another manuscript of this chapter, Hartshorne states, "I have presented a theory of the ontological bearings of these terms, and my reasoning stands or falls with this theory." For one statement of Hartshorne's theory of modal theory, see his article "Real Possibility," *Journal of Philosophy* 55, no. 21 (1963): 593–605. See also George L. Goodwin, *The Ontological Argument of Charles Hartshorne* (Missoula, MT: Scholars Press, 1978).

3. For Peirce on modality, see *The Collected Papers of Charles S. Peirce*, ed. C. Hartshorne and Paul Weiss (Cambridge, MA: Harvard University Press, 1932–1935), 2.323, 3.527, 4.972, 6.6, 6.185.

4. Editors' note: Shakespeare, *Henry IV*, part 1, A.3, scene 1.

5. Editors' note: See, for example, "What Did Anselm Discover?" in *Insights and Oversights*, 93–103.

6. Editors' note: This list can be compared to a similar one in *The Logic of Perfection*, where Hartshorne speaks of "ten marks of contingency" (74–75).

7. Editors' note: See John Hick, "A Critique of the 'Second Argument,'" in *The Many-Faced Argument*, ed. John H. Hick and Arthur C. McGill, 341–56 (New York:

Macmillan, 1967); see also Hartshorne's reply, "John Hick on Logical and Ontological Necessity," *Religious Studies* 13, no. 2 (1977): 155–65.

8. David Braine, "Review of *Anselm's Discovery*," *Mind* 77 (1968): 447–50.

9. *Creative Synthesis and Philosophic Method*, chap. 14.

10. Editors' note: Peirce says, "In respect to the ideal world we are virtually omniscient." See "The Nature of Mathematics," in *Philosophical Writings of Peirce*, 146.

11. Editors' note: In another essay, Hartshorne quotes Findlay as saying, "God must be lord over possibility as well as actuality." See "Our Knowledge of God," in *Knowing Religiously*, ed. Leroy S. Rouner, 55 (South Bend, IN: University of Notre Dame Press, 1985). As a reference for this quotation, Hartshorne cites Findlay's "Can God's Existence Be Disproved?" in *New Essays in Philosophical Theology*, 52. However, the closest that Findlay comes to Hartshorne's phraseology is this: "God mustn't merely cover the territory of the actual, but also, with equal comprehensiveness, the territory of the possible."

CHAPTER ELEVEN. CATEGORIES, TRANSCENDENTALS, AND CREATIVE EXPERIENCING

1. The exact quote is, "Philosophy, accordingly, finds its place and function as a criticism of the categories," James Edwin Creighton, *Studies in Speculative Philosophy*, ed. Harold R. Smart (New York: Macmillan Company, 1924), 154. James E. Creighton (1861–1924) was a Canadian-born philosopher, professor at Cornell University, coeditor of *Philosophical Review* (1892–1902), American editor of *Kant-studien* (1896–1924), and cofounder and first president of the American Philosophical Association (1902).

2. Editors' note: *Process and Reality*, 35.

3. Editors' note: Ibid., 166.

4. Editors' note: Ibid., 21.

5. Editors' note: Whitehead's exact words are "The truth itself is nothing else than how the composite natures of the organic actualities of the world obtain adequate representation in the divine nature. Such representations compose the 'consequent nature' of God, which evolves in its relationship to the evolving world without derogation to the eternal completion of its primordial conceptual nature" (*Process and Reality*, 12–13).

6. Editors' note: For Whitehead's references to God as nontemporal, see *Religion in the Making*, 90 and 94, chap. III, parts 3 and 4, and *Process and Reality*, 7, 31, 32, and 46. Whitehead says that the everlasting nature of God is "in a sense non-temporal" in *Adventures of Ideas*, 208, chap. XV, section 6. Whitehead speaks of the consequent nature of God as "moving onward and never perishing" (*Process and Reality*, 346).

7. *Creative Synthesis and Philosophic Method*, 100–101.

8. Editors' note: "A Revision of Peirce's Categories," reprinted in *The Relevance of Charles Peirce*, ed. Eugene Freeman (La Salle, IL: Monist Library of Philosophy, 1983), 80–92, also as Chapter 7 of Hartshorne's *Creativity in American Philosophy*.

9. Editors' note: Central to Lequier's work is the phrase "to make, not to become, but to make, and in making, to make oneself." See *Œuvres complètes*, 71. Sartre quotes a briefer version of this phrase but without mentioning Lequier's name. See *Les écrits de Sartre*, Ed. Michel Contat and Michel Rybalka (Paris: Gallimard: 1970), 655; see

also Sartre's introduction to Mallarmé's poetry *Poésies* (Paris: Gallimard, 1989), 14. For Whitehead's references to "self-creation" see: *Symbolism: Its Meaning and Effect* (New York: G. P. Putnam's Sons, 1959 [1927]), 36; *Process and Reality*, 25, 69, 85, 289; *Adventures of Ideas*, 195, 199, 236, 238; *Modes of Thought* (New York: Free Press, 1968 [1938]), 152, 166.

10. Editors' note: See Russell's *Introduction to Mathematical Philosophy* (New York: Dover, 1993), 44–45.

11. Editors' note: According to Whitehead, "it belongs to the nature of a 'being' that it is a potential for every 'becoming'" (*Process and Reality*, 22).

12. See Chapter One, note 4.

13. Editors' note: Peirce wrote, "Those that have loved themselves and not their neighbors will find themselves April fools when the great April opens the truth that neither selves nor neighborselves were anything more than vicinities." See *Collected Papers of Charles Sanders Peirce*, ed. Charles Hartshorne and Paul Weiss (Cambridge, MA: Harvard University Press, 1933), 4:45.

14. Henry Stapp, "Whiteheadian Approach to Quantum Theory and the Generalized Bell's Theorem," *Foundations of Physics* 9 (1979): 1–25.

15. Editors' note: Hartshorne discusses the views of Paul Tillich (1886–1965) in a number of places. For example, see: "Tillich's Doctrine of God," in *The Theology of Paul Tillich*, ed. Charles W. Kegley and Robert W. Bretall, 164–95 (New York: Macmillan, 1952); "On God and His Attributes (Hartshorne's Question to Tillich and Tillich's Reply)," in *Philosophical Interrogations*, ed. Sydney and Beatrice Rome, 374–75 (New York: Holt, Rinehart, and Wintson, 1964); "Tillich and the Non-Theological Meaning of Theological Terms," in *Paul Tillich Retrospect and Future* (Nashville: Abingdon Press, 1966), 19–30; *Creative Synthesis and Philosophic Method*, chap. VII; *Creativity in American Philosophy*, chap. 23. For more on Hartshorne and Tillich, see Edgar A. Towne, *Two Types of Theism: Knowledge of God in the Thought of Paul Tillich and Charles Hartshorne* (Frankfurt am Main: Peter Lang, 1997).

16. Heinrich Scholz, *Metaphysik als strenge Wissenschaft* (Darmstadt: Wissenschaftliche Buchgesellschaft, 1957), 178–81.

17. Editors' note: Hartshorne is here referring to the argument that Georg von Wright gives in *Time, Change and Contradiction* (Cambridge: Cambridge University Press, 1968). If becoming is continuous, then either moments of zero duration have definite characteristics or some temporally thick processes have contradictory characteristics. With von Wright, Hartshorne rejects both disjuncts of the consequent; it follows that becoming is not continuous.

CHAPTER TWELVE. THE HIGHER LEVELS
OF CREATIVITY: WIEMAN'S THEORY

1. Editors' note: The quoted sentence is Hartshorne's summary of Berdyaev's ethic of creativeness. See Nicholas Berdyaev, *The Destiny of Man* (New York: Harper and Row Publishers, 1960), especially chapters 3 and 4.

2. Editors' note: Hartshorne either misremembers or intentionally changes the phrase with which Emerson ended his poem, "Give All to Love." Emerson wrote, "Heartily know, / When half-gods go, / The gods arrive."

3. Henry Nelson Wieman, *Man's Ultimate Commitment* (Carbondale: Southern Illinois Press, 1958), 76.

4. Editors' note: Whitehead occasionally spoke of "mutual prehensions" within a nexus (e.g., *Process and Reality*, 76, 194, 230, and 253). Hartshorne considered this way of speaking to be in tension with Whitehead's notion of the causal independence of contemporary occasions by virtue of their lack of physical prehensions of each other (*Process and Reality*, 62, 123). Early in his career, Hartshorne did not hold to the mutual independence of contemporaries, but he eventually came to accept what he understood as Whitehead's view on this issue. See Hartshorne's *Whitehead's Philosophy: Selected Essays, 1935–1970* (Lincoln: University of Nebraska Press, 1972), 3.

Index of Names

Anselm of Canterbury, 29, 96, 104, 110, 112, 151
Aquinas, Thomas, 23, 95, 116, 120
Arnauld, Antoine, 53
Aristotle, xi, 1, 5, 16, 22, 23, 24, 36, 45, 47, 48, 49, 51, 53, 58, 81, 89, 94, 95, 96, 99, 103, 104, 112, 115, 117, 120, 122, 123, 124, 126, 150
Augustine, 68
Austin, J. L., 25
Ayer, A. J., 66

Bahm, Archie, 122
Bentley, Arthur F., 134
Berdyaev, Nicholas, 95, 117, 130, 141, 143, 153
Bergson, Henri, 1, 3, 5, 11, 13, 14, 15, 17, 21, 22, 23, 47, 71, 77, 101, 114, 115, 116, 119, 121, 125, 128, 135, 140, 141, 143
Berkeley, George, 3, 14, 23, 24, 26, 56, 59, 60, 61, 99
Berlin, Isaiah, 25
Blanshard, Brand, 20, 48, 57, 119
Bochenski, Jozef, 5, 125
Bohm, David, 60
Bohr, Niels, 140
Bosanquet, Bernard, 14, 24, 68
Boutroux, Émile, 71, 140
Bradley, F. H., 14, 20, 24, 48, 49, 57, 65, 67
Bradley, R. D., 81, 90
Braine, David, 108

Bridgeman, Percy Williams, 110
Brightman, Edgar Sheffield, viii, 141
Buchler, Justus, 121, 122, 124
Burger, Herman, 68

Campanella, Tommaso, 116
Canetti, Elias, 147
Čapek, Milič, 49
Carnap, Rudolf, 25, 45, 48, 81, 93, 95, 106, 107
Carneades, 107
Charlesworth, Max 105
Clifford, W. K., 68
Collingwood, R. G., 122, 123
Comte, Auguste, 107
Confucius, 46
Cornford, F. M., 98
Creighton, James E., 113, 152
Croce, Benedetto, 14, 24

Dante, Alighieri, 8
Democritus, 36, 37, 147
Descartes, René, 17, 18, 22, 23, 43, 58, 127
Dewey, John, 23, 24, 25, 26, 34, 71, 132, 134, 135, 140
Ducasse, C. J., 37
Duns Scotus, John, 23

Edwards, Jonathan, 125
Einstein, Albert, 25, 60, 71, 72
Emerson, Ralph Waldo, 23, 153

Index of Subjects

actual entities, 3, 4, 115, 118, 149
actus purus, 2, 111, 126
abstract and concrete, 18, 19, 33, 42, 55, 58, 59, 61, 64, 117, 125, 137; and continuity, 123; logical relation with the concrete, 45, 53, 121; see *concrete*
abstraction, two forms of, 35, 75
abstractness, levels of, 29, 106, 121, 122
afterimages, 14
afterlife, 8
agnosticism, 95, 96
analytic, narrow (formal) and broad (meaning) senses, 108
appearance and reality, 36, 42
astrology, 132
asymmetry, and symmetry, 49, 66, 118; logically more basic than symmetry, 52, 120; prejudice in favor of symmetry, 90
atheism, 94, 96, 98; empirical v. *a priori*, 105, 109

beauty, 8, 48, 98, 113, 116, 117, 132, 150; divine, 7, 146
becoming, 6–7; more obvious in audition than in vision, 114; in contrast to being, 113; as inclusive of being, 114, 122; creative-cumulative view of, 71, 77; and no de-becoming, 85; as epochal, 5, 23; as piecemeal contingency, 45; as particularization, 120; units of do not change, 114; von

Wright's argument against continuity of, 153
Bell's Theorem, 120
big bang, 99
bivalence, of truth values, 81
block universe, 127
body, cells theory of, 13, 100; perception of, 36, 38, 39; as composed of lesser minds, 99
bracketing (*epoché*), 18
Buddhists, 5, 40, 49, 50, 56, 107, 114, 126; Theravada and Mahayana, 6, 67, 69, 118, 124, 125

categorical contrasts, 117
causation (cause and effect), 19, 26, 40, 41, 45, 67, 77, 104, 138; asymmetrical and symmetrical views of, 119; cause as defining possible effects, 76; more information content in effect than in cause, 73; effect as including its causes, 117; effects as premises, 75–76; as social aspect of freedom, 141
cells, 33, 34, 39, 40, 60, 62, 79, 129, 140; as feeling, 3, 13, 14, 16, 39, 40, 51, 78, 99, 100
chance, 5, 22, 46, 52, 117, 119
Christians, 56
common sense, xi, 4, 33, 34, 39, 41, 42, 49, 51, 59, 60, 85, 87
communism, 143
compatibilism, 119, 140

laws of nature, 45, 52, 71, 75, 85, 109
logical positivism, 25; as opposed to *positivism*, 47
love, 6, 52, 116, 131, 138, 141, 153; divine, 7; as what moves the world, 8; as social relatedness, 42

materialism, 3, 47, 50, 51, 57, 61, 68, 77; and emergent dualism, 50; methodological, 44
matter, 47, as active, 4, 51, 60; as inert stuff, 60; as mindless, 13, 17, 24
metaphysics, xi, 43, 104, 122; as descriptive science, 11; error as in denials, 96; and formal logic, 123; neglect of, 30–31; neoclassical, 115; Principle of Contrast, 2, 5, 45, 49, 53; cannot be replaced by science, 132; truth by coherence, 45; truth as mean between extremes, 2, 49; truths as all positive, 1, 31; truths as informally analytic, 108; unity of contraries, 2
memory, 3, 4, 15, 16, 18, 21, 26, 28, 35, 38, 40, 50, 55, 57, 62, 76, 77, 79, 103, 104; 115, 123, 126–127; personal and impersonal, 42
method in philosophy, 117–118
mind, 17, 37, 40, 44, 51, 55, 56, 59; and body (or matter), 9, 17, 24, 37, 39, 57; Buddhist "mind-only" doctrine, 114; as excluded from much of nature, 51; criteria for the absence of, 60; as excluded from science, 44; as inextended, 68; as on both sides of ultimate contrasts, 58–59; as including and as included, 68; as mirroring nature, 13; *see* other minds, problem of
Mitwelt, 17, 24
modalities, 53, 108, 126; *see* necessity
monism and pluralism, 48, 124
mystics and mysticism, 98, 107

necessity, 30, 44, 45, 49, 52, 64, 86, 88, 89, 90, 95, 96, 101, 104, 105, 108, 110, 111, 117, 119, 123, 138; causal, 43, 73, 77; *de dictu* and *de re*, 103, 108, 126; distributive rule concerning, 53, 97, 120; as what is common to all

possibilities, 53, 106; of necessary and nonnecessary connections, 97
negative facts, 27, 47
negative theology, 126
nominalism, 6, 21; two forms of, 121
nonbeing, impossibility of, 29, 43, 44, 46–47, 106, 110, 111; impossibility of nonexistence of some nondivine beings, 125
nontheism, 8, 97, 108; *a priori*, 108; and atheism, 95
novelty, 117, 131; levels of from atoms to humans, 129

omnipotence, 43, 44, 98; pseudo conception of, 105
omniscience, 42, 44
ontological argument for God's existence, 107, 125; and existence and actuality, 106, 111; as refutation of empirical atheism and theism, 105; entails impossibility of nonbeing, 106; positivist's objection to, 107; not sufficient in itself to establish theism, 105, 109
ontological parity, 121
ontological principle, 117
optimism and pessimism, 130
other minds, problem of, 28, 39

pain and pleasure, 13, 22, 24, 38, 39
panpsychism, *see* psychicalism
past, xii, 3, 4, 5, 6, 15, 17, 24, 30, 35, 42, 52, 63, 71, 72, 77, 78, 80, 84, 86, 89, 90, 99, 103, 106, 115, 116, 119, 120, 122, 123, 124, 127, 139, 141; as actual, 7, 20, 25, 26, 43, 147; beginningless, 110; derived cognitively by subtracting novelty, 75; given in present experience, 40, 50, 76; not created by present experience, 57; permanent reality of, 7, 22; remote, 50, 79, 85, 140
pathetic and apathetic fallacies, 40–41
Peircean Firsts, Seconds, Thirds, *see* Firstness
perception, 3, 4, 12, 18, 40, 50, 51, 55, 59, 68, 74, 79, 104, 120, 129; as of the body, 14, 26, 36, 38, 79; causal and acausal theories of, 41, 56; as

Made in the USA
San Bernardino, CA
15 May 2019